AF370457

THE FENRIS WOLF

ISSUE NO. 4

EDITED BY CARL ABRAHAMSSON

TRAPART books

The Fenris Wolf, issue no. 4

ISBN 978-91-986242-8-1

Trapart Books
P.O. Box 8105
SE-104 20 Stockholm
Sweden

info@trapart.net
www.trapart.net
www.patreon.com/vanessa23carl

The Fenris Wolf, issue no 4
Contents

The whys of yesterday
are the why-nots of today
(A foreword)

Our perception of chronological time is remarkable and must truly be one of the cornerstones of the term "subjectivity". We can rationally note that an objective consensus-time has passed but may still feel that no time has passed at all. This latter sentiment is what I'm feeling right this moment, and I ascribe all virtues and truths to that feeling.

So, basically no time has passed since the latest issue of *The Fenris Wolf* was published in 1993. But still, I feel it's high time a new one is published. I do hope you agree.

Although the previous issues were joint efforts in many ways, they also very much reflected my own interests and inclinations. I don't think that has changed. In fact, very little has changed. When I started the project, it was in part a continuation of my work with various subcultural fanzines in Sweden, and in part an indulgence in my own budding metaphysical interests. The concept of "Occulture", as codified by Thee Temple Ov Psychick Youth and its protagonist Genesis Breyer P-Orridge, was indeed a very fitting headline. The first three issues of *The Fenris Wolf* are basically three facets of the same rough (philosopher's?) stone – the occultural one.

In my preparation of the fourth issue (and yes, I have to admit it: it did take a long time in the chronological sense!), there were many bursts of inspiration and effort. Approximately one every three years or so. I wanted to maintain an eclectic and open-minded editorial attitude (I still do) and collected material from all corners of the globe. But my own interests in regard to the hocus pocus stuff had changed somewhat. After the initial rush of youthful enthusiasm and enchanting meetings with many remarkable men and women, I noticed that my own mind was working overtime seeing patterns and similarities on more general levels. We live in a decidedly magical world and most of the people on this planet perceive it that way. And yet our own supposedly civilized culture seems unwilling to acknowledge that fact. This was well worth some attention.

As I had absolutely no intention of going back to university, I simply developed my already existing "Institute of Comparative Misanthropology" to a similar one preoccupied with "Magico-anthropology". That was that and it still is. *The Fenris Wolf* was slightly pushed to the back of my mind though, as the Institute embarked on its first major expedition/project. In 2000, the book *Bardo Tibet* was issued by the Swedish publishing company Fischer & co. It's basically a photo book by the talented Max Fredrikson, but with a lengthy introduction by myself and ICM colleagues Henrik Bogdan (nowadays an academic superstar in his own right) and Danish adventurer extraordinaire Peder Byberg. We traveled for two months in Northern India in 1996 and then for another two months in Nepal and Tibet in 1999. The work focussed on magical aspects of Vajrayana Buddhism, and we interviewed a great many people – monks, nuns, lamas, lay people, etc. The fruits of this labour, in the substantial textual sense, have yet to be tasted. But they will be.

Anyway, the interesting and stimulating detours of life kept *The Fenris Wolf* slightly at bay, and I wasn't really happy about that. Then, in 2009, I was invited to speak at the Equinox-gathering of minds in London. It was a fine opportunity to meet up with old friends and make some new ones. I realised that there was indeed still interest in *The Fenris Wolf* as an open-minded and eclectic source of challenging thoughts. And so, here we are.

You may have heard of the "Internet"? At times, I was tempted to jump overboard, abandon the printed matter-ship and give myself wholly to the demons of contemporary digiculture. But instead, I also tricked these demons: by dutifully sticking to my devotion to book-making, while at the same time serving them with new and perhaps more non-esoteric matter "online".

I have more or less lost track of everyone I ought to thank during this winding chronological process, so I won't even attempt it. Current kudos are in order though: first and foremost to all the contributors to this issue, for keeping a well-needed Promethean spirit alive, to Fredrik Söderberg especially for the cover art and for the donation of the series of 23 original drawings to the project, to Genesis Breyer P-Orridge for sparks and fuel, Margareta Abrahamsson, Sofia Lindström-Abrahamsson, to Mikael Prey for transcription help, Kenneth Anger, Brian Butler, Camilla Hyldal and the Danish Film School, Lars Top-Galia, Henrik Møll, Simon Kane, Raymond Salvatore Harmon, The Equinox-festival, Sylvie Walder, to Annabel and Michael Moynihan for invaluable help in so many ways, to Klett-Cotta for allowing me to publish Ernst Jünger's classic LSD-account (for the first time ever in English!), also to Insel Verlag, and to Blanche Barton, Peter Gilmore and Peggy Nadramia for being there and fanning the flame so well. Thank you all very much!

Thanks and respect are also due the following extraordinary gentlemen, who moved onwards during this period of time: Timothy Leary, William Burroughs, Anton LaVey, Robert Anton Wilson, Paul Bowles, Ernst Jünger, Albert Hofmann, Conrad Rooks, Jhon Balance, Peter Christopherson, Kenneth Grant and Owsley Stanley. "You can check out anytime you want, but you can never leave."

This issue is dedicated to genuinely creative, bold and daring individuals. I wonder: are you still out there?

Vade Ultra!

Carl Abrahamsson, Editor
Stockholm-Monstropolis, Vernal Equinox, 2011

THE EXECUTION

Hermann Hesse

Translated by Michael Moynihan

The Master made a journey from the mountains down to the valley, together with some of his disciples, and approached the walls of a large city where a great crowd had gathered at the gates. As they got closer, they saw a scaffold had been erected and the executioner was at work dragging a man, weak from imprisonment and torture, from the tumbrel and hauling him up to the block. The mob surged about the spectacle, mocking and spitting at the condemned man and awaiting his beheading with boisterous lust and excitement.

"Who is he?" the disciples asked one another, "and what could he have done that the mob should so ravenously desire his death? There is not a single one who has pity or weeps for him."

"I think," said the Master somberly, "it is a heretic."

They came closer in. When they met with the mob, the disciples compassionately inquired among the people after the name and the crime of the man whom they were just then watching kneel down at the block.

"It's a heretic!" cried the mob angrily. "Look, he's laying down his cursed head! Down with him! Verily, this cur wanted to teach us that the City of Paradise has only two gates, but we all know there are twelve!"

Bewildered, the disciples turned to the Master and asked, "How could you have known all this, Master?"

He smiled and walked on.

"It wasn't hard," he said quietly. "If he had been a murderer, a thief, or a criminal of some sort, there would have been pity and sympathy from the folk. Many would have been weeping, some would have protested his innocence. But one who has a faith of his own: he will be pitilessly slaughtered by the people and his corpse will be thrown to the dogs."

Black and White Meditations 1-23

Ink drawings by Fredrik Söderberg

With his skilful technique and magnificent visionary abilities, Fredrik Söderberg has established himself as an artist of intelligence and integrity. His majestic large paintings of psychic-psychedelic symmetries, of magical history, his smaller watercolours of heathen lore, as well as his stripped yet detailed drawings of eternal symbols, all point in the same direction: Söderberg aspires, ascends, ascertains and acquires, to be able to filter and then share the vistas of discovery on his path.

Initially, Söderberg positioned himself in the midst of his favoured sources of inspiration. From that privileged position he has diligently roamed onwards, both in the inner and outer, only to find that both levels are essentially the same. When the soul meets the eye that then meets the hand, Söderberg's *tour de force* begins and we are left, literally spellbound, to see ourselves in his miasmic mirrors.

This series, *Black and White Meditations 1-23*, was made specifically for *The Fenris Wolf* in 2011, and in many ways presents the essence of Söderberg's highly admired psychic symmetries.

– Ed.

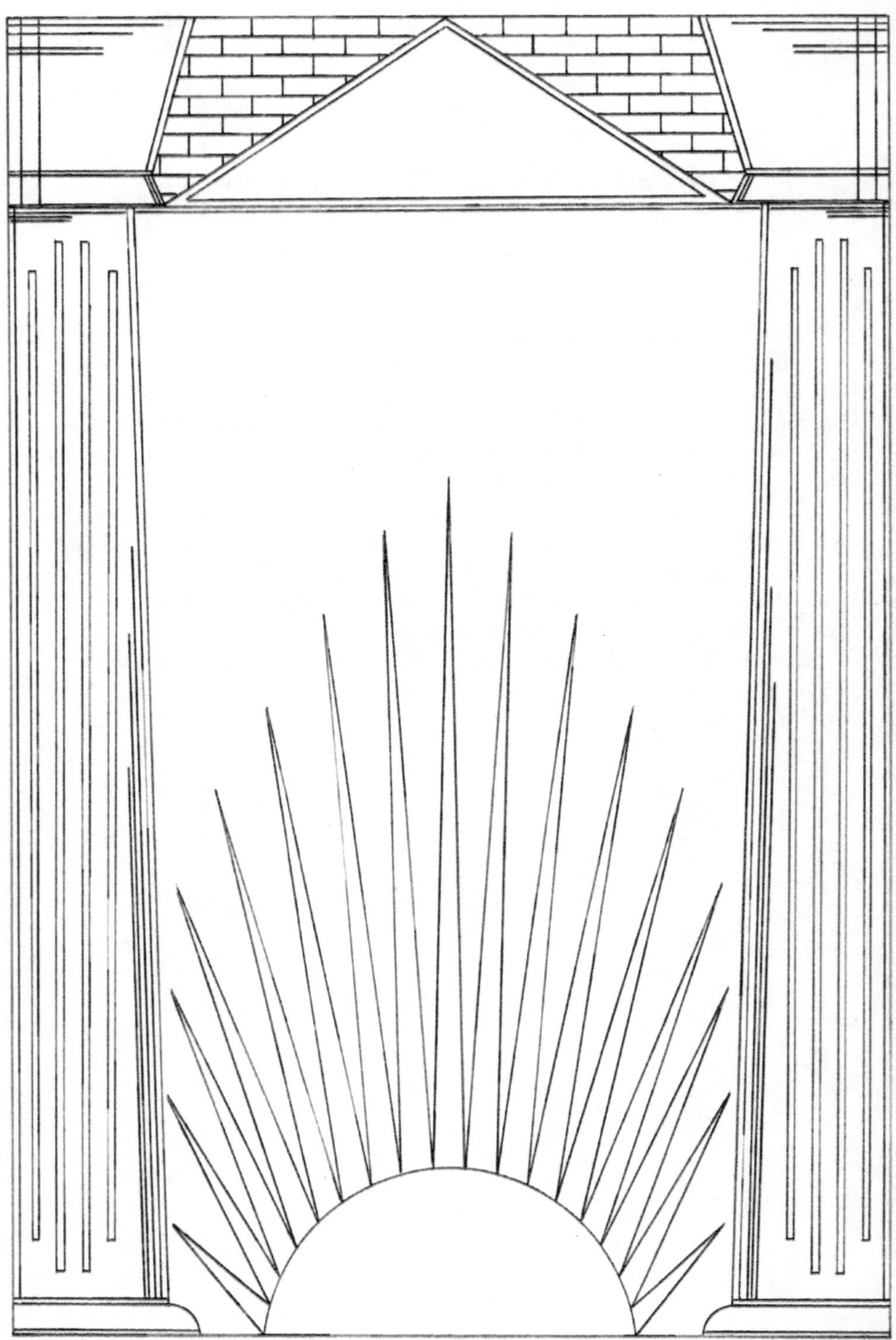

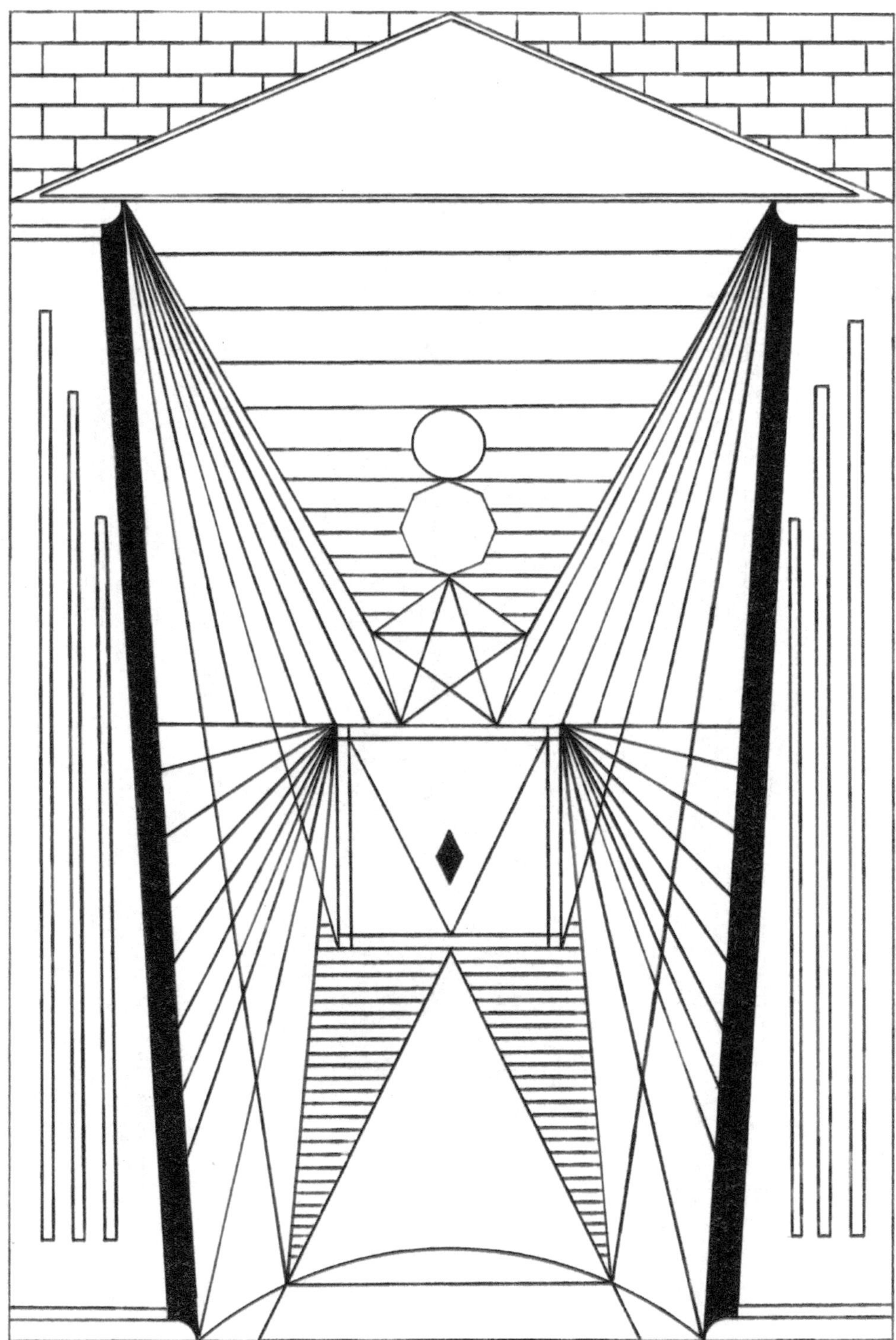

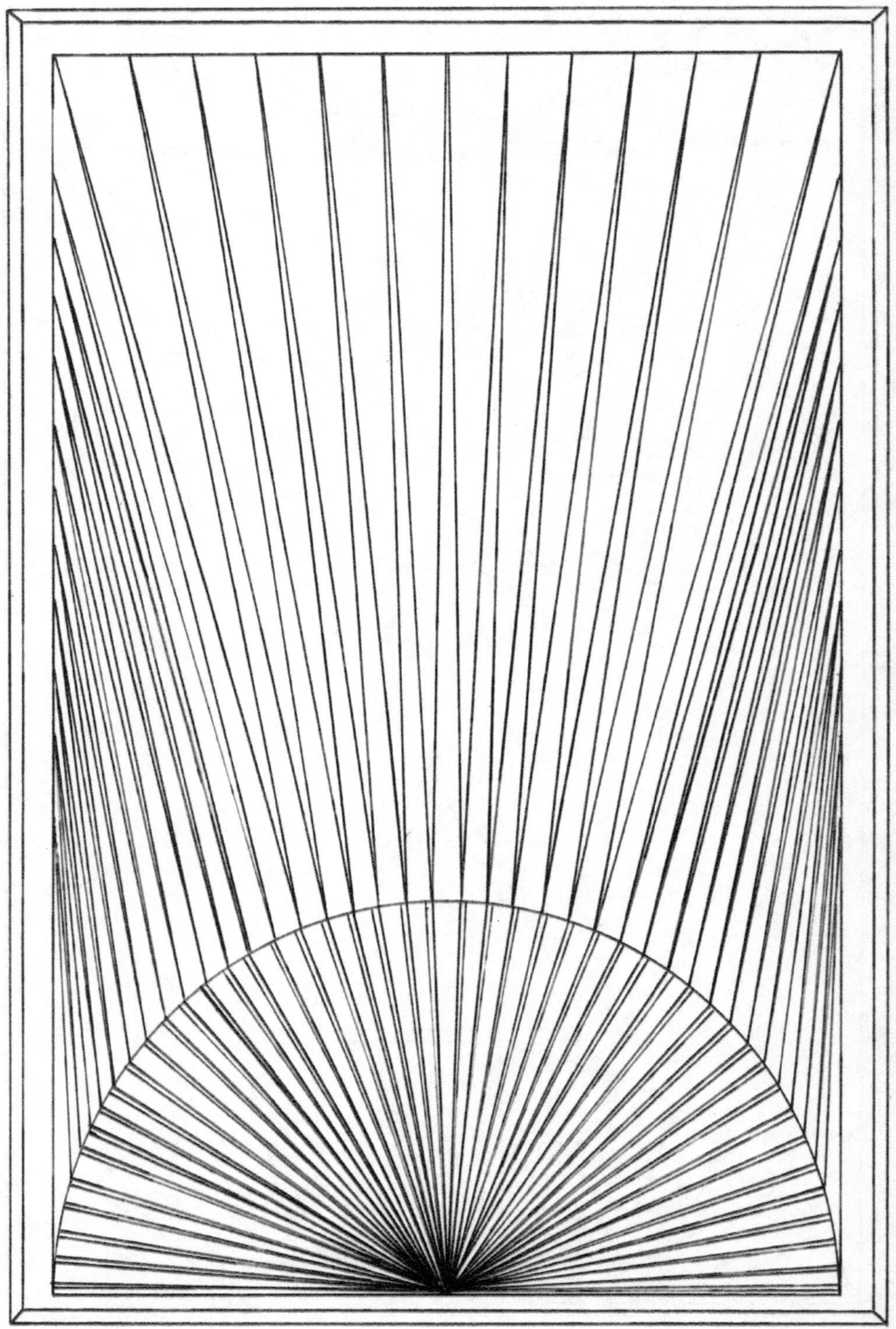

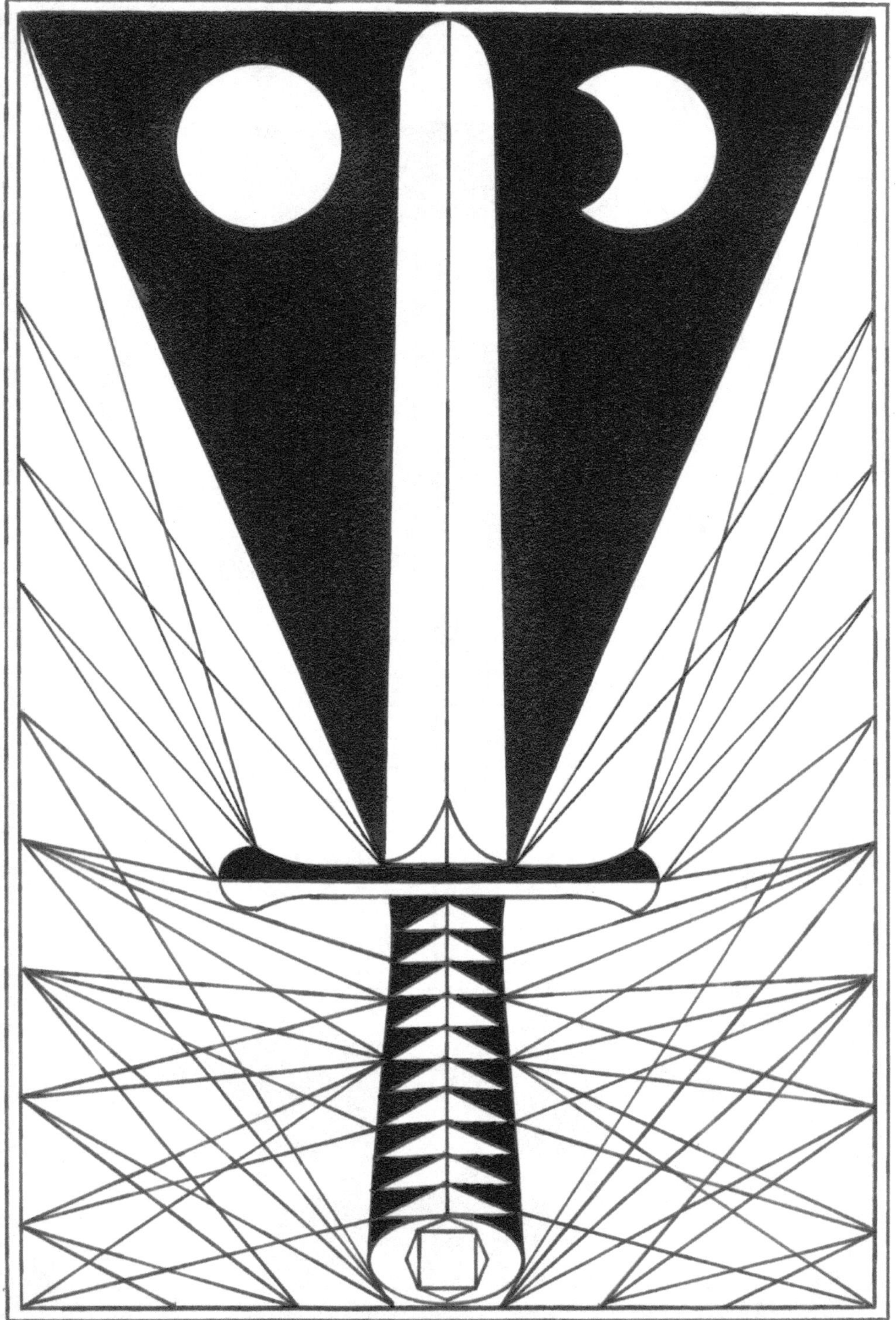

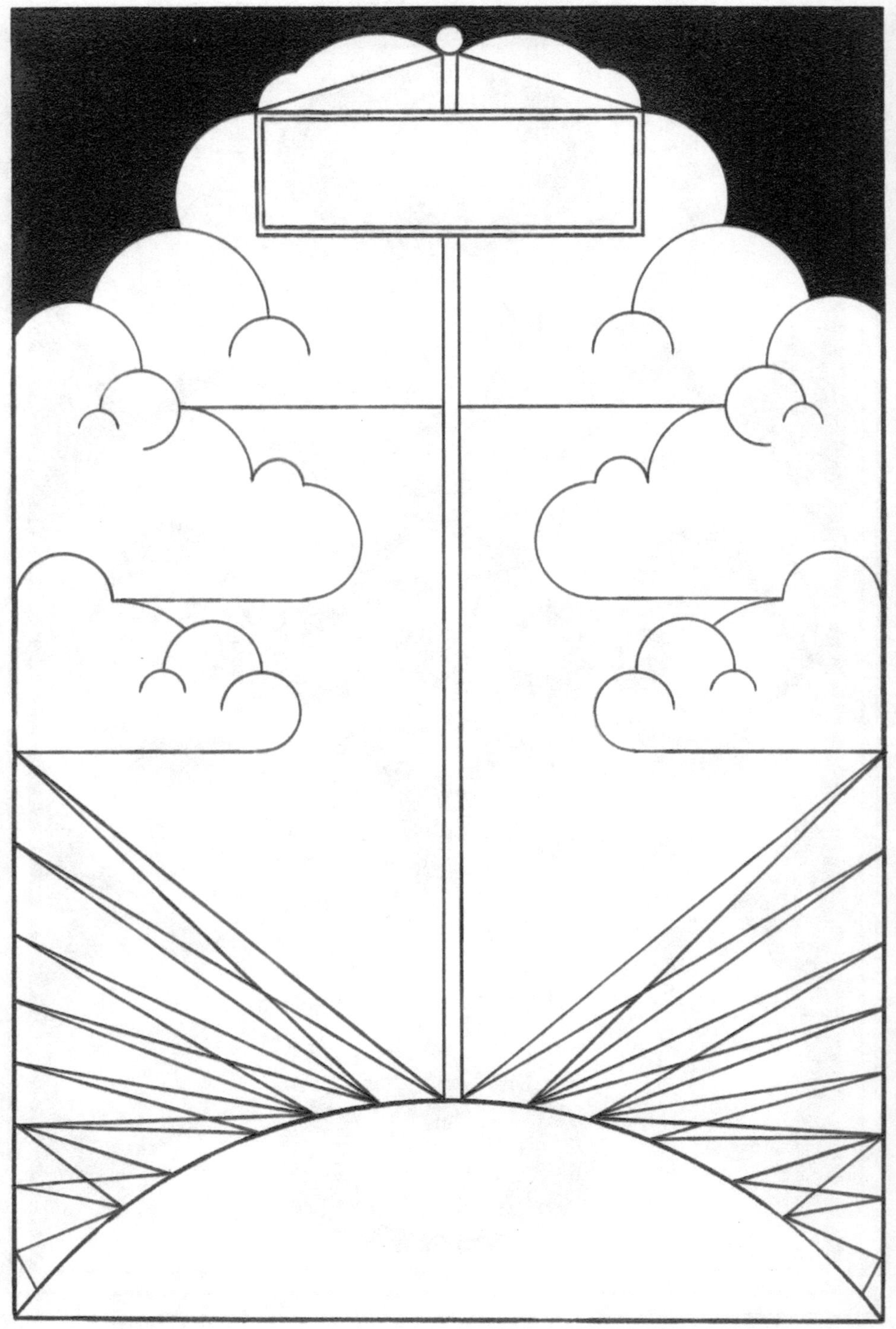

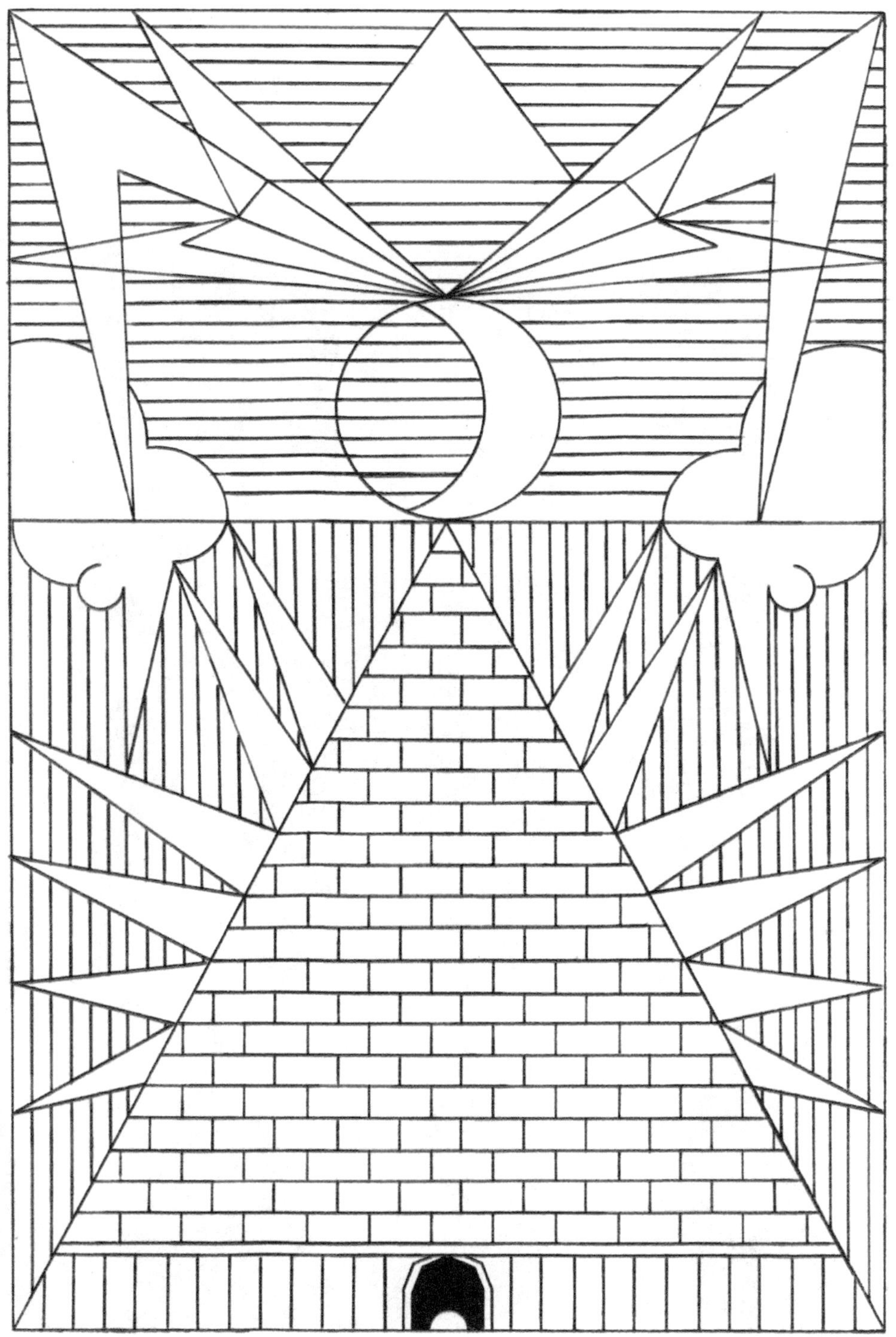

EVERY MAN AND WOMAN IS A STAR…

Peter H Gilmore

…Yet each is of a unique type and magnitude. But, how many have the wisdom to honestly recognize their particular role in the cosmos?

Each individual consciousness may be likened to a black hole, a form of gravity lens. But this lens is not one that focuses and pulls in the existing components of our material Universe; it is one that pulls in and focuses time. The present is an "event horizon," the eternal moment in which we live. It is the domain of our awareness. That which is whirling into the hole is the yet-to-be-realized future, the events that might happen. Amongst this nebular cloud of possibility (which is finite, with greater particles being more likely probabilities) are the Is-To-Be's that will become reality once they reach the present. These are the consciously desired future events established by the magical Will of a Satanic Sorcerer. Once these things pass through the Now, they fall into place in the linear progression that is the past of each individual. Motile possibility becomes actuality and is frozen as the past. History is thus made.

Most people's consciousness is continually focused upon their past—the events of which are like a row of tableaux on a foggy plain, receding into the distance and becoming less clear as the present moves further away. People are thus walking backwards into their future, each step a second in time. One second per second. They are thus rather blind to the events that will soon come into their Now and then be locked into their history as past experiences.

The Satanic Magician attempts to turn around, to be hyper-aware, so he is walking forward into the future, and before him is that swirling smoking mirror of the possibilities that his Will attempts to make actuality when they pass through the eternal Now. The Satanic Magician projects his visions for his Is-To-Be's upon this nebula, and they coalesce, begin to take form and definition of ever greater clarity as they move through the whirlpool and come closer to the event horizon. The important point is that the Satanic Magician's Is-To-Be's do not only go through his own event horizon, but through those of certain other individuals as well, to strengthen the reality his vision creates. This is a metaphorical perspective for viewing the mechanisms of Greater Magic.

Time travel is an attempt to look backward and bring those things that have passed and are distant in memory/time into sharper focus—to leapfrog over interim experiences and experience chosen past moments afresh. Some of these events have a tie to the eternal Now of consciousness, which allows that consciousness to jump immediately to these past tableaux, skipping all other less significant events in one's linear past. The cable that binds the consciousness to these ever-visible mountain peaks is emotion.

Emotion apparently comes from the "oldest" part of the brain (that which was earliest to evolve), and is an instantaneous instinctual deep evaluation of a situation that is being experienced in the Now. It adds what could be viewed as a "color" or tonality to that situation, so that it is eternally marked in the consciousness and is thus hierarchically ordered in the past.

A Satanic Magician can thus attempt consciously to emotionally "tint" or harmonize events from the linear past of others (which collectively is referred to as history). By making a "time travel journey" to them he may absorb them into his own past through the "virtual reality" experience which a rite of time travel can bring to this past event.

The gateway which one must open in order to toss his Is-To-Be's into another's gravity well is that oldest "reptile" part of the brain that can only be accessed via very strong emotion. In essence, the Greater Magic described by Dr. LaVey is a process wherein one creates these coalescences taken from possible future events and focuses them into the one you want to happen. You must feel the need for it to happen with the deepest emotions of which you are capable, and it is by giving vent to this need in the ritual chamber that you open that trap door and throw these Is-To-Be's out there into the future possibilities of other consciousnesses, to become a need that will fall into the gravity wells of individuals who have a bearing on the matter, who thus will feel compelled to move their purview according to your Will.

Of course, Lesser Magic is simply the day-to-day charm and glamour the Satanic Magician uses to manipulate people into doing what is wanted. In order to be successful at this, first he must be consummately skilled at reading people, to be able to determine what it is that they are seeking. But then, the Satanic Magician must be willing to role-play, to be a chameleon and an actor of exquisite skill to be able to push those buttons and throw the switches in that target individual to make him do as you desire.

Some jejune people balk at that, saying, "I want people to know the real me!" But they fail to realize that most people are far too crass to actually "see" them and too narcissistic to even care. They only see what they solipsistically project on others. The Satanist chooses to be protean, a person of mystery, and only those whom he really cherishes ever get to look behind the myriad masks to see the substance of the individual who sports them. Each Satanic Magician naturally adopts a general persona that is often reflective of chosen elements of his essence. He is satisfied with his knowledge of his personal nature and so has no fear in adopting different guises. He is emotionally secure enough not to care that many people will know him only as the selectively projected façade. And really, why should he care, if these folk have done as is required by his Will?

So my fellow sorcerers, let the rabble observe your passage through their constellations, noting your magnificent gravity and superior stellar magnitude while being dazzled into following the orbits you have plotted for them. The successful Satanic Magician has a presence that can sweep galaxies of lesser celestial objects in his wake. With his highly attuned awareness, he controls his own destiny by consciously selecting his desired future, motivating many satellites into roles supportive of his sublime vision of self-deification.

Barbarians at the Gates

Peter Grey

There is always a moment at the end of a civilisation when it becomes aware of the imminence of its own demise. A moment when the truth can no longer be concealed however immersive the illusions have become. The lie cannot be propagated that all is as it ever was. Progress is not a jackbooted march into forever. Celebrities are not demi-gods. Ever larger screens cannot prevent what is creeping into our peripheral vision. The seas are fished to extinction, industrial agriculture is destroying bio-diversity, the degrees creep towards burning and the mass of mankind are reduced to serfdom. Our future is looking more medieval and apocalyptic than we want to admit. Most of Homo Urbanus inhabit a photoshopped existence of corporate branded blandness. They have mistaken noise for signal. The grimoires offer a way out of this illusory world through the smoke and mirrors of spirit contact. This is something that can only make sense to magicians.

The resurgence of the grimoire tradition comes at a critical moment, and as conjurers we should view the publication of the grimoires as a magical act, with both consequences and causes in our physical world. There are portentious events which are being relayed to us by hard science as well as the hoarse voices of the spirits. The events are inexorably linked, and we should take heed of both and act accordingly.

Magicians have intellectually understood the Aeonic shift of precession, but only those with a connection to the living world can read the warning signs in nature, rather than twittering away their attention with digital blither, hunchbacked over laptops. Many of the spirits of the grimoires are nature spirits, lost gods, and the vital essence of threatened plants, species and environments. It is little wonder that they are communicating to us with urgency. The magician understands that you cannot replicate and release books without consequences. An entire spiritual ecology is thronging in the storm of pages, taking to quarter-bound leathery wings. All the spirits of the grimoires share a practical nature. They are here to get things done, and arriving in legions. The seals of the spirits are alive. In contrast, interrogating corporate logos with the vapid smartness of pop-occultism reveals only dead-eyed dollar signs.

An unprecedented number of small presses are publishing texts with intent, often at the behest of individual spirits rather than simply Mammon. In particular it is the grimoires, both medieval and modern, that are captivating the current generation of magicians. Texts which have been long unavailable are suddenly in idle hands. This means something, this reveals something, and we must be able to divine from these omens if we wish to count ourselves as magically aware.

The grimoires are becoming more physical, more manifest. They are built to last on acid-free paper and section sewn. Without an ISBN they cannot be tracked down and slaughter discounted on Amazon. They lurk in specialist bookshops and are issued direct by the printers and binders and writers. The artists and artisans have taken back control to produce objects of malevolent beauty. It is a revolutionary opposition to mass production that has arisen spontaneously and been embraced by practitioners who understand the magical nature of the book itself. The utilisation of the skills of the bookbinders and letterpresses are what we like to call *A Vision of William Morris in Hell*. It is very fittingly a return to the arts and crafts which the grimoire spirits promise to teach. The cherished book will endure longer even than the Scientologists who are sinking their archival bunkers deeper into the desert than Manson ever dreamed. The book becomes an ever more talismanic and magical object. It becomes dangerous again.

There is of course the suspicion that we are simply becoming gentlemen collectors, lured by the perversions of fine binding and the solitary pleasures of bibliophilia, that these are simply books, status objects taking the place of ritual prowess. So we must ask, are there magical changes occurring as a result of the grimoires being opened? Does this represent a decadent phase that follows the rush to xerox, zine and spiral bind of the Chaos scene?

The popular book is ceasing to exist as a physical object, it is a ghost echo of what a book should be. Industrial glue tenuously holds bleached tissue paper to flimsy cardstock. Production shifts to the Far East where slave labour is the law, and the pollution pours into our global water cycle. In many ways it is as cynical an object as all the other consumer un-durables, perishing as the pages turn, soon to be replaced by the anti-sensual zenith of kindle or i-book. But the paperback can also ignite with its short fuse, in the way that the bibliotheque bleu pamphlets did as they swept across Europe. We cannot afford snobbery. In the war of ideas, we must fight by any means necessary. The word must get out to those who are not already lit up.

The weight of correspondence and records of practice now being laid before us suggests that radical change is taking place. Something is coming through these books. The culturally persistent idea of the magical book is taking phoenix form out of the still warm ashes of the ages. We must not forget that these are books of knowledge which people have been burned for, and with good reason. They work.

Academia has in many cases led the work with grimoires, and we should acknowledge that. There are many appealing features for academics, a body of texts all out of copyright, the lure of the forbidden, and now that the subject is considered safely dead, corpses to pick over with impunity. The work of the academics has added to our understanding, though not necessarily to our knowledge. We should never trust sex manuals written by celibates. Many magicians now speak deferentially around the subject of grimoires for fear of being savaged by these little dogs. Worse still is the creeping academic dress-up of material by practitioners, and the criticism of received or inspired work. Who exactly are the experts here? Who is it that conjures these spirits? As necromancers our advice is that the academic pathologists should stand a little further back, as things can become more animated than their analysis admits. The grimoire tradition lives, and it evolves.

A collapse of certainty is occurring in more than the field of quantum physics. Capitalism and consumerism have passed the tipping point. Freedoms are being stripped from a passive populace. Magic is undergoing a resurgence in this unstable environment. Richard Dawkins would perhaps argue that this represents a rise of superstition against reason. A popular attempt to make sense of a post-modern world emptied of meaning. With this reading the grimoires in their garbled state are a fleeing back into unreasoning and infantile fantasy. But we are not the same as the cretins who argue against evolution and suggest god forged and buried fossils to test the faithful. We have found something compelling in the pages and practice of these neglected books, and it is something which science has not measured. The grimoires represent an ingress of spirits that man has sought communion with since the stone age and whose voices many have stopped hearing.

In one sense grimoires do offer certainty in that they answer the burning question of the neophyte; How do I do magic? The grimoires are replete with practical information from the ritual equipment to purification, prayers, invocatory formula and of course spells. But very quickly it becomes apparent that the texts need careful reading to extricate the hidden meanings and need to be understood in relation to each other. What is more, the grimoires are "results magic" they work in this world rather than being a "no-effect magic" swathed in obscure mystical bullshit. The spirits have tasks and expertise which, like the Nephilim, they will teach the daughters of men. If our society is indeed on the verge of collapse, whether catastrophic, or a sludgy descent as we pass peak oil, should we be surprised that the spirits are returning to instruct us in arts as diverse as horse thievery, handicrafts and masonry?

Grimoires have been the backbone of the magical revival, though ivy leaves and egyptiana can obscure these facts. Gerald Gardner's *Ye Bok* and the whole Wiccan tradition is founded upon the *Key of Solomon* (plus the Crowley cut and paste) rather than any direct witch lineage. The case can be made that the force and fire of both the Golden Dawn and Thelema is to be found in the *Lemegeton*, *Abramelin* and Enochian material rather than the Masonic play acting and Qabalah. Even *Liber AL Vel Legis* can be considered a grimoire of sorts, as it is a hodgepodge of recipes, spells, prayers and spirit communication.

Perhaps the importance of Thelema and the Golden Dawn will be finally judged to be in the grimoire material and the spirits which passed through them. Many magicians in the thrall of Crowley have pronounced the grimoires "Old Aeon" the kind of newspeak denunciation which shows very limited thinking. Crowley was of course indebted to the grimoires for the major milestones of his magical progress. He sought traffic with the spirits and produced grimoires of his own, with *Liber 231* gaining increasing notoriety and use by modern practitioners often in combination with the *Goetia* and/or *Le Dragon Rouge*. Here we can see the vitality of the modern grimoire tradition, as it embraces new material in its coils recognising it as its own. Individuals such as Thomas Karlsson and Johnny Jakobsson are to be commended in this respect, even if we do not always agree with their conclusions. Inclusivity has always been a mark of the grimoires, they are wild and voracious texts.

It is Kenneth Grant who intuitively grasped this and plunged with vertiginous wonder into the *Typhonian Trilogies*. His central tenet of direct spirit contact is in complete accordance with the grimoires. His green language readings and creative etymology may be criticised, but they demonstrate the skills a magician needs to decipher the often deceptive simplicity of the grimoires. As a result the numerically small Typhonians have produced the most creative occultism post-Crowley. No magical book is ever written straight, or without the spirits whispering in the scribe's ear. Grant added material, in his case Massey, Lovecraft et al and in doing so was true to the grimoires, which are a palimpsest, that is, they are never written on virgin parchment however hard you scrape. In one sense the grimoires Lovecraft dreamt of and Grant made flesh are a longing for a reconnection with the taufer books of the European tradition, and they have manifested.

What Grant and Crowley missed were the full array of grimoire texts rather than their butchered remnants wrapped in greaseproof paper for us by AE Waite and Idries Shah. We are in a unique, if perilous position in history where the texts are available, and they make fascinating reading. The working notes and hand copied mistakes of our forebears can teach us more than the reductive filter of the Golden Dawn. Though we can and indeed must take modern influences, we would do well to remember that what distinguishes the spirits of the grimoires is that they have been extensively worked with. These well worked spirits include a trinity of Lucifer, Beelzebuth and Satan, as well as the demonic divine feminine in Astaroth. We cannot forget that the Devil remains as ever the patron of the printing press and that as publishers we are doing his work. This is our Western tradition of spirit work, not something we have to hunt for in Haiti. The same spirits crop up across the texts and with name, seal and description can be called and worked with in many ways rather than the scream and demean method which is (wrongly) seen to characterise Solomonic magic. The operating system is something which has been bolted onto the spirit lists and can and must be upgraded, just as new spirits are added when we encounter them.

The grimoire revival shows that the Golden Dawn era of magic has ended. There has been a loss of credibility in the claims of exclusive knowledge cloistered within the orders. The secrets have been published, and not only that, a whole avalanche of material which was not available to the Victorian occult revival is ours. We no longer believe in a world teacher, whether Krishnamurti or Crowley or Christ. The sex magic of William Blake now seems more developed than that of the OTO. The grimoires are enabling individuals to practice magic by going direct to the spirits rather than to be imparted the Hebrew alphabet by the concealers of wisdom. The orders are deflating in numbers and relevance like a rather sorry looking colostomy bag on a dead patient. The knowledge is in the books, if you are cunning enough to get it out.

The search for magical authenticity has begun again, and it is leapfrogging both Crowley and the Golden Dawn to the medieval and renaissance mages. Here we have a lineage of lone necromancers, renegade priests and copyists working with the magical books they have tracked down and secreted away. There are examples of both christian and diabolists, conservatives and radicals, aristocrats and agriculturalists all using the same material. In fact, the same bewildering diversity of practitioners as there are spirits. What we do not find are ten degree stepping-stone orders, and any edicts of secrecy are there to prevent the imprisonment or state sanctioned murder of the practitioners. The game has changed.

In part this leapfrogging and need for authenticity explains the popularity of the Cultus Sabbati and their faux archaic style. They are knowingly creating modern grimoires from both appropriated folklore and their imaginations. Though to be applauded for their aesthetic values, the mannered style of expression they have adopted can seem out of step with the cunning traditions they reference which will have spoken and written simply, even when concealing meanings.

There is a stylistic shift in modern writers on magic towards expressing themselves in grimoire terms. Though often carrying elements of Crowley with them such as the titular use of 'Liber', which in itself shows how magical texts accumulate past knowledge and carry it with it like junk DNA to be deciphered by esoteric scientists in the future. Many of the modern works are acts of self-enchantment and highly personal systems rather than group orientated, undoubtedly this references Austin Osman Spare, but it is also the method of the classical grimoires. It is a multiplicity of individuals whose work is making the difference to the practice of modern magic and the multiplicity of spirits they traffic with.

Intriguingly, a study of the grimoires leads us back to the very roots of magical practice. Jake Stratton-Kent makes a highly convincing case that the structure, format and even spirits of the *Grimorium Verum*, a relatively late period text, can be traced back to the *Graeco Magical Papyri* and the figure of the Goes. My own (as yet) unpublished work with the *Goetia* confirms this. The splinters I have encountered in the *Goetia* contain the missing elements of Western magic, such as devotional spirit work, ancestor worship, a reconnection with the dead, full possession, and a history which Christianity attempted to erase and effectively demonised.

The search for authenticity also comes from a sense of cultural dislocation, the impermanence and uncertainty already discussed. Magic has always looked back to a mythic past. What intrigues me is the extent to which it is colliding with the now. McKenna's Omega Point, RAW's information doubling, the Cup of Babalon, even the 2012 hypothesis are all describing an event which we are witnessing unfolding. The return or the overlap of the grimoires is one aspect of this collision of magical realities. Perhaps this is our last chance to talk with and listen to the spirits again.

HALLELUJAH

John Duncan

How am I – with each attempt to go forward, I ask myself why. In my heart I feel the need for a companion, a lover, and by now I know that I will cause whoever comes to suffer. So my New Year Resolution is to live alone until this nightmare ends. Which I truly hope will be soon, in one way or another. At this point, I really don't care how. Out of habit, I make a sustained effort to be polite to everyone – despite the ridicule of friends and the hostility of strangers, which the books I read tell me I create... Each step takes me more deeply into the Nightmare, someone else's, some "higher authority" that by now seems more lost than I. In my dreams I hold an Israeli Uzi machine pistol in my hands. After destroying a wall covered in wallpaper with Rorschach patterns made of my blood, I point between my eyes and fire with joy...

Perhaps this is "letting go"...

We'll see.

In the meantime, I continue moving forward. Trying to laugh, especially in front of the mirror, at "negativity" – or is it "reality'"? – and above all at the concept of the power of prayer. I pray to die, certain that they will never be heard and that sooner or later it will happen anyway: the swine that we call "god" incapable of anything apart from eating everything within reach... It will happen when it happens. Hallelujah.

In the meantime, I try to respond to the Muse and support friends as well as possible – "friends" in the most naïvely optimistic sense imaginable. When the end does come, I hope to be ready – to laugh at the end of this suffering and delusion, at those who come to fight among themselves over the things they find here.

Happy New Year,

John

ALLELUIA

John Duncan

Come sono – con ogni tentativo di fare un passo avanti, mi chiedo perche. Sento dal cuore il bisogno di aver una compagna, un'amante, e ormai so che la faccio soffrire chiunque chi viene. Quindi il risoluzione di 2006 è di vivere completamente solo finche finisce quest'incubo. Spero proprio presto, in un modo o l'altro. A questo punto, non me ne frega come. D'abitudine, provo di essere gentile con tutti – nonostante i ridi dagli amici (Morbin) e l'ostilità dagli sconosciuti, che i libri che leggo dicono che creo io... Ogni passo va più profondo ad un incubo, un'incubo d'un altro, un "higher authority" che ormai sembra anche più perso che sono io. Nei i miei sogni ho una pistola automatica israeliani Uzi in mani che, dopo aver distruto un muro coperto dell'immagine del mio sangue in forma di wallpaper in desegno Rorschach, punto fra le miei occhi e sparo con gioia...

Forse questo è "letting go"...

Vedremo.

Nel frattempo, continuo fare i passi. Provo ridere, particolarmente allo specchio, alla "negatività" – o forse è realtà? – e inanzitutto al concetto della potenza della preghiera. Pregho di morire, sicuro che non ascoltarà comunque e che primo o dopo succederà: quello stronzo che chiamiamo "dio" incapace di fare altro che mangiare tutto davanti... Succederà quando succede, e basta. Alleluia.

Nel frattempo provo di rispondere alla musa e sostenere gli amici lo meglio possibile – "amici" nel definizione più naivamente ottimistico immaginabile. Quando arriva il fine, spero che sarò pronto – di ridere alla fine di questa sofferenza e delusione, a tutti che vengono di lottare fra loro sulle cose che trovano qui.

Buon anno,

John

Democracy Is Dying of AIDS

Ramsey Dukes

I have a problem with my immune system. I detest its politics.

When a virus enters my body, it is only doing what any living thing would do, looking for a comfortable environment in which to multiply. But my immune system goes into "red alert" – raising a fever, violent sneezing, runny nose, local inflammation and all the reactionary responses of a military regime. If a few cells in my body break out from their daily drudgery and decide to do something creative, they will be immediately ostracised, cut off and ejected as a potential cancer in the body corporate. Some day I'll need hip replacements – my legs will really need them and yet they will only be passed by my antibodies if sweetened by a significant shipment of drugs. I cannot even enjoy a cup of coffee on an empty stomach without a severe purging from my over-vigilant system.

It is not easy to point a finger, for the immune system comprises a highly complex symbiotic culture of local interests dispersed throughout my body, and yet I can identify a common thread of xenophobia, dogmatism, reactionary values and the militarism of a police state linking all those parts. I hate its politics and detest the way that, just like a military state, the immune system demands enemies to keep it from degenerating. Bored soldiers will inevitably get drunk and find some joint to trash – and in my case it is the joints of my fingers. Arthritic auto-immune attacks on the hands of a writer are unwelcome, and I resent them.

So, am I saying that I do not like my immune system?

No! Please don't get me wrong. As a relatively healthy 65 year old I respect and deeply appreciate everything it has done for me. When I witness old friends and those around me suffering the torments of cancer or a defective immune system I am heartily grateful for my own vigilante force and its relentless purging of so many invaders and rebels. Like a quiet white South African neighbourhood in the apartheid days, the health of my body owes more to border patrols than political correctness. I cannot help feeling grateful, but still don't like its politics.

I do however have a sneaking admiration – and it is hard to admit this in polite society – for the HIV virus. We have all tasted rejection at some time in our lives, but the feeling is especially poignant for a little known author. Haven't I yearned at times to be able to outwit the publishing industry's own immune system, to break through its defences and infect some editor with a madness that will force them to reach into the reject bin, pull out my manuscript and scream "This is brilliant! A seminal work of genius! How much can we afford for a truly headline-grabbing advance!"?

I admire the HIV virus because, for those of us who detest the politics of the old regime, it stirs up dreams of revolution, creative new beginnings and accelerated evolution as the barriers of prejudice and conformity are broken down. And yet, as with so many rebellions, I am appalled at what eventually follows.

I need to explore this ghastly paradox, and yet I cannot bear to explore further within me, for I am a little squeamish about bodily functions. I wish my body could be as some vegetable – an apple or pumpkin – just flesh all through without all those smelly internal organs. So I'll turn my attention to society's immune systems instead.

Democracy is a major player in a society's immune system, evolved in ancient Greece to keep tyranny at bay. But virus evolve fast and even from early times new types of tyrant have exploited the democratic process itself to get into power – Hitler being the prime example of our times. But democracy is still only one factor within a highly complex system.

Britain in the 1950s was a severely wounded nation, convalescing from the sickness of war. But we had our pride and would boast that "Hitler could never have happened here". At the time, I do believe we were right, for Britain still had an exceptionally strong immune system then. But 20 years later Thatcher came into power under the same "law and order" banner used by Hitler decades earlier, and we began to witness how HIV works its wretched spell.

No, we did not actually see it, for the virus works by misdirection. The very broad front of any immune system requires an equally broad attack, and that calls for a campaign that remains unrecognised until too late. Misdirection leads the eye away by raising popular campaigns elsewhere.

Although integrated over a broad front, the assault must be analysed part by part. Begin with the trade unions, the part of the immune system that monitors and confronts the many potential tyrannies of management and working conditions. Of course the unions had the usual vices of any immune system – xenophobia, militancy, reaction etc – and it was easy to find stories of highly motivated workers being forced to "work to rule" and so on. So it was not difficult to win support, especially in the management classes, for union reform and, when that invoked the expected militant reaction, to use that as an excuse to escalate the attack into "breaking the unions".

But why was this allowed by the working classes? Because they were too busy cheering on campaigns elsewhere in the system. There was plenty to attack in the City with the stock market's version of the "closed shop", the old boy network and walls of discretion. Its politics stank just as foully, and yet it takes the wisdom of hindsight to recognise that the old boy network and public school values did offer some measure of immune response to the sort of excesses that led to economic collapse once finance was de-regulated and opened to the wide (and not so old) boys. And the City itself was too busy applauding the breaking of the unions to offer much resistance.

Newspapers also play a key immune role as a watchdog against corruption. But in the late 70s the media were paid off with favours from the government in return for their support. While Murdoch's and Thatcher's systems each congratulated themselves that they were winning control of the other, in retrospect it is clear that both were succumbing to the same viral infection.

How parents cheered when it was suggested that the waywardness of youth was not their fault at all, but could all be blamed on a defiant teaching establishment stuck with discredited educational theories from the 1960s – a part of the immune system that aimed to protect society by teaching its members to think instead of repeat by rote. So Britain let her schools and culture of education be discredited because it was too busy applauding the assault on single mothers as the true cause of all ills...

And so the assault on the immune system progressed. Each part of the whole such an easy target, so easy to win support for an attack on its many vices – the closed shops, the elitism and militant reactionary tendencies. No part of Britain's immune system was above criticism from the reformers and yet, as a whole, it was what had once allowed us to say "Hitler could never happen here" and it did keep many other such diseases at bay. The system, so needing to be reformed and revitalised, was instead eroded or dismantled until even the very thing it existed to protect and maintain, namely "society", was itself dismantled and deemed to be an illusion.

For those who did not heed the longer term implications of the neocon, neolib, Thatcher virus, it was fun while it lasted. So many rotten reactionary institutions being broken up or rendered impotent, that it was all too easy to overlook what they had evolved to protect and what they were created to resist.

After the revolution, after HIV has done its work, then comes full blown AIDS – a new government from a party that had once been part of the immune system but now itself upholding the values of the invading virus. Legal processes against corruption are now subject to financial interests, and the case against arms dealer corruption was quietly shelved by the Prime Minister.

Look further afield and we see so many other establishments in their dying throes. In South Africa the very antibodies created to fight corruption are used to lever the more competent or scrupulous operatives from their posts. There used to be a Buddhist saying "If the finger is pointing at the Moon, look at the Moon, not the finger"; in politics it should become "if a finger is pointing, just look at the pointer". If society is not actually sick it is only because it no longer exists.

I feel angry. To be more specific I feel reactionary, militant, dogmatic and something akin to a form of xenophobia against all ideas alien to common humanity.

I would appear to have embodied the very politics that I so detest. I am no more part of society, for I am an individual – and yet the immune system that once stood to defend society has found a refuge within my soul.

This paradox is widespread. We live in a time when, in an inversion of the Platonic ideal, the masses are becoming more ethical whilst the rulers grow increasingly corrupt.

Fellow rebels – should such exist – let us unite!

THE TECHNOLOGY OF CIVILIZATION X
AND THE ASTRAL MACHINE

Timothy O'Neill

Illustrations by Rev Elder Mech

Legends of an incredibly ancient and wise civilization existing tens of thousands of years before the Sumerians, Babylonians, Egyptians or Greeks have a long pedigree, reaching back to Plato's story of Atlantis in the *Timaeus* and Greek legends of Hyperborea. The Egyptians spoke of others who had preceded them; the "Gods" who had built such astonishing anomalies as the Great Pyramid and the Sphinx. The ancient Egyptians understood that they had no ability to construct such things.

Beginning in the 1960s, Erich Von Däniken and then Zecharia Sitchin among many others believed that the wonders of this very ancient world were built by or under the influence of extraterrestrials. Atlantis became a spaceport and Hyperborea a landing pad.

Long before the ancient astronaut thesis, during the 1920s, the legends of incredibly ancient Lemuria, the Atlantis of the Pacific, were advanced in a series of books by James Churchward. Richard S. Shaver's tales of Elder Gods, ancient Mantong languages and degenerate Deros operating Elder God ray machines emerge from the atavistic strata of a time around 12,000 B.C. His tales of Elder Gods leaving Earth because of deadly radiation from the Sun speak to worldwide myths of primeval chaos and the Wars of the Gods. He refers specifically to their machines and rays, their control of human genetics and their manipulation of flesh to evolve more quickly. H.P. Lovecraft's Mythos speaks of creatures so ancient as to defy imagination with battles between more human Elder Gods and eldritch indescribable Great Ancient Evil ones. Charles Fort collected clippings of anomalies revealing technological objects far too old to have possibly existed and of an archeology depicting a mankind very different from the one in the textbooks. In his books, there were giants in those days. The legends persist and have been growing every year.

Most of these myths refer to an alien element entering Earth's sphere of influence to plant the seed of such incredible accomplishments and this is by no means impossible. Yet, for the sake of our argument, let's assume that Mankind had the wherewithal to invent an advanced technology, paleo-physics and mathematics on their own 40,000 years ago. That is a staggering enough thesis without bringing in Serpent People from Ophiuchus!

The growing evidence of a very advanced civilization existing some 40,000 years ago hinges heavily on one extraordinary anomaly in the history of archeology. The core evidence for this civilization exists most strongly in Egypt, the traditional source of all Mysteries. Various theories of the use of the Great Pyramid of Giza as a huge machine to produce power have been advanced by various writers within the past two decades (Malinkowski, *Ancient Egypt 39,000 BCE*, Farrell, *The Giza Death Star* and Dunn, *The Giza Power Plant*). The nature of that power has been speculated to be maser driven[1], water driven and sound driven. The uses of that enormous power have been suggested as a vast interplanetary weapon (Farrell) an agriculture enhancing and evolutionary machine tied to the entire complex of Nile Delta Pyramids (Malinowski) and more of a question mark for Dunn, who entertains the idea of beaming power by microwave to an orbiting spaceship… Implied to be one operated by the Egyptians!

The core hypothesis of all of these researchers has been that we do not need to seek for extraterrestrials to explain an advanced technological culture in the far distant past. The Megalithic Elders' knowledge of Nature's forces and Sacred Geometry were sufficient to explain their tremendous achievements. Along similar lines, a group of "super-yogis" in the Indus Valley existing tens of thousands of years ago has been advanced (Geoffrey Ashe, *The Ancient Wisdom*) as the source of the advanced technology described in the *Mahabharata*, with its Mercury-powered Vimanas or flying discs. It was their spiritually based knowledge of the secrets of Nature that allowed them to create such mastery over gravity and the elements.

When we speak of the Elder technology we are speaking of a technology that consisted of stone, metals, crystals and minerals, water and light, rather than smoking combustion engines and Earth-depleting machines. It was in many ways far more advanced than what we can achieve with our engines and motors. The Elders lived by a core sense of harmony with the subtle electro-fluid that fills all space and time: the celestial "fire" of Heraclitus. They understood space, time, matter, light and mathematics in ways that we still do not and they were able to sustain that vision for tens of thousands of years. They created a resonant harmony with Nature and that was their vision… Working under Nature's guidance rather than conquering her like some harlot. There was a deep respect for the Feminine aspect of Nature among the Elders and that translated into finding ways to enhance Nature's own restorative and evolutionary forces.

It struck me, while reading these books, that the core Science, Art and Occultism of Civilization X that I am describing above was really one thing and not three. The split did not happen until much later, after the descent into barbarism that signaled the end of the Elders. There are worldwide legends of a great war of the gods, which may have involved human colonies on nearby planets in our solar system. That may be the cause

---

1. MASER = Microwave Amplification by Stimulation Emission of Radiation, like a Laser but operates in the microwave range, rather than visible light.

From *Wikipedia*: "The maser is based on the principle of stimulated emission proposed by Albert Einstein in 1917. When atoms have been put into an excited energy state, they can amplify radiation at the proper frequency. By putting such an amplifying medium in a resonant cavity, feedback is created that can produce coherent radiation."

The theory is that the King's Chamber is geometrically structured to create such a resonant cavity and that it was producing coherent microwave emissions. It is difficult to imagine what they might have been used for. I much prefer the theory that the Pyramids were used to stimulate water from the Nile to be used for irrigation and agriculture. It is simpler and makes much more sense. Viktor Schauberger, the "Water Wizard" of Austria, demonstrated that water can carry intensified life-force under certain conditions.

of the end or it may be the simple decline of a very old culture. Until we put all of the pieces of this jigsaw puzzle together, it will remain a mystery.

I strongly believe that the unitary wisdom of Civilization X survived into antiquity and then into our own era. It was disguised by riddles and conundrums, but it is all there for those with eyes to look. We know it as Alchemy, the Circular Science; the work of children.

Now the spiritually oriented ideas of Alchemy and Technology seem to be far apart. How is it that we can link the alchemical idea of enhancing evolutionary forces with the technology of Civilization X and what did that technology look like?

I. THE IDEA OF MACHINES

> "A machine is a device that uses energy to perform some activity. In common usage, the meaning is that of a device having parts that perform or assist in performing any type of work. A simple machine is a device that transforms the direction or magnitude of a force." (Wikipedia)

The word "machine" is derived from the Latin word "machina," which ultimately derives from the Greek "mechos" which means, "expedient or remedy." There is almost a medical sense to this, in which natural forces are re-ordered to produce results above and beyond what Nature Herself can create. At root, then, the use of forces existing in Nature to better Nature's own ways are at the root of the Alchemical and trans-formative Science of the Paleoancient Technologies. There is a sense of unforced advancement along normative paths rather than of a manipulative desire to master through the imposition of force.

The Elder sense of machine did not focus upon intricate moving parts or complex assemblies. A machine could be as simple as two different types of stone placed together under tremendous pressure to create a piezoelectric effect. It could be as simple as creating a simple suction pump to circulate water around specific geometric causeways. Researchers have proven that sheer mass of certain types of stone can create unique electromagnetic properties in the surrounding landscape.

That Civilization X could move these stones is one of the greatest mysteries. Some of the stones at Giza weigh 200 tons. Perhaps the miracle of Ed Leedeskalnins' Coral Castle in Florida teaches us that one man with a unique intuitive understanding of electromagnetic fields and where the center of mass of a large stone is located could move huge megalithic stones by hand. It is science, but it is a science still not understood by official culture. It won't be understood until certain erroneous ideas in Physics are corrected and that may take a generation or two more! James Clark Maxwell's original Quaternion equations hold many mysteries for those with eyes to see! (See Joseph P. Farrell's *Secrets of the Unified Field*)

The Great Pyramid as a Machine for evolution is not as preposterous an idea as it might seem, as contaminated by New Age fol-de-rol as it has been. The very word for alchemy, "Khem" derives from the rich black alluvial soil of the Nile Delta. Malinowski's idea that the Great Pyramid transmitted enhanced subtle energy, aka "prana", back to

the other pyramids in the Nile Delta to increase agricultural production rings true with research that has shown that megalithic monuments the world round tend to gather electromagnetic forces that enhance seed growth in the surrounding countryside. The initial work of Alchemy is Spagyricism, the work of plants.

As is clear from the preceding, the definition of "Machine" is evolving and dependent upon advances in technology and science. There is a simple core idea that a machine is a device, something designed, although we can also speak of machines occurring naturally. In a sense, the entire Cosmos is an engine, shifting heat and cold in order to produce motion and change. The essential idea is that of work being done through the application of energy.

2. THE INFINITE CONTINUUM OF MACHINES

We are all familiar with machines in the physical plane of existence. We can also speak of physical machines whose purpose is to tap into subtle forms of energy. Most spiritual traditions have the concept of such subtle energies, calling them Prana, Chi, Vital Life Force, Aether, Vril, Zero Point Energy etc. There have been many who have sought to tap into these forces in order to achieve access to infinite supplies of clean energy. Many have found this energy to behave like an electric fluid or fire filling all Space and have sought inspiration in the behavior of Water in order to understand how it operates. Many have felt that Water itself carries large amounts of this subtle energy.

Designing machines based upon this principle has met with mixed success, since the subtle energy field of the operator has been the key factor. Operators with strong fields have great success, those with weak fields fail. What I am most interested in is the next stage in the concept of machines; machines which operate purely in the subtle fields and which have no physical basis whatsoever. This kind of machine involves a different and

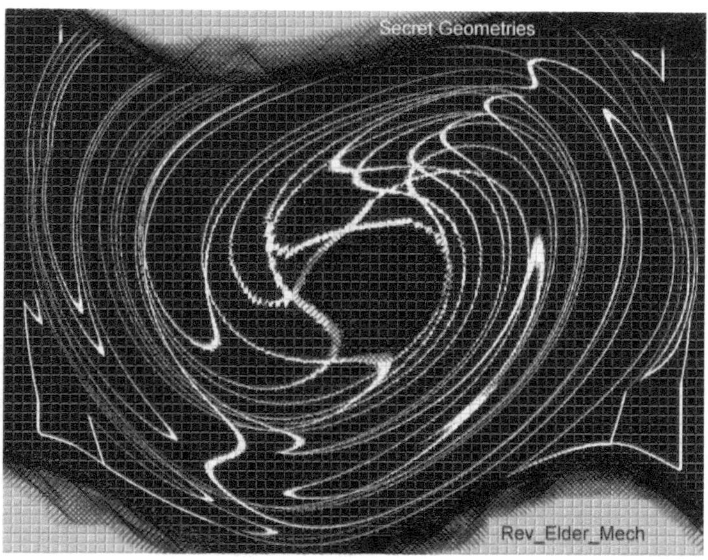

more open relationship between machine and operator.

One of the key concepts of Chaos Magick was the creation of "Servitors," computer-program like entities whose sole purpose is to accomplish some goal in the subtle planes which would hopefully reflect back into the Physical World. It is the operator's intentionality, energy and focus which provide the servitor with their motive power and direction. This is a way of thinking about astral machines which provides us with an insight into how alive and self-willed they may become.

THE THEORY OF THE ELDER MACHINES

There is an infinite continuum of machines, filling all time and space, some accessible to certain operators and some not. They operate upon all levels of existence.

There are three axes of defining force that allow these machines to operate:

1. The Continuum from Sub-Physical Matter to Monadic Matter
2. The Continuum from Creativity to Destruction
3. The Continuum from Space to Time

Each is infinite but can be accessed at various x, y, z type coordinates where all three intersect.

Each Elder Machine will exist at such a coordinate point, which defines its purpose and intention. Not every coordinate contains an existing machine. Some exist only in idea and some cannot exist for various reasons. So, while there are a large number of possible machines, not all possibilities are active or ever will be.

In Alchemy, Tantra, Kriya and Taoist Yoga (all survivals from the Elder age) we learn that it is the rotation of prana or life-force around an axis that mirrors the rotation of

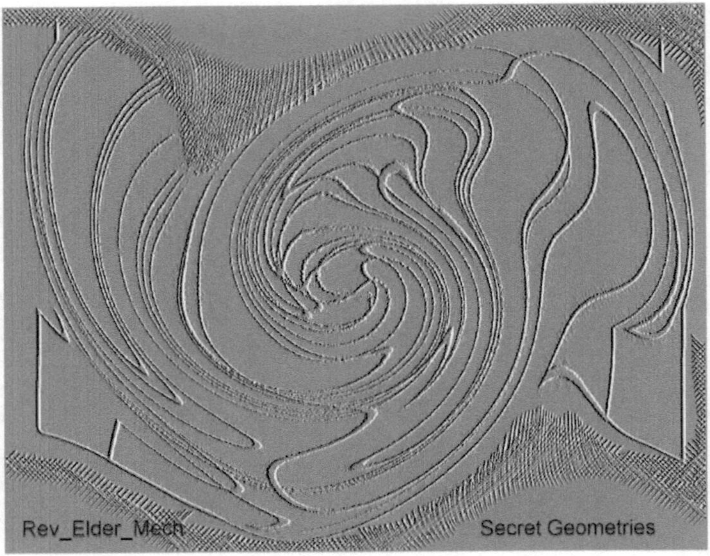

the Earth around the Sun which produces change and transformation. Each year on Earth is a step in universal evolution, closer by an infinitesimal amount to the ultimate goal of full realization. The Elder Science sought to speed this process... The source of Shaver's ideas about the Growth Rays and Stim Rays! Modern Pulp Sci-Fi meets the real Elder Tradition!

The waterfall or swiftly moving current with its eddies and currents is another model of pranic force moving in an enhanced way to create power and change. Viktor Schauberger studied water deeply and came to some amazing conclusions about its ability to tap into forces of Nature that are normally invisible and unreachable. He believed that the Null Point was accessible through highly rapidly circulating water in a pump. The first thing we learn in the Rosicrucian teachings is that water is the key to advancement and evolution. It contains a particular pranic force that can heal, change, evolve and teach.

Alchemy is the science of taking an impure, low vibrational rate and turning it into a highly scintillating healing, evolving force and this is the very basis of the science of the Elders.

The pranic energy is purified at the same time that it is strengthened. Such an alchemical machine is defined by four elements: the input, the rotary mechanism, output and the operator. It is the operator's intention and will that are the key to the successful operation of the device. When John Worrell was building his multi-ton machines that operated off the energy in one teaspoon of water, it was discovered that the machines would only work while he was the operator. He was so tuned into the machines that no one else could possibly operate them.

On earth, pranic machines such as radionics, null-point and the mechanisms responsible for the incredible operation of UFOs are restricted by the laws of physics to lower amplifications of the rotational cycle. On the Astral plane, those restrictions are

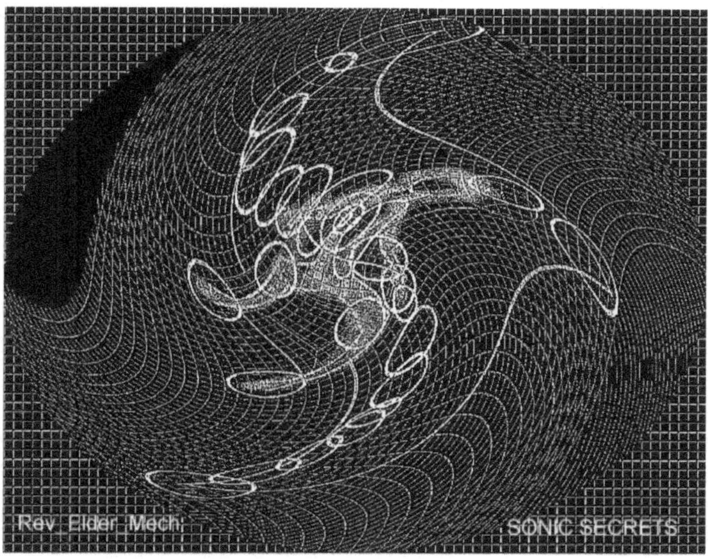

lifted tremendously and then even higher rates are possible in the Causal and Monadic planes. Machines are much easier to build in the Astral than the higher planes, so we will focus on that aspect here.

Design

The simplest Elder Machine is an alchemical pump, designed to enhance the circulation of prana in such a way that it is moving much more quickly than normally possible in a physical machine in a focused way, thus achieving great creative potential force.

Using our knowledge of astral matter in the sense that it operates as a higher form of our physical light and electro-dynamic fluid, we can see that our earthly models need to be highly modified for such a device to work on the Astral Plane.

As with any pump, there must be an intake, a device for collecting the impure light/electro-dynamic living energy (aka Prana). While on Earth we are limited by the laws of materials, the Astral is ruled more by the realm of ideas and geometry pure and simple. We can tune our input to specific geometries possible only on the Astral Plane to "catch" precisely the energy we wish to work with.

Our second design element is the rotor, which controls and fuels the tremendously high rotational rates of the circulating prana. The key element here is geometry. It is the specific harmonic geometrical forms that produce the alchemical change. Without a geometry based upon Nature and the Divine, we are working in the dark upon infernal machines! We are not limited to the simple uni-plane geometries of Earth. We can imagine complex spheres with delicately rotating sub circles which feed specific elements of energy out of and back into the sphere with the purest non-euclidean force.

As astral mechanic or operator, our machine can be constructed out of pure geometry and energy or we can use subtle metals like astral lead and gold existing in pure mono-atomic crystalline lattices. The sky is the limit, but there are still limits even when working with Astral Machines.

The final design element is the output; the way we conduct the rotated and cycled alchemically purified energy toward our desired purpose. This needs to be carefully considered for if it is incorrectly tuned to the intent and purpose of the machine, all of the alchemical rotation of the rotor will be for naught. We can picture healing or simulating "rays" bathing our subject and producing tremendously beneficial results. The output is best thought of as an antenna with delicate tuning capabilities, much like a radio.

What becomes clear is that to design a successful astral machine requires the same sort of knowledge, care and intuition that is brought to bear upon the construction of earthly machines. Knowledge of sacred geometry and its relationship to fluid dynamics is essential. It is the basis for all of it, much as it was for the Elder race when they created such wonders as the Great Pyramid. We must consider the purpose of the machine, its scale, functions, internal relationships, location and internal and external motive forces. I have spoken of our machine as though it just operated itself. It requires the will of an operator with clear and unshakable intent to operate such a machine. It requires a person skilled in yogic discipline and mental visualizations as well a person whose own energy and thoughts resonate with Nature. Such a person is rare, hence the rarity of such machines! People skilled in Remote Viewing will have some of the qualities necessary to design such machines on their own.

It is the combination of the operator's will, the Suchness or Infinite Potential, aka the Zero-Point field, and the coordinate of the Infinite Continuum chosen to operate upon that define how the work proceeds and the energies necessary to accomplish it.

I am imagining a point in future time when the practice of astral machinery becomes more commonplace and something approached by large numbers of people working in common. The possibilities are endless. True Astral Servitors like complex robots or Artificial Intelligences.

This also brings up the ethical issue, which I have studiously avoided until now. It is true that there will be Astral Weapons and destructive devices designed, but that is the nature of the Cosmos and it may explain the end of the great Elder Race. They may simply have taken their technology a few steps too far and that is a lesson for all of us.

BIBLIOGRAPHY

Dunn, Christopher, *The Giza Power Plant*, Bear & Co., 1998

Farrell, Joseph P., *The Cosmic War*, Adventures Unlimited Press, 2007

Farrell, Joseph P., *The Giza Death Star*, Adventures Unlimited Press, 2001

Farrell, Joseph P., *The Giza Death Star Deployed*, Adventures Unlimited Press, 2003

Farrell, Joseph P., *The Giza Death Star Destroyed*, Adventures Unlimited Press, 2005

Malinowski, Edward F., *Ancient Egypt 39,000 BCE: The History, Technology and Philosophy of Civilization X*, Bear & Co., 2010

Sitchin, Zecharia, *Journeys to the Mythical Past*, Bear & Co., 2007

Santillana, Giorgio and Von Dechend, Hertha, *Hamlet's Mill*, David Godine, 1969

Childress, David and Shaver, Richard Sharpe, *Lost Continents and the Hollow Earth*, Adventures Unlimited Press, 1999

Runyon, Poke, *Beyond Lemuria: The Shaver Mystery and the Secrets of Mount Shasta (DVD)*, Maelstrom Press, 2007

McClure, Rusty and Heffron, Jack *Coral Castle, The Mystery of Ed Leedeskalnin and his American Stonehenge*, Ternary Publishing, 2009

Cobbald, Jane, *Viktor Schauberger: A Life of Learning from Nature*, Floris Books, 2006

Burke, John and Halberg, Kaj, *Seed of Knowledge; Stone of Plenty: Understanding the Lost Technology of the Ancient Megalith Builders*, Council Oak Books, 2005

Religion and Science, Romanticism and Enlightenment: The Way of the Left Hand Path as Synthesis and War of Two Fronts

Thomas Karlsson

The American researcher Pascal Boyer claims that religion works as a cognitive parasite that sponges on our brains. This kind of argumentation against religion has seen a renewed interest after having been abandoned, to a great extent, during the early 20th century. Anti-religious natural scientists, like the zoologist Richard Dawkins, have received great attention for the criticism of religion in books like *The God Delusion* (2006). Religion is placed against science, as two incompatible and fixed monoliths. The new criticism of religion received further advance after the 9-11 attack against the World Trade Center. The fear of both Moslem terrorism and the arms-wielding, American Christian right got numerous opionion-makers to declare, in the spirit of Dawkins, that religion is something evil. Religion is described as an authoritarian teaching in which the individual submits to a despotic god.

Is religion something that belongs in history's junkyard and that is incompatible with freedom and modern science? There are certain basic problems in the starting points of Dawkins and his followers that speak against this view of religion.

To begin with, religion is not a homogenous phenomenon but a joint description of a number of phenomena. Religion can be a collection of social behavioural patterns closely related to a secular Christmas celebration or to rock concerts. To many people, religious groups constitute economic networks, where reliable caravan buyers is an equally important factor for religiousness as the communion. To some, religion is a mystical personal experience of a higher kind of reality.

Dawkins' mistake is, among other things, that he ignores the fact that religion isn't necessarily monotheistic, but can, as in Hinduism, encompass a great amount of gods or, as in Buddhism, no (ultimate) god at all. The next mistaken premise is that religion is always authoritarian and conservative, which is not the case. Religious positions have motivated uprisings, fights for social improvements and, not least, research. It was with an hermetic-religious view of the world that Giordano Bruno stood up against the Church, declared heliocentrism and was thereby burnt at the Campo di Fiori in Rome in the year 1600.

Organised monotheistic religion has persecuted and murdered dissidents both within and outside of their own religion all through history. An example of the first would be the persecutions of the Gnostics during the first centuries of the Christian Era, or the executions of Cathars and Knights Templar during medieval times, or the Church's resistance towards esoteric Christianity even in our own days. As for attacks on foreign religions, we can count the destruction of pagan temples, and the crusades, the burnings of witches, and forced conversions at the times of the colonialisations. In our own days, it's current in the attempts of the organised monotheistic religion to ban criticism against religion (as in the suggested resolution in the UN). It has been presented by Moslem dictators who, in this manner, wish to avoid a criticism of their own regimes.

The language of religion seems unsurpassed in giving humans a meaning in life, but is it possible to unite religion and science and can religion serve a purpose in a modern society?

THE ESOTERIC TRADITION

Esotericism has sometimes been brought forward as a third path between religion and science. Esotericism is a tradition of thought that has its roots in the Hellenic mystery cults and the neo-Platonic philosophy. It was developed during the renaissance by humanistic thinkers like Marcilio Ficino, Pico della Mirandola and Paracelsus. Esotericism is characterised by that the human beings and the universe are regarded in a holistic way, as mirrors of each other, which means that the human individual can receive knowledge of God and nature by studying her own inner life. And also vice versa: that studies of nature and theological issues help the human being to reveal truths about her own inner life. Esotericism is furthermore characterised by the fact that this process of knowledge takes place gradually through different steps of initiation. Western esotericism can be regarded as a third current of thought, by the side of Greek rational thinking and Judeo-Christian faith, the two major traditions of thought on which Western culture rests. Within Western esotericism there is a resistance both against rational thinking and dogmatic faith.

As an undercurrent within esotericism exists "the left hand path" (LHP) or "the sinister path". It's constructed of partly different premises than many forms of Western esotericism. Although the LHP has grown in the West during modern times, traditions like Indian tantra, archaic Greek philosphy, shamanism and traditions of witchcraft are usually referred to. Dr. Alberto Brandi shows, in his recently published book *La Via Oscura. Introduzione al sentiero di Mano Sinistra* (*The Dark Way. Introduction to the Left Hand Path*), that one can distill two forms of the LHP: 1) Traditions that belong to the LHP both in method and goals. Among these, Brandi mentions Tantric LHP and heretic and qliphotic kabbala. 2) The traditions that only use the methodology but lack the initiatory perspectives. As examples of this, Brandi mentions Petro Voodoo and Palo Mayombe, which focus on the exchange between the worlds of the dead and the living.

DRAGON ROUGE AND THE LHP

20 years ago, I founded the esoteric order Dragon Rouge, which is the leading Nordic LHP-organisation. During this period of time, we have on several occasions been involved in the discussion about religion and science. Dragon Rouge is religiously un-

committed and has members of different religious affiliations. The majority of members have views on this that are imbued with a late, modern Zeitgeist which questions dogmatic religion. Dragon Rouge emphasizes academic studies and many of its members rely on a scientific view of the world, which co-habits with notions about magic, different worlds and occult phenomena that are hundreds (sometimes thousands) of years old. This combination means an affirmation of the critical methods of science, but also a questioning of the scientific nihilism that from time to time is distributed from the universities. In the same way, this combination can bring with it an embrace of the language of religion but a questioning of its dogma. This combination is not unique to Dragon Rouge, but exists within the esoteric tradition since way back in history. For the practitioner of the LHP – within Dragon Rouge also called the Draconian Way – this is taken to its extreme because it also means a questioning of certain principles that have been taken for granted within conventional esotericism.

Dragon Rouge belongs primarily, according to Alberto Brandi's categorisation, to the first form of LHP, the one that works both with the dark forces as a method and with the goal of achieving deification and individual development. Dragon Rouge is somewhat of an anti-religion. To the extent that religion can be defined as duties, rules and behaviours that help the religious to reconstruct the order of an originally lost ideal state, the LHP strives to accomplish the events that threw the human being out of that original order. The original order, as we face it in, for example, the myth of the garden of Eden, describes a static child-like original existence in submission before God. Instead of appeasing God to return to this state, the adept of the LHP instead follows the serpent that offered the fruits of knowledge, which led to that the human being was driven out of Eden but that also awoke her sexuality. Through desire for knowledge, sexuality and an uprising against God, the human path towards becoming God begins, which is something the serpent promises. Some even mean that it's the will of God, because God has made the human being in his own representation and actually wants the human being to become existentially grown up and like God, and that the adepts of the LHP thereby better accomplish God's desires than all those who merely obey and pray to God.

The LHP is associated with the goal to become a god, which means existentially grown up, to achieve free will, assume one's own responsibility, acquire knowledge and gain power of existence. The adept of the LHP doesn't beg for mercy but assumes his own responsibility. Dragon Rouge doesn't mean that man is a god but that this is an ideal goal. The term "god" can be understood as a creative principle with an acausal will. Man's terms are to a great extent determined, but through the initiatory work on the LHP the adept can liberate his capacity and gradually acquire free will.

What makes this path different from, for example, forms of hermeticism which also stress god-becoming and knowledge, is the emphasis of the dark and the left. To basically all cultures the left side represents the forbidden, abnormal, exclusive and divergent, and within esotericism it's associated with the magic that goes against the decrees of religions and gods. The LHP celebrates dark and revolutionary characters from the myths, like Lucifer, Loke, Kali, Hekate, Prometheus, Azazel and the fallen angels, to mention a few. The LHP is antinomic and breaks cultural, religious and, not least, existential taboos. It's not about any form of criminal practice, or about performing shocking or provocative deeds, but about breaking unconscious patterns that determine the existence of man. The antinomic breaks the unconsciousness and makes us consciously take a look at our own existence and our prerequisites and, based on that, make free choices and assume responsibility. The greatest existential taboo is our own non-existence, our death, something that the adept of the LHP confronts by examining darkness. Through the meeting with our non-existence we can grow and breathe the air through which we can become as gods. The LHP is a meta-tradition that's characterised by 1) the goal to become a god and 2) to explore the dark.

THE LHP AND SCIENCE

How do esotericists in general and particularly practitioners on the sinister path look upon science and religion? For a long period of time, esotericism was regarded skeptically or even with hostility, by both science and religion. The theologians perceived the esoteric doctrines as heretical and the natural scientists considered them unscientific. The researcher Frances Yates (1899-1981) claimed, in opposition to earlier notions, that esotericism (or what she called the "hermetic tradition") had been instrumental in the development of the values of the enlightenment, libertarian movements and modern science, a thought that the Swedish historian of ideas, Johan Nordström, brought forth already in the 1930s. That the renaissance occultist Pico della Mirandola played a definitive part in the growth of individualism and humanism is beyound doubt. The philosophers of the enlightenment fought justly against the authoritarian and superstitious religions doctrines of those days, but have now, in today's Western society, wrongly come to be linked with materialism. As an esotericist, one then finds oneself in an idelogical war with two fronts against, on one hand, a scientism that makes science a dogm that denies all spiritual values and, on the other, censorship-loving, authoritarian religions.

Practitioners of the LHP differ from practitioners of white magic and the right hand path, by celebrating revolutionary forces like Lilith, Lucifer, Loke and Prometheus. In different ways, these forces represent freedom and knowledge. The fallen angels give knowledge to human beings, Satan (or was that possibly Lilith?) sneaks into Eden and shares the fruits of knowledge, and Prometheus steals the fire from the gods and gives it to the humans. The message of these stories can be interpreted as a warning about the dangers of knowledge, which is the religious interpretation, or as an imperative to receive knowledge and dare to question the over-gods, which is the sinister interpretation. The LHP celebrates, based on these mythological motifs, the human being's free search for knowledge and the free sciences. The practitioner of the LHP would rather identify with the mad genius – a Frankenstein or a van Gogh – than with the obedient parishioner, the pious monk or the politically correct collaborator. When Rabbi Lööw creates a golem in the Jewish ghetto of Prague, it can be interpreted, by the religious, as a warning of the consequences of imitating God, while the dark magician looks at it as an exemplary act of creation.

At the same time, the revolt must never be an end in itself, as within the more vulgar interpretations of dark philosophy. The revolt should serve as an inititaion, self development, maturity and an increase of knowledge. The sinister revolt is not that of the defiant child against the parents, but rather the researcher's attempt to constantly widen the knowledge, or the adventurer's lust to exceed his ability. It's a Luciferian driving force that must be polished and refined in an initiatory context, in the same way that schools and universities should develop the students' abilities, or the athletic club its members' results.

ROMANTICISM AND ENLIGHTENMENT

The LHP is a third way beween religious faith on one hand and materialistic scientism on the other. In the same manner, the dark spirituality is a third path between the philosophy of enlightenment and the world view that grew within romantic and gothic traditions.

Karl Marx meant that religion is opium to the people, and he regarded religion as a tranquilizer that sedates people into passivity and an illusion of safety. The ruling classes have used religion to rule people and make legitimate the power as God's will. The argument could from this side be: "We rule you because God wants it, so don't rebel or you'll end up in Hell!" This way of looking at religion is old and we find critics of religion already in the days of antiquity. It acquired its modern form during the enlightenment of the 18th century, when philosophers like Voltaire fiercely attacked the Church. The project of the enlightenment was about spreading education and to propagate reason. The vision said that if people were only rational enough, they would liberate themselves from superstition and oppression and become free, self-ruling individuals.

Then followed the French revolution and a little more than hundred years later the Russian Communist revolution. Both these revolutions were driven, despite their differences, by the vision to fight oppression, end religious superstition and they meant to stand for reason and a scientific approach. The French revolution led to the mass executions of the terror reign and finally dictatorship under Napoleon, while the Russian revolution would bring Stalin and genocide. In the traces of these revolutions, thinkers questioned whether reason is always reasonable. After the French revolution, romanticism grew within art, literature and philosophy, and brought a criticism against the values of the enlightenment.

Reason can't be everything, the romantics said. Life is too big, as is the universe, too immense to be able to be understood rationally. Reason can't explain love or the meaning of life. Intuition, artistic creation, feelings and spiritual experiences could, for the romantics, better catch the spirit of life than rational thinking could. Although romantic keyfigures, like the Shelleys (known for works like "Prometheus unbound" and "Frankenstein"), were anarchistic atheists, the romantic criticism of the rationalistic faith of the enlightenment would also be used by conservative religious thinkers.

In our own times, the values of the enlightenment are often called upon in a superficial manner and posed against religious thinking. Most of the philosophers of the enlightenment believed in a spiritual reality, but were opposed to what they perceived to be a blind faith and an oppressive priesthood.

The Draconian current and the LHP can be said to represent a synthesis of the ideals of the enlightenment and the world view of the romantics. What enlightenment is and what romanticism is, researchers could debate in eternity, but if we make a simple categorisation and define the ideals of the enlightenment as an accentuation of individualism, rationalism, education and man's ability to free himself from oppression and to create his own situation, then the Draconian current represents values of the enlightenment. If we, by a romantic world view, mean that there are a number of things reason can't explain (like the meaning of life), and that there is more than the everyday world we have around us, then the Draconian current is very much related to romanticism. But when the values of enlightenment land in materialism, nihilistic individualism and rootless modernism, then the Draconian current moves in the opposite direction. In the same way, the Draconian current is against those sides of the romantic that are fanatic or escapistic. The Draconian current is vigorous and pro-action.

SUMMARY

The Draconian current starts out from the position where there are phenomena that won't be explained by reason or won't be proved with the aid of science. Within the Draconian current is also the concept of the Draconian vital principle, which means that the totality is more than the sum of the parts. In that respect, the Draconian current stems from a spiritual and non-materialistic view of the world. The Draconian current and the LHP celebrate dark and revolutionary figures that are associated with autonomy and knowledge. In that respect, the LHP is an esoteric and metaphysical elevation of science. When humans eat of the fruits of knowledge, they carry out the first scientific action, a first experiment, and are thereby punished by God. To the religious, the goal is to return to Eden, while the adept of the LHP strives for a continued exploration of the hidden knowledge, to achieve yet higher levels of certainty and autonomy. In that respct, the LHP is a synthesis of religion's striving for a higher spiritual reality and science' will to free research. The LHP is both a synthesis between the striving for knowledge and freedom of the enlightenment and romanticism's visions of the sublime that opens up beyond the limits of reason. As the Draconian current doesn't strive for an absolute and almighty harmonious view of the world, this synthesis paradoxically doesn't mean that the adept of the LHP mediates between religion and science, enlightenment and romanticism, but rather that the adept, voluntarily or involunarily, finds him- or herself in a war of two fronts against a dichotomy that characterizes modern society.

Bloodsongs:
The Cult of the Blutleuchte and Kosmic Necromancy

David Beth, Hierophant Fraternitas Borealis, 2009

The blood-radiance is an uninterrupted, profoundly disturbing access of awe. A dark strangeness throbs and ferments within hidden hovels. Wild, raucous cries blend with the crashing of the storm. Being speaks in a demonic voice out of the murky twilight; but the glowing crimson of a winter sunset is encircling the world, and a blazing fire engulfs the pursuing powers. The smoke flares into the holy night like the flame of the hearthfire before the forces of the wind. Blood-radiance is Eros and child, is the golden unity of life, and through the eyes of the child, it gazes into radiant visions (...). In the blood-radiance, the mysteries of the maternal universe are revealed.[1]

Blood of human beings potentially contains immense cosmic powers. The activation of these forces becomes a central goal of a kosmic initiate working within the Fraternitas Borealis (F.B.). The Gnosis of the F.B. is a Gnosis of Life. Not life as mere existence, but powerful, shuddering and passionate Life, empowered by death, that leads to Absolute Being. A radiant life suffused with erotic energy, ecstatic and cosmic rapture which culminates in the mystical Cult of the Blutleuchte or Blood-Lamp, Blood radiance! To experience this we need to bring about kosmic symbiosis between the inner Life (with its seat in the Blood) and the outer androgynous All(Father-Wotan: the all encompassing). An adept of the F.B., as he gradually advances along the kosmic path, eventually becomes an initiate of the Blood and erects within his soul and through his body a temple to True Life! The unfolding Blood Gnosis is not a profane blood mysticism in the racial sense, this must be very clear. It is a universal cultus to whom those are admitted that are able to activate the hidden powers of the blood and the soul. As we will see, these secrets of the Blood are intimately connected to a unique form of heathen necromancy and a Weltanschauung fiercely opposed to the orthodox dogmas of the abrahamic desert religions.

---

1. Ludwig Klages, *Rhythmen und Runen*

BODY, SOUL AND SPIRIT

> It is not man's spirit but his soul that is liberated in ecstasy; and his soul
> is liberated not from his body but from his spirit.[2]

The Fraternitas Borealis works in the kosmic tradition and thus acknowledges a trinity of body, soul and spirit in the human being where body and soul form the polarities of life. Unlike orthodox Christianity and most of philosophy however, we do not believe that life only fulfills itself by the higher principle of spirit, whose influences to absorb and to communicate to the body is the designation of the soul. On the contrary, we see the unrefined spirit not as sacred but as an adversary and destroyer of Life itself. The spirit, as shown by Aristotle, Schopenhauer and Klages, broke into Life as an a-cosmic power to de-soul the body and to de-body the soul and wage war against and destroy all Life within its reach. Ludwig Klages, in his groundbreaking work *Der Geist als Widersacher der Seele (Spirit as Adversary of the Soul)* collected compelling evidence in this regard and showed how historical time is a gradual conquering of the forces of spirit over the soul and life. The true corruption of life began with the onset of Judaeo-Christianity in its orthodox sense and a historical viewpoint which makes rational will paramount and de-actualizes the world. Through a gnostic fall into historical time the Light of the pagan mythical golden age or paradise was dispersed into darkness. With Christianity and the other abrahamic religions moving the center of existence into a transcendental realm like Paradise, Heaven or Hell, they are the minions of the demiurgical spirit who wants to seperate Man from life itself through inner and outer dualism, promising a treacherous reward. This inner duality, in which spirit grows in power and continually suppresses the soul, steadily leads people into a metaphysical stupor and spiritual poverty.[3] Especially in the modern world we can see the results of an unrestrained egomanical arbitrariness of the measuring, calculating, solely analytical spirit. We see a continuous devolution of mankind that has led to the current Kali Yuga or Age of the Wolf. The result of a mankind chasing the phantom of dualism and transcendence will be and already is a growing hollowness, a soul-less world, mechanical being without the animation of the soul and the cosmic life force until, in the future, the mask of transcendence will be dropped as well and what will be left is the Man-Golem, utterly alienated and enslaved.

To break the spell of the destructive spirit, to alchemically refine the spirit so that he becomes supportive of life, guided by the wisdom of the soul, this is one of the goals of an initiate of the Kosmic Gnosis, a path which leads to a kosmic resurrection. We must achieve an equilibrium of soul and spirit where spirit clarifies growth, not impends it, where spirit ceases to be an instrument of the will but becomes animated by life through the soul. The Northern, Apollonian, male *Lichtheld* (light-hero), who can bring deification, must be guided by the fertile womb of the Dionysian female, and chthonic, tellurian South.

---

2. Ludwig Klages, *Sämtliche Werke*
3. Every modern human being contains within himself the trinity of body, soul and spirit wherein body and soul constitute a unity with the spirit trying to seperate man from Life itself.

THE CULT OF THE BLUTLEUCHTE

> Separated by a condition of the blood from the mainly rational man, the truly kosmic ecstatic man, the blood luminary, once again will follow the song of his blood into orgiastic, primordial life, creative ecstasy and the mysteries of the flesh.[4]

As initiates of a Hyperborean and Saturnian Order, we see ourselves as lonely wanderers on a mysterious path. With the great poet Novalis we understand that "the mysterious path leads within. In us, or nowhere, lies eternity with its worlds, the past and the future".[5] But only through devotion to and contemplation of the phenomenal world can the eye of spirit be opened, whereby it can perceive amid the appearances the soul to whom they appear; and in the same way it can recognize in the outer world the inner life that expresses its ever-changing vitality there. Novalis was right when he wrote that it is "in the seat of the soul where inner and outer world meet".[6]

In the soul alone we are no individual, no ego; in the soul we are a cosmic storm and through it we can experience universal and All-Life. The F.B. teaches that it is the blood which contains the soul essence and thus is the spring of all creative and visionary power. The soul essence is understood as a fiery glowing substance, of electrons, shining in a continuous explosive Hieros Gamos of polarities. However, in our world and time this metaphysical essence in humanity is dead or degenerate, inactive. It is one of the main goals of our Kosmic Fraternity of the North to re-activate, to recharge and develop this cosmic blood essence which we initiates call the Great Telesma. A master of the F.B. will become a true aristocrat of the soul, a carrier of true metaphysical blue blood. Kosmic vitality and true Life pulses through this divine blood. Such a man will be able to break the chains of the spirit and to erupt into true being, bringing the alchemically refined spirit into a constructive symbiosis with the soul – the great god of individuation, Apollo, undergoes symbiosis with the wild hunter, the god of the heroic, erotic rush, Wotan-Dionysus.

> Separated by a condition of the blood from the mainly rational man, the truly kosmic ecstatic man, the blood luminary, once again will follow the song of his blood into orgiastic, primordial life, creative ecstasy and the mysteries of the flesh. The pores, the mouth, anus and sexual organs are magical portals to this realm! [7]

Only through the ignition of the Blutleuchte, the blood-lamp, will the blood become metaphysical blue and divine blood. To achieve this the initiate must undergo complex transformations and alchemical transmutations. He must stop the continuous evacu-

---

4. David Beth, *Hymns of Blood – the esoteric importance of Blood in the Fraternitas Borealis*, unpublished paper of the Fraternitas Borealis.
5. Novalis, *Blütenstaub*
6. Novalis, *Blütenstaub*
7. David Beth, *Bloodsongs – the esoteric importance of Blood in the Fraternitas Borealis*, unpublished paper of the Fraternitas Borealis.

ation of soul substance from his esoteric organism and slowly begin to strengthen his soul by a variety of esoteric and spiritual methods[8] so that the tyranny of the unrestrained spirit, which reigns without and in most people also within, is broken.[9] Once the soul is empowered and the devolution stopped, the blood may awake! The experience of the Telesma and the activation of the Blutleuchte is deeply cosmic and erotic in character. Ludwig Klages describes it thus:

> The blood-radiance is an uninterrupted, profoundly disturbing access of awe. A dark strangeness throbs and ferments within hidden hovels. Wild, raucous cries blend with the crashing of the storm. Being speaks in a demonic voice out of the murky twilight; but the glowing crimson of a winter sunset is encircling the world, and a blazing fire engulfs the pursuing powers. The smoke flares into the holy night like the flame of the hearthfire before the forces of the wind. Blood-radiance is Eros and child, is the golden unity of life, and through the eyes of the child, it gazes into radiant visions (...). In the blood-radiance, the mysteries of the maternal universe are revealed.[10]

The activation of the Blutleuchte goes hand in hand with the reconnection of the soul essence within the blood with cosmic essences. The impact of these rays from the androgynous All-Father/Mother are felt as cool shivers from the Cosmos while their continuous explosive exchange or Hieros Gamos with the blood-essence, that living entity, is experienced as "hot".[11] A deep state of awareness results. Substance becomes essence in ecstatic moments of intoxication whether they are purely erotic, eroto-heroic or eroto-magical. This Orphic Eros that is so far removed from profane eroticism is also called Eros Cosmogonos. Klages explains that this

> ... Eros is not the pleasant, blind animalistic lust; this only feeds him. Eros is that lust which is simultaneously visionary. The one inhabited by Eros-Dionysus becomes a Daemon while he yet remains a Man. He gazes through the shadow body of things into the flaming night of the image. He himself is destiny, he is gorgonic dread. The streams of the earth, the storms of heaven and the starry vault above are all within him and his power reaches beyond Saturn.[12]

An individual who is seized by this type of cosmic and elemental Eros experiences it as a pulsating, inundating stream of electricity.

---

8. Methods as have been handed down to us within the Cult of the F.B. range from esoteric active imagination to sexual magical rites, to shamanistic practices and sorceries.

9. The Ecclesia Gnostica Aeterna, which also works in the kosmic current, brings about this transformation (the strengthening of the soul and refinement of the spirit) through the gnostic sacraments and gnostic-esoteric practices.

10. Ludwig Klages, *Rhythmen und Runen*

11. Here we may find a connection to the Points Chauds or Hot Points of esoteric Voudon, a connection which has been overlooked until now.

12. Ludwig Klages, *Rhythmen und Runen*

KOSMIC NECROMANCY

We shall return. We are not dead.
Limbs that are swimming in primal red.
We speak, and our blood is the living page,
Husks of the sinner in purple rage.
When the time has rushed in a passionless red
When time is rotten and full of dread
We come again, through pain and fear.[13]

This Cultus of the Blutleuchte and Eros Cosmogonos in the Fraternitas Borealis is symbiotically linked with unique teachings on Necromancy. Through our secret teachings we understand that only the Dead are quintessential Life! Unlike in Christianity, the souls of the Dead are not being banished into the "beyond", the place of no connection to our realms. We do not seal the soul essence in Heaven and thus prevent the return of the Dead.[14] On the contrary, in our Gnosis the Dead are ever present and are being experienced in the Telesma of the living. The soul essence of the Dead renews itself in the organism of the kosmic initiate where it activates and empowers the Telesma within the metaphysically aristocratic and luminous blood.[15] It is not the profane personal soul or "I" which crosses the threshold of Death but the essence of the soul that is being released back into the aether. Thus, what remains are the essential moments of a past soul which reveal and manifest themselves through transfiguring images of the blood-visionary. The soul essence of the Dead when released into the aether of the All after death forms the core of a powerful cosmic cell of pulsating energy – the Death Lamp. It is this animated cosmic energy of the Dead which the initiate of the F.B. is able to receive into himself as an ultimate empowerment of rejuvenation and transformation! The essence of the soul of the Dead symbiotically unites with the soul of the living. This union takes place foremost in the blood where the soul essence pulses through the organism. The more accomplished and perfected a person becomes in his esoteric development, the more powerful his soul essence becomes. The soul experiences life through visions and images, and the more powerful the soul becomes the more intense, empowering and transforming are the visions. Such a person potentially also becomes more powerfully experiential, empowering, even immortal after his Death by returning to Life through the visions and empowerments he provides to a living initiate of the soul and the blood, like a master of the Fraternitas Borealis. The transfiguring images are the form in which the "Dead" meld with the Living.[16]

---

13. Alfred Schuler, quoted from Raymond Furness, *Zarathustra's Children: A Study Of A Lost Generation Of German Writers*.

14. People weep for the Dead believing they weep FOR them while in fact they unconsciously only pity themselves for being eternally seperated from the deceased.

15. As well as in other bodily secretions

16. The experiences of reincarnation or "past lives" may indeed be the revealing of soul essence of a deceased in a living person whose soul still is capable of receiving it. Obviously most theories of reincarnation and past lives as we see them popular in new age and big religions are results to package such fundamental kosmic-pagan experience and gnosis into escapist and materialistic religious frames which deny this necromantic exchange and empowerment.

Such an initiate will achieve the Elemental Vision which Ludwig Klages describes thus:

> The elemental vision equals rebirth; within us, the element recalls its limitlessness amid the primordial flux, as element and flux devour themselves anew: the winds, the trees, and the stars now speak. Through immeasurably distant ages, death and birth greet the soul of man in the wavering blade of grass, and they hear the dark inner night of the blood of man in the falling rain, as it trickles through the leaves outside. [17] [18]

Like in the esoteric paganism of ancient times, the poles of Being are present and past rather than present and future like in the abrahamic religions. The *Weltall* (the universe or World-All) is seen as past and thus stands for the world of the Dead and thus it is the past through the continous empowerment of the Dead which to us is the focus of renewal![19] Those mighty legions of the necropoles and catacombs sanctify all of our work, our liturgies, our feasts, initiations and illuminations!

Through our sorceries, rites and initiations, the Dead are forever standing within life and endlessly dispense their blessings on the initiates of our Fraternitas. Collapse of cosmic awareness and creativity has two main causes: weakness from within and infection from without. But an initiate in whom the Blutleuchte blazes with its mystic fire stands at the summit of his vitality, he becomes invulnerable. In this moment of kosmic resurrection, within this awareness, "... man is invulnerable... stronger than external destiny. No one and nothing can slay us!" [20]

---

17. Ludwig Klages, *Die Geschichte seines Lebens, Band 1*, translated by Joe Pryce
18. As has been shown for the first time in my recent book *Voudon Gnosis*, the Elemental Vision of the Fraternitas Borealis equals the esoteric interpretation of the Prise des Yeaux in Esoteric Voudon.
19. The past, golden age of the heroic and pagan cultures which provided all rejuvenation and metaphsyical links stand in stark contrast to the futurism of the abrahamic religions and resulting materialism which promises a vague escapism of a future "good".
20. Ludwig Klages, *Rhythmen und Runen*

LIBER ASTRUM

Payam Nabarz

To the Stars

WITH holy voice I call the stars on high,
Pure sacred lights and genii of the sky.
Celestial stars, the progeny of Night,
In whirling circles beaming far your light,
Refulgent rays around the heavens ye throw,
Eternal fires, the source of all below.
With flames significant of Fate ye shine,
And aptly rule for men a path divine.
In seven bright zones ye run with wandering flames,
And heaven and earth compose your lucid frames:
With course unwearied, pure and fiery bright
Forever shining thro' the veil of Night.
Hail twinkling, joyful, ever wakeful fires!
Propitious shine on all my just desires;
These sacred rites regard with conscious rays,
And end our works devoted to your praise.[1]

In Plato's *Timaeus* the view of the planets and heavenly bodies containing gods is discussed as the necessary force that moves the planets around the earth. The Greek cosmology viewed the movement of celestial bodies to be "resembling as closely as possible the perfect intelligible Living Creature". The laws of Newtonian physics have long ago replaced the need for gods as the necessary force for movement of stellar bodies, thus astronomy has taken over from astrology.

Yet, when walking on a clear night and staring at the stars, something does capture one's imagination. It may be the simple beauty of the stars and the planets, or perhaps a religious meme that compels one to head out night after night in the footsteps of the modern and ancient stargazers. It is not only the full moon that turns people into lunatics and poets; there are other subtle forces there too that inspire us; the constellations. There has been much written about the magick of the sun, moon and the planets, yet the gentler streams of the constellations largely remain unspoken of. The constellations

---

1. *The Hymns of Orpheus* translated by Thomas Taylor, 1792.

that are popular are the twelve signs of the Zodiac, which are seen as part of the celestial powers that influence us from birth. However, in modern astrology, the interaction with the constellations is a reactive rather than proactive relationship, viewed as a unidirectional flow of energy from the heavens to us; this is referred to as "divinatory astrology" by the Swiss mystical writer Titus Burckhardt in his book *Mystical Astrology according to Ibn Arabi*.[2] The field of divinatory astrology is well covered by thousands of books on the subject and it is part of popular culture, with many newspapers printing daily horoscopes. The divinatory astrology is a practice which goes back centuries. For example, in the Persian *Shah Nameh (Epic of Kings)* circa 1000 AD we read:

> When Feridoun had thus opened his lips he called for the book wherein are written the stars, and he searched for the planets of his sons. And he found that Jupiter reigned in the sign of the Archer in the house of Silim, and the sun in the Lion in that of Tur, but in the house of Irij there reigned the moon in the Scorpion. And when he saw this he was sorrowful, for he knew that for Irij were grief and bale held in store. Then having read the secrets of Fate, Feridoun parted the world and gave the three parts unto his sons.[3]

Another example is the well known testing of astrologers by Roman Emperor Tiberius (42 BC – AD 37). His method of testing was:

> Whenever he (Emperor Tiberius) sought counsel on such (astrological) matters, he would make use of the top of the house and of the confidence of one freedman, quite illiterate and of great physical strength. The man always walked in front of the person whose (astrological) science Tiberius had determined to test, through an unfrequented and precipitous path (for the house stood on rocks), and then, if any suspicion had arisen of imposture or of trickery, he hurled the astrologer, as he returned, into the sea beneath, that no one might live to betray the secret. (Astrologer) Thrasyllus accordingly was led up the same cliffs, and when he had deeply impressed his questioner by cleverly revealing his imperial destiny and future career, he was asked whether he had also thoroughly ascertained his own horoscope, and the character of that particular year and day. After surveying the positions and relative distances of the stars, he first paused, then trembled, and the longer he gazed, the more was he agitated by amazement and terror, till at last he exclaimed that a perilous and well-nigh fatal crisis impended over him. Tiberius then embraced him and congratulated him on foreseeing his dangers and on being quite safe. Taking what he had said as an oracle, he retained him in the number of his intimate friends. [4]

---

2. *Mystical Astrology according to Ibn Arabi* by Titus Burckhardt, Beshara Publications, 1977.
3. *The Epic of Kings* by Ferdowsi. Translated by Helen Zimmern, 1883.
4. 6.21 *The Annals* by Publius Cornelius Tacitus. Translated by Alfred John Church and William Jackson Brodribb, *The Complete Works of Tacitus*, 1942.

However, the focus of the work in this book (i.e., Payam Nabarz' *Stellar Magic* – Ed.) is on divinatory astrology's less popular cousin, which Titus Burckhardt refers to as 'spiritual astrology'. The aims of following stellar workings are to make such relationships a bidirectional flow of energy and to honour the constellations in the same way many modern Pagans honour earth, moon, sun and the planets. To draw down powers of the constellations as some modern Pagans draw down the moon or the sun, or as some magicians work with planetary hours and days of the week for the ideal time in which to achieve their aims or create talismans as we see in works like the "Picatrix" or "The Key of Solomon".

In following the approach of using star lore for spiritual astrology and not just divinatory purposes, we are in good company, as this is in line with *The Chaldæan Oracles*:

> Theurgists fall not so as to be ranked among the herd that are in subjection to Fate. The Oracles also tell us: Direct not thy mind to the vast surfaces of the Earth; for the Plant of Truth grows not upon the ground. Nor measure the motions of the Sun, collecting rules, for he is carried by the Eternal Will of the Father, and not for your sake alone. Dismiss (from your mind) the impetuous course of the Moon, for she moves always by the power of necessity. The progression of the Stars was not generated for your sake. The wide aerial flight of birds gives no true knowledge nor the dissection of the entrails of victims; they are all mere toys, the basis of mercenary fraud; flee from these if you would enter the sacred paradise of piety, where Virtue, Wisdom and Equity are assembled. [5]

The point is succinctly made by W.W. Westcott in his introduction the Chaldæan Oracles:

> Although destiny, our destiny, may be 'written in the Stars' yet it was the mission of the divine Soul to raise the human Soul above the circle of necessity, and the Oracles give Victory to that Masterly Will, which:
> Hews the wall with might of magic,
> Breaks the palisade in pieces,
> Hews to atoms seven pickets . . .
> Speaks the Master words of knowledge!
> The means taken to that consummation consisted in the training of the Will and the elevation, of the imagination, a divine power which controls consciousness. [6]

In other words, the initiates have to exceed the total sum of their programming, and using their spiritual training, go beyond the boundaries set at time of birth, be they social, intellectual, physical, astrological, or religious boundaries. Initiates at all times aspire consciously to improve themselves, and, for example, as Sufis aim to become an

---

5. *The Chaldæan Oracles Attributed to Zoroaster*. Edited and revised by W.W. Westcott, 1895, pp 45-46. Sure Fire Press, Edition 1984.
6. Ibid, p 21.

"Insan Kamil" (a perfect or complete human). An intellectual study of the occult and mysticism on its own is not enough. Let us look at magical arts and witchcraft. The word art is important here, magic can be an art like any other art; witchcraft is a craft like any other craft. When someone practices an art or craft, be it painting, academic research, music, gardening or sport etc, they are all going on a similar skill journey to their fellow magical arts practitioners. It is the journey, the trials, approbations, and continuous overcoming of obstacles and pushing oneself to improve that makes the difference and can result in making contact with your divine spark, the higher self or, according to Greek philosophy, your Daimon or the Holy Guardian Angel in the Christian and Zoroastrian religions. The rough Ashlar stone becomes smooth or the grape turns to the Sufi's wine of ecstasy, the cosmic transformation and metamorphosis. What is interesting is when someone masters their art or craft or sport; their piece of music, or performance, or spell or rite, or painting etc. This transforms them, and also influences others in a major way too.

The Chaldean Oracles encourage us to:

> Explore the River of the Soul, whence, or in what order you have come: so that although you have become a servant to the body, you may again rise to the Order from which you descended, joining works to sacred reason… Every way unto the emancipated Soul extend the rays of Fire… Let the immortal depth of your Soul lead you, but earnestly raise your eyes upwards… Who knoweth himself, knoweth all things in himself.

This is a highly significant text, which draws upon Neo-Platonism and other teachings; therefore the whole text of *The Chaldean Oracles* is part of the recommended reading and bibliography.

"This magical and religious approach to the constellations is not a new idea; indeed it can be viewed as the root of many ancient religions. Prof Franz Cumont, in his *Astrology and Religion among the Greeks and Romans*, raises the issue of "the idea that the primary source of religion was the spectacle of celestial phenomena and the ascertainment of their correspondence with earthly events, and he (Dupuis) undertook to show that the myths of all peoples and all times were nothing but a set of astronomical combinations."[7] The field of archaeo-astronomy has shown us numerous religious structures since the megalithic age that had cosmological roles and were aligned to the stars, the moon or the sun. For example, from the period, Callanish in Scotland, Stonehenge in England, the Pyramids of Giza in Egypt, and Newgrange in Ireland.

The central role of the stars in the roots of religions is echoed in our time also in a myriad of manifestations; from Star Gate-fans, to UFO enthusiasts, to fanatical Solar Temple cult followers. From the ancient stargazers to modern astronomers and New Age astrologers the stars still inspire – the thoughts of the Magi still resonate today.

The place of stellar magic in modern occultism is best seen in works of Rudolf Steiner and Aleister Crowley. Aleister Crowley talks of the Star Goddess Nuit in his *Book of the Law (Liber AL vel Legis)* in depth, indeed the first chapter of this book is

---

7. *Astrology and Religion Among the Greeks and Romans*, Franz Cumont, 1912.

of Nuit speaking directly to the reader; for example, she states: "I am the blue-lidded daughter of Sunset; I am the naked brilliance of the voluptuous night-sky. And Had! The manifestation of Nuit, The unveiling of the company of heaven, Every man and every woman is a star."

He also refers to Nuit in a number of his other works, for example:

> It is written in The Book of the Law: Every man and every woman is a Star. It is Our Lady of the Stars that speaketh to thee, O thou that art a star, a member of the Body of Nuith! Listen, for thine ears become dulled to the mean noises of the earth; the infinite silence of the Stars woos thee with subtile musick... For inasmuch as thou hast made the Law of Freedom thine, as thou hast lived in Light and Liberty and Love, thou hast become a Free-man of the City of the Stars...[8]

Rudolf Steiner, the founder of Anthroposophical Society, also developed a stellar-based approach and philosophy, and, in 1913, built the first Goetheanum, a physical temple, so to speak, to connect to the stars. In his words:

> The stars once spoke to man.
> It is world destiny that they are silent now
> To become aware of this silence can be pain for earth humanity
> But in the deepening silence
> There grows and ripens what human beings speak to the stars
> To become aware of this speaking
> Can become strength for Spirit Man.

In his view the stellar connection was a crucial step in one's spiritual journey: "Steiner explained that to know the human being, one must take ... the heavens and the earth as your province and discern the rhythm that beats between them."[9]

My own interest in theurgy and stellar magic is rooted in the Mithraic Mysteries. In this stellar religion, the individual's soul is seen to have descended from the starry heavens to earth and at death the soul makes its journey upwards again into the firmament, a vision similar to vision of Jacob's ladder. The initiatory system allowed the neophyte to become familiar with the cosmos, and learn the star "signposts" which would have allowed his return journey to be smoother and reach a state of henosis. The cave-like temple, (called a Mithraeum) was a representation of the universe; here the initiate ascended through various planetary degrees and learned about the constellations and their meanings. The Mithraeum is an authentic microcosm, literally a model of the heavens. Roger Beck describes the Mithraeum as an "image of universe". The Planetary initiates were:

---

8. *Liber CVI*, Aleister Crowley.
9. *Speaking to the Stars: In consideration of Cosmic Ritual* by Mary Stewart Adams in *New View*, Winter 2006/7 p 50.

Mercury (Corax/Raven)

Venus (Nymphus/Bee chrysalis or male bride)

Mars (Miles/Soldier)

Jupiter (Leo/Lion)

Moon (Perses/Persian)

Sun (Heliosdromus)

Saturn (Pater)

According to the Porphyry, in *On the Cave of the Nymphs:*

> Thus also the Persians, mystically signifying the descent of the soul into the sublunary regions, and its regression from it, initiate the mystic (or him who is admitted to the arcane sacred rites) in a place which they denominate a cavern. For, as Eubulus says, Zoroaster was the first who consecrated in the neighbouring mountains of Persia, a spontaneously produced cave, florid, and having fountains, in honour of Mithra, the maker and father of all things; a cave, according to Zoroaster, bearing a resemblance of the world, which was fabricated by Mithra. But the things contained in the cavern being arranged according to commensurate intervals, were symbols of the mundane elements and climates.[10]

The central iconography of Mithraism (for full details, see *The Mysteries of Mithras: The Pagan Belief That Shaped the Christian World*, by Payam Nabarz) is called "Tauroctony" or the Bull Slaying. This was a representation of the night sky and structure of the Mithraeum building lends itself to contain all the symbols of macrocosm. The scene shows that Mithras, while facing away from the bull, has one leg on the back of the bull, one hand holding the bull's head, and the other hand stabbing the bull in the neck, where blood pours forth. Around him are a dog, a raven, a scorpion, a snake, a lion, and a cup. From the tip of the bull's tail, a shaft of wheat is growing. The cloak of Mithras is the night sky with stars; the signs of the zodiac surround the whole scene. The symbols of the seven planets are present; the two torchbearers of Mithras stand at either side of the bull-slaying scene. One of the Mithraic mysteries is that the bull slaying scene is a representation of the constellations the Perseus (Mithras), Taurus (bull), Canis Minor (dog), Hydra (snake), Corvus (raven), and Scorpio (scorpion). The wheat is the star Spica (the brightest star in the constellation Virgo); where the knife enters the bull, is the Pleiades; the life giving blood of the bull is the Milky Way. The two torchbearers,

---

10. *On the Cave of the Nymphs* in the Thirteenth Book of the *Odyssey* from the Greek of Porphyry, translated by Thomas Taylor, 1823.

Cautes and Cautopates, symbolise the equinoxes. Cautes' torch is pointing upward: the spring equinox. Cautopates' torch is pointing downward: the autumn equinox.

Several key images around the central Tauroctony scene are important because they contain a creation story. In the beginning Mithras is asked by the Sun to kill the first bull, but he is reluctant to do this. The Raven, messenger of the Sun, comes to him again with the message. Mithras goes into the field and captures the bull, and with his might, lifts the back legs of the bull over his shoulder and drags him to the birth cave. The crescent moon over the bull suggests its connection to the moon. As Mithras kills the bull, from his blood comes wine and all the plants that cover the earth. The tail becomes wheat, which gives us our bread. The seed and the genitals of the bull are taken to the Moon Goddess and purified, giving rise to all the animals. Hence, by this slaying of the first bull, life comes onto the earth. The new life on Earth is growing very slowly, due to drought. Mithras, as the mediator between Heaven and Earth, is asked to solve this problem; however, this means a conflict with the Sun, who has been burning the land. The battle between Sol (the sun) and Mithras results in Mithras overcoming the planetary sun and becoming the Invincible Sun. Sol kneels in front of Sol Invictus while Mithras holds the constellation the Great Bear in one hand. This emphasizes his power as the stellar god, one who moves the cosmic pole as well as causing the precession of equinoxes. Mithras and Sol then become friends and shake hands with their right hands. Mithras is referred to kosmokrator (ruler of cosmos) and also rules the movements of the earth and the seasons, as his number is 365, the number of days in a year.

In making their Hermetic ascent, the Mithraic initiates were magical cosmonauts, making astral journeys and making preparations for their final destination; returning to the Milky Way. The Neoplatonic based ideals allow the ascent of the soul through the planetary spheres, an initiatory voyage to purify the divine aspects, hidden in mankind, from its contact with matter from birth.

This is indeed the basis of Aleister Crowley's saying of "Every Man and Woman is a Star", and we all aim for our one star in sight. A view that we have inherited from the Ancient Greeks, as we see in Plato's *Timaeus*:

> Thus he spoke, and once more into the cup in which he had previously mingled the soul of the universe he poured the remains of the elements, and mingled them in much the same manner; they were not, however, pure as before, but diluted to the second and third degree. And having made it he divided the whole mixture into souls equal in number to the stars, and assigned each soul to a star; and having there placed them as in a chariot, he showed them the nature of the universe, and declared to them the laws of destiny, according to which their first birth would be one and the same for all,-no one should suffer a disadvantage at his hands; they were to be sown in the instruments of time severally adapted to them, and to come forth the most religious of animals; and as human nature was of two kinds, the superior race would here after be called man. Now, when they should be implanted in bodies by necessity, and be always gaining or losing some part of their bodily substance, then in

the first place it would be necessary that they should all have in them one and the same faculty of sensation, arising out of irresistible impressions; in the second place, they must have love, in which pleasure and pain mingle; also fear and anger, and the feelings which are akin or opposite to them; if they conquered these they would live righteously, and if they were conquered by them, unrighteously. He who lived well during his appointed time was to return and dwell in his native star, and there he would have a blessed and congenial existence. [11]

According to the classical writers it is not only the human souls that originate in the stars and strive to return to them. The gods too have their origins among the stars, in the *Hermetica* (the Greek Corpus Hermeticum) we read about the birth of the universe and life and a creation story which is centred around the stars:

In the deep there was boundless darkness and water and fine intelligent spirit, all existing by divine power in chaos. Then a holy light was sent forth, and elements solidified out of liquid essence. And all the gods (divide the parts) of germinal nature. While all was unlimited and un-formed, light elements were set apart to the heights and the heavy were grounded in the moist sand, the whole of them delimited by fire and raised aloft, to be carried by spirit. The heavens appeared in seven circles, the gods became visible in the shapes of the stars and all their constella-tions, and the arrangements of (this lighter substance) corresponded to the gods contained in it. The periphery rotated (in) the air, carried in a circular course by divine spirit. [12]

11. *Timaeus* By Plato Written 360 B.C.E Translated by Benjamin Jowett. New York, C. Scribner's Sons, 1871.
12. *Hermetica: The Greek Corpus Hermeticum* and the *Latin Asclepius* in a New English Translation, with Notes and Introduction by Brian P. Copenhaver, 1992, p 13.

Unveiling the Mysteries
of the Process Church

Hiram Corso

With the publication of Timothy Wyllie's book on The Process, a new perspective of the group has emerged which reveals a radically different view from all that has been written about to this point – the majority of the books and articles having enmeshed The Process into a conspiratorial role by connecting to the Manson family, Son of Sam or postulating other nefarious activities that they imagined they could be involved in. This article aims to reveal and dispel the mysteries of The Process and is presented from a non-conspiratorial perspective. The Process developed into an extremely intelligent, creative and innovative system of psycho-therapy which produced shocking results in its effectiveness and beneficially changed the lives of those involved in its methods.

While the sociological impact evidenced by The Process upon any widespread mainstream audience was minor, those who utilized their therapeutic methods found them an effective way to tap inner reservoirs and many aspirants were enthralled by the apocalyptic philosophy espoused by Robert de Grimston. Many of de Grimston's writings are heavily steeped in rhetoric and combine the approach of philosophic logicians with the bombastic apocalyptic style of A.O. Spare. The Process represented many different things to each of its adherents. It served a myriad of simultaneous functions to those that it attracted and was a unique organization that was much more multifaceted than merely being an offshoot of Scientology. The Process was a sociological experiment that pushed the boundaries of what was achievable in a group dynamic. It continually evolved and changed from its early period in 1966 to the schism in 1974, at which time it ceased to be known as The Process. They initially emerged as a psychotherapeutic group but eventually evolved more religious overtones to their decrees. After their journey to Xtul, the direction of the group had thoroughly changed.

The Process articulated and promoted a doomsday message concerning an approaching Armageddon. The extremeness of their message being espoused regarding the unity of Christ and Satan, although it was concerned with the reconciliation of opposites, may have been seen as extreme for those who first encountered them. The Process believed that the world was coming to an end, but that it would be saved if they could assist both Christ and Satan in their reconciliation.

Robert Moore and Mary Ann MacLean met while both were deeply involved in the exploration of the methods of Scientology. After becoming "clear", Mary Ann influenced Robert (during their sessions as auditors using the E-meter) to deviate from the standard practice of auditing by following their own line of questioning designed to uncover points of contention, which were spiritual and psychological blocks in those participants. Mary Ann found a complimentary partner in Robert, and aided by a powerful chemistry that developed, they were able to evolve techniques which came to be used in Compulsions Analysis. Robert changed his last name to de Grimston because of its occult significance. They continuously revised and improved upon their therapeutic techniques and probed the minds of their inner circle in lengthy brain-probing sessions and produced oftentimes startling results.

In 1962 Robert Moore and Mary Ann MacLean joined the Scientology center located in London on Fitzroy Street. After quickly rising through and acquiring considerable skills as Scientology auditors, they grew weary with the unquestioning adherence to Hubbard's doctrine and began to develop their own methods for auditing. They resigned their positions in the Scientology Organization and began to combine the concepts of Adler regarding compulsive goals with techniques taken from Scientology. Continually refining their methods and producing dramatic results with their clients, in 1963 they announced their own psychotherapeutic group known as Compulsions Analysis. Its methods were designed to rid the patient of compulsive behaviors. They used the E-meter as a powerful tool to measure emotional charge and produced effective results through their adept usage. As the therapy sessions continued, a deeper sense of spiritual purpose began to emerge from the group of participants under the guidance of Robert and Mary Ann, and this manifested in the formation of the Process Church. The name Process was chosen as a reference to the change that occurred through the transformative means of their influence. They relocated to 2 Balfour Place in the Mayfair District in London and emanated a professional demeanor in this upscale neighborhood. After lengthy deliberation, it was ascertained that the group should travel to Xtul in the Yucatan Peninsula. While living at Xtul, the group weathered a severe hurricane, and de Grimston experienced a direct contact with the gods. This encounter dramatically changed his approach to writing, as the majority of books written thereafter were all channeled by the gods. The members experienced a rebirth and realized a fundamental theology level of purpose and significance, and the group set course on a spiritual odyssey. The Omega drifted further from reach after this early period and were soon only seen by those in the innermost circle.

As The Process's theological ideologies developed, de Grimston interpreted three basic forces which he designated as God, Lucifer and Satan – Christ was presented as the unification principle of these divergent energies. Because Satan was included amongst these primordial energies, it was easily and purposely misconstrued by those who had accused The Process of being involved in Satan worship, animal sacrifice and venerating the principles of evil.

The Gods and Their People clearly delineates the four paths held within The Process and how each may be described. It provides a thorough account of the role of the gods and how they manifest in our lives and may be better understood and used to one's advantage. This eventually evolved into a system of higher and lower aspects of each of the four divisions. The four gods of The Process represent basic underlying personality types which at their core can be observed to have four distinct and unique attributes. Although some Process members treated them as actually existing in a non-corporeal sense, others conceived them as theoretical archetypes, a combination of which makes up the human psyche. By properly understanding the subconscious drives and desires that are motivated through the interactions of the gods, man may come to realize the structures that control our behavior and attain to the aspirations of one's higher self. Each individual leans more to one particular god, although all four are present in the self to varying degrees. JEHOVAH represents strength. He is the wrathful god of vengeance and retribution, demands discipline, courage, ruthlessness and a single-minded dedication to duty, purity and self-denial. LUCIFER the light bearer urges us to enjoy life to the fullest, to value success in human terms, to be gentle, kind and loving and to live in peace and harmony with one another. (This defines the ethos which characterized the 60s into the 70s generation.) Lucifer has always held a special occult significance within magic and secret societies – Blavatsky and the Theosophical Society, Nazi occultism, and Freemasonry have all recognized the primary importance of the mythological role of Lucifer. He is exemplified by an awareness of the physical aesthetics of beauty and body image, hedonistic indulgence, free will, and material success. In the film *Lucifer Rising*, Kenneth Anger embodies this image and spirit of Lucifer as a representation of the energies which had been emerging. SATAN represented separation and was perceived as an adversary. He is the receiver of transcended souls and corrupted bodies; he instills in us two directly opposite qualities – at one end, an urge to rise above all human and physical needs and appetites – to be all soul and no body; at the other end, to sink beneath all human codes of behavior and to wallow in a morass of violence, lunacy and excessive physical indulgence. CHRIST is the unifier and is the emissary of the gods. He plays a pivotal role in the salvation of humanity through his task of unifying the universe. He is the reconciler of opposites and the transcender of conflict. Many rituals were devised to bring Process members into communion with each of these gods. It played a major importance for Processeans to realize that they were subject to the will of the gods.

Several books play an especially important role in conveying the message of The Process. *EXIT* is a book of teachings of The Process which were originally intended only to be read by Internal Brethren. It consisted of a series of letters called BI or Brethren Information. It includes: BI 7 – *The Universal Law*; BI 5 – *The Cycle of Ignorance*; BI 13 – *The Separation*; BI 14 – *The Self*; BI 16 – *Control is Contact*; BI 19 – *The Game of the Gods*; and BI 20 – *The Lie*. Other important writings include: *Humanity Is The Devil*; *The Gods and Their People*; *As It Is*; *The Gods On War*; and *The Unity of Christ and Satan*. In *The Game of the Gods* the role of the gods is explained, as they interact and are reflected in man. Satan's role is explained, as is the purpose of evil—if he didn't exist as a form of separation, the Game wouldn't be able to be played. It is through this cycle that union and harmony is maintained. *Humanity Is The Devil* explains that man has faltered in blindness and deception and taken on the role of the Adversary. It is an admonishment upon man given in a time of retribution so that man may be able to change his fate. *As It Is* is a pronouncement of mankind's impending calamity– salvation may be found for those seeking to banish fear and ignorance and live in unity with one's god. It is written for those who desire to break the pattern of reality perpetrated as a lie and to live life as it really is. Each issue of the Process magazine dealt with subjects with great emotional impact – *On Death, On Sex, On Fear, On Love*, etc.

The Grey Forces, which are often referred to in Process literature, signify: conformity, mediocrity, repression, weak will, resentment, futility, compromise, and the spirit of all that hinders progress and evolution.

At its peak period in 1971, the Process consisted of about 250 members. People were attracted and drawn into the fold through a number of means. Donating was a practice usually done by messengers and prophets. They were expected to donate and to bring money into the organization, and often functioned on minute amounts of sleep. They hit the streets with a stack of Process magazines and other literature and had a goal of raising as much money as possible selling the Process materials. Oftentimes, celebrities were encountered while donating and sometimes were enticed into appearing in photos and interviews that ran in the Process magazines. Occasionally, they were even curious enough as to attend meetings to discover what The Process were all about. The money collected was rigorously tallied and all statistics were kept track of by higher level members. In the coffee houses run by The Process, they advertised classes and group encounter sessions where their psychotherapeutic techniques were demonstrated. In the Telepathy Developing Circle, a group of participants sat in a circle in a candle-lit room facing one another and once they had chosen a subject of focus, they conducted a meditation in which they vividly imagined subjects that were focused upon. After this process, they discussed and analyzed the images that had appeared. In some instances, prescient information would be gleaned of events that hadn't yet transpired and sometimes a course was set in motion based upon these messages. One such message led to the group traveling to Xtul. In the Midnight Meditation Sessions, which were held every Friday and Saturday at midnight, a ritual was conducted, led by a single priest serving as the Sacrifist. Subjects were decided upon and suggested by the patrons that attended. This consisted of two opposing concepts. The focus was that a resolution of conflict is achievable by fully reflecting upon both sides of an issue or idea and recognizing the underlying connection that comes into play in a more occluded level. Interspersed between these meditations, Process hymns were sung.

Progresses were educational and therapeutic classes were held for Initiates, Disciples or Messengers. These superseded the Communications Course originally held by Compulsions Analysis. In addition to the study of Processean teaching, a series of exercises were practiced which pushed beyond the limits of sensitivity and interpersonal communication and broke through self-restricted levels of personal comfort in the participants. The study of Intention/Counter-Intention served to accelerate the evolution of consciousness in the members. The P-Scope or Process E-meter was used in the early period of Compulsions Analysis but began to be phased out in the early period of The Process. Photo-identification cards were made for and distributed to all members.

One revelation in Timothy Wyllie's book *Love Sex Fear Death* is that although Robert was the out-front part of the Omega, Mary Ann was very much the one in charge and had groomed Robert in his role of the Teacher and helped choose for him the message that was transmitted and the form in which it was presented. Robert was influenced and controlled by Mary Ann and was the one following her plans the majority of the time. She was the one who had been gifted with the power to see into the deepest regions of one's personality as well as having incredible powers of persuasion and a dominant will that was able to manifest that which she set her mind to. It was generally known to those in higher ranks that although Robert wrote much of the doctrinal publications, Mary Ann was the one who wielded the power. Together Robert and Mary Ann formed "The Omega" – Robert served as "The Teacher" and Mary Ann "The Oracle".

In reading Robert's accounts in *Initial Sketch for an Autobiography* it is clear that Mary Ann was his muse and that he was fully willing to serve to her needs. He felt that she was an incarnation of a goddess. To quote from *Initial Sketch*:

> "Mary Ann is a God figure for those who can't find God within themselves. And everyone needs God, either inside or outside, and very few can find it inside."

> "She was after my soul. She wanted to drown my individuality in her own. She wanted to encompass me completely, starve my reality and replace it with her own. She'd done this with countless other people and she'd do it with countless more. I was just another candidate. There was an alternative she'd settle for. If she could drive me away – on my decision – that would also be a victory – not so great a triumph as owning me, but a triumph none the less. If I couldn't take what she handed out and still stay with the game, she'd have won by my default. But that was second best. The first and foremost goal was to have me believing everything she believed, and with as much conviction. As credit to the extent of her power of suggestion, I must admit that there were many times when she almost succeeded. It shouldn't have been hard to attribute to Mary Ann the infallibility of God."

> "Basically, Mary Ann was the real drive in the situation, I was the intellect. She had the certainty; I had the answers. She had the eye for an opening; I had the means to navigate it. She knew the move to make; I knew how to make it. Without her, I'd have been too uncertain to plunge ahead. But between us we had the essential elements and in no time at all we were in business."

Celebrities played a role in getting the message of The Process transmitted and able to be received by a receptive audience. Mick Jagger and Marianne Faithful were prominently visible on the cover of Process magazines and were also featured in interviews. George Clinton featured two of de Grimston's writings on his Funkadelic albums – *America Eats Its Young* contained a short piece called *America* and *Maggot Brain* has an essay that had been taken from the *Fear* issue of the Process magazine. Many important and influential celebrities crossed paths with The Process and received their publications. Timothy Wyllie met Tim Leary and was able to give him heartfelt advice and a Processean perspective to help him deal with the weighty issues that he had been struggling with. He had previously met William Burroughs through Ian Sommerville in Tangier in the 50s. A Process band was organized in Toronto and often played at the local Process coffee house. It came to be known as The Process Version and featured Wyllie on lead guitar. They recorded ten songs in a Toronto recording studio but hopes were quashed by Mary Ann who hadn't liked the music, so nothing further became of the recordings. Another foray into the media was attempted by Malachi, who had been invited to appear on a nationally syndicated talk show. He was told he was to receive a fair time allotment to explain his ideology, but instead, the opportunity was used to put him on the spot and publicly scrutinize The Process.

Sex was used as a means of control within the group. Although celibacy was practiced by Processeans within the lower strata because it thwarted the natural flow of sexual energy, sex was viewed as a powerful force which one must come to terms with so as to not allow it to dominate one's behavior and thinking. The Process experimented with sex couplings with members of the group. Some members were paired together in Process unions and sexual relations were allowed with these members. However, no one owned each other in The Process and the concept of adultery didn't exist within the group. Group sex was indulged in at experimental gatherings that had been orchestrated by the Omega – but mostly was directed by Mary Ann. Members were encouraged to go beyond the bounds of societal restrictions and one's own inhibitions and connect with their sexual energies at the root of their being. They acted out their deepest fantasies. Normally, the Omega did not actively participate in them, although Mary Ann did couple herself with Timothy in one incident. Sex seems to have played a factor in the dissolution of the marriage of Robert and Mary Ann – she seemed to encourage him to physically express his attraction to Mother Morgana and afterwards to have used this against him in a manipulative power play that disposed him from his position in the Omega and from his role as Teacher as well.

Children that were born and brought up in The Process community were cared for by nannies in the group whose chief duties were to attend to them. They sometimes were sustained in small quarters under somewhat harsh conditions and were treated with rigid authority.

The original mode of dress or P-Gear was a long black cape with a cowl hood worn over all black attire. The badge of Mendes, which consisted of a black triangle with its point facing downward and the Sabbatic goat of Eliphas Levi in the center also adorned the uniform. This struck an intimidating image to those who first encountered a Processean. After 1971 this uniform was changed to a more moderate grey leisure suit, designed to change the public perception of members. Eventually it was determined that the greys were too bland (and may have been too similar to representing the grey forces) so they were changed once again to medium blue. The Four P Cross, created by Mother Sibyl, consisted of four lines which joined at 90 degree angles and formed a square in the middle. It had a similar look to that of a Nazi Swastika. The four P's represented in the Process symbology follow a four-fold tetragrammatical approach and are also reflective of the earth, air, fire, water division of nature as symbolized in ceremonial magic. The next Four P Cross was designed by Robert and was more stylized in its conception and had a similar look to a German Iron Cross. It was the icon most prominently displayed with Process material and the one that they became most recognized by. Another symbol designed by Robert was the conjoined Alpha and Omega symbol. It is referred to as the Sign of Union and has both mystical and sex-magical overtones to it. The Unity Cross consists of a large silver cross with a coiled red serpent whose body is contained within the cross. It represented the coming together of Christ and Satan and was a powerful symbol worn by many members. After Robert left the group, the P Cross was replaced with a six-pointed Star of David with two F's, one upside-down facing the other, which were conjoined.

Scientologists considered Process members to be "fair game" and although it can't be proven to have been orchestrated by them, while in Toronto, Timothy experienced a series of pranks. On one occasion, 200 pizzas were sent to the Toronto chapter. In another, a ton of sand was dropped at the doorstep of the chapter and they met with an irate driver who demanded payment.

On March 23, 1974 a schism occurred which resulted in Robert being asked to step down from his position – both as half of the Omega and as the Teacher. This order came from the Council of Masters. Several months after, Robert's writings in their entirety were dropped from the curriculum. Lawyers for the church advised that this would be best to avoid any claims that Robert may try to make concerning The Process. Within a short time, the name of the group was changed to the Foundation Church of the Millennium. At this juncture it was decided to do away with the four god system, removing Lucifer and Satan and deemphasizing Christ. The restructuring adhered only to Jehovah. The negative press received from an association with Charles Manson and the satanic bend of a portion of the literature were contributing factors in the setup of this new order. It was determined to distance The Process from these past influences as much as achievable. At this critical point, leadership within the group took on a much more authoritative tone and this drove a segment of the membership away over time. Robert attempted to continue along on his own. He turned to the New Orleans chapter, which he felt to be most important, and attempted to set up a program to teach courses and start a Process college, but was unable to stir enough interest in the project. He wrote "The Matthew Commentaries" which was a commentary on the New Testament. He then traveled to Toronto, and then on to Boston, where he began working with a fledgling group which he began to refer to as the Waltham Group, but unfortunately there wasn't enough potential in the group and nothing got off the ground. By 1979, he had given up any further hope of continuing a Process group under his leadership and withdrew any further contact with these past associations. After this series of futile attempts, Robert chose to return to the world of the grey forces and took a series of mundane jobs. He tried to propose a legal settlement from the Foundation considering all that he had contributed since its inception but was unable to work out any sort of deal. The Foundation Church took on a more acceptable public appearance and worked in the area of healing and led a series of courses. They began Psychic Workshops, Focus and Forum, which replaced Telepathy Developing Circles and Progresses. They eliminated the original axiom of the Unity of Christ and Satan, stopped using the church emblems, and discontinued singing many of the hymns. In their new structure, which was more spirituality based, they believed that a messiah was coming but hadn't yet arrived. Timothy realized, after having revealed a life-changing meditational experience and then sharing this with Mary Ann, and receiving little feedback or any value on the experience, that she considered that to focus any attention on it would be a threat to her position of authority. Mary Ann became more tyrannical and intolerant in her leadership after the schism had occurred. In 1975, the name was once again changed to the Foundation Faith of the Millennium. In 1976, a healing ministry was begun in New York. After a dispute with upper-level members, Timothy and seven others chose to leave the group to begin an autonomous sub-chapter of The Foundation known as The Unit. This was met with legal wrangling by members of the Foundation and after less than a year, The Unit dissolved. After several less than profitable years had passed, Foundation members relocated to Kanab, Utah in 1984 and decided on another dramatic reinvention by eliminating all religious affiliations held by the group. The name Foundation Faith was dropped and changed to a non-profit business known as Best Friends Animal Sanctuary. Since its inception in the late 80s, it has continued to expand and thrive and is now one of the most successful sanctuaries in the country. It even has its own television show on National Geographic called *Dogtown*, which is recorded at Best Friends.

Mary Ann died on November 14, 2005. Reportedly she had been in a coma prior to her death. A rumor mentioned by Wyllie is that during an evening stroll at Best Friends, she was attacked by a pack of wild dogs that ripped her throat out and tore her apart. A fitting mythology for a woman who styled herself as the goddess Hecate. She was married to longtime Process Master and Best Friends administrator Gabriel De Peyer at the time of her death.

The best book written about The Process from an academic perspective is *Satan's Power* by William Bainbridge, published in 1978. It gives a thorough account of the activities and philosophy of the group and follows their history up to the period of the Foundation Faith and is presented from a sociological point of view. It was written with the assistance of Robert de Grimston so it may have a slight bias towards his view of how events transpired. In this book, the names and orders were given pseudonyms to protect the confidentiality of those involved. Quite unfortunately, this book was never re-published after its first printing and is scarce to come across but is infrequently seen on the collectible book market.

A chapter of Ed Sanders' subjective and highly speculative book on Manson, *The Family*, drew unfounded connections between Manson and The Process merely because one of the Process headquarters was located in close proximity to where the Manson family were residing. Some of Manson's notions of incarnating the energies of Abraxas and going beyond good and evil were similar to de Grimston's thesis of the reconciliation of opposites – the dissolution of the enmity between God and Satan. While this drew unwanted attention to The Process (in subsequent printings of the book, this chapter was removed due to litigation by the Process who successfully sued the publisher, E.P. Dutton) the connection had been made in the court of public opinion between Manson and The Process. Members of the group even went so far as to visit Manson in prison, and in a subsequent article in the *Death* issue of the Process magazine, a brief article contrasted Manson's writings on death with that of the Christian author Malcolm Muggeridge. While this may have been seen as taboo to associate with Manson and present his writing, it nonetheless presents a thought-provoking perspective, and its inclusion was quite bold and daring at the time. However, the mere inclusion and association with Manson drew the ire of those who had already viewed The Process with trepidation and held fear of the unknown which they represented, and this provided easy fodder with which to draw a loose connection between The Process and the nefarious activities of the Manson family – a guilt by association mentality. Manson espoused that he was both Jesus and the devil. This is similar to the Process concept of the Unity of Christ and Satan, or in other words, coming to terms and uniting both extremes of one's personality so that rather than being at odds with one's nature, they are able to achieve a unity in one's being.

In chapter five of the first edition of Sanders' *The Family*, he states that The Process appeared in LA in early 1968 and retained a prominent presence until several days before the shooting of Robert Kennedy in June 1968, at which time they dropped out of sight. He quotes de Grimston from *Jehovah on War*: "Release the fiend that lies dormant within you, for he is strong and ruthless and his power is far beyond the bounds of human frailty." By this, he implies that Robert is advocating the acceleration of bloodshed and violence and that once this has transpired, The Process would be the chosen ones who shall lead the way in the post-Armageddon. Sanders purports that the Process magazines eulogized Hitler and that its graphic content spilled forth with gore and mayhem. He includes sections from an interview with Brother Ely (a.k.a. Victor Wild), who had been recruited into The Process in LA. Ely explains that as The Process swept through different parts of the world, they attracted converts and that by a multi-god approach, the appeal broadened as certain individuals gravitated toward a particular god – either Jehovah, Lucifer or Satan depending upon their predisposition. The Satanists are depicted as the goons with a streak towards violence. Sanders attempts to link The Process to a network of death cults operating in California and through this to suggest that Charles Manson was involved in this. In a jailhouse interview, when asked whether Manson was familiar with Robert de Grimston, he remarked, "You're looking at him." Although both Process members and Manson were known to have hung out at the Spiral Staircase in Topeka Canyon in Malibu and that both had resided on Cole Street, it was at different times and their paths never directly crossed. Sanders further speculates that The Process may even have been an influence on Robert Kennedy murderer Sirhan Sirhan. While some of the historical accounts in Sanders' research seem to be accurate and to have been gleaned from Process magazines, the conclusions drawn from his research seem to have been gathered from his mistaken beliefs from reading de Grimston's apocalyptical writings and taking them far too literally. It was quite fortunate that this chapter was removed after the first printing due to the erroneous information it contained, after legal action was taken by the Process.

Just as in Sanders' book, there is also a chapter in *The Ultimate Evil* by Maury Terry entitled "The Process". Terry was a part of the Satanic Ritual Abuse (SRA) hysteria which was in full force in 1987, a new scare in the media that was also known as a Satanic Panic epidemic. This book is one that set the foundation for the hysteria being perpetrated and was often cited when referencing unconfirmed accounts of satanic activity. The insidious factor that set the precedent in this book was the theory that there exists a covert, highly orchestrated satanic organization which trafficked in murder, child pornography, drugs, human and animal sacrifice and that it threatened the very fiber of modern society. In Untermeyer Park located in Yonkers, skinned German Shepherds were discovered – Berkowitz was known to have been in the area shortly before they had been discovered. The Process were known to be fond of the Alsatian breed of German Shepherd. Terry implies that perhaps the sacrifices could have been initiated by a fringe group within The Process. In Berkowitz's letter to Breslin, he refers to a group that took credit for the murderous mayhem known as the "Twenty-Two Disciples of Hell". Terry perceived The Process to be a "cult", so in researching the group he already imagined all sorts of sinister abominations lurking behind every corner. Terry spoke to Sanders while researching this book, so it should be kept in mind that much of the information provided regarding The Process came through the filter of Ed Sanders – who was an advisor for this book. It presents his slanted, biased view that The Process was a sinister satanic cult.   Terry saw them strictly as a satanic group rather than a four-fold equilateral system that was focussed on a union of opposites. Once again, as with Sanders, Terry took the writings of de Grimston literally as easy fodder to present his view that The Process was a cult bent on hastening the end of the world through means of chaos and murder, in order to cleanse the world of the grey forces so that they could rebuild a satanic empire in the new world order. Another de Grimston quote that Terry seized upon was the statement, "My prophecy upon this wasted earth and upon the corrupt creation that squats upon its ruined surface is: THOU SHALT KILL" (taken from *Jehovah on War*). It should be remembered that in this tumultuous period the Vietnam War raged on daily and student protests sought a way out of the senseless slaughter being perpetrated in the name of freedom.

Terry asserts that Manson had been heavily influenced by The Process and that he shared an affinity to the idea of a duality of Jesus/Satan which he believed he was a living example of. Similarities between the Process writings on Fear and Manson's concept of "getting the fear" is viewed as more than mere coincidence by Terry. The Process magazines *Fear* and *Death* he viewed as being chock full of Nazi and other forms of forbidden imagery – the union of the Lamb of God and the goat of Satan was described by Terry as an "unholy alliance". He reveals that all members of The Process, regardless of their affiliation with a particular god, were required to undergo a long stretch of Satan worship supposedly involving blood rituals and sacrifice. He states that Stanley Baker admitted that he was a member of a Process offshoot in Santa Cruz known as Four Pi or the Four P Movement. Baker stated that the group practiced ritual human sacrifice and that he was a cannibal and had ritually sacrificed dogs as well. One murder that he had been convicted of occurred in O'Neil Park in the Santa Ana Mountains. The group of which Stanley was a member was said to possess a portable crematorium to dispose of any evidence of their crimes. Terry goes on to speculate that Berkowitz was simply a hitman for the Four Pi. In the updated epilog to the 1999 edition, Berkowitz admits that he was a member of Four Pi and he had witnessed German Shepherds being sacrificed. The "occult superstar" hitman Manson II has his identity revealed to be Bill Mentzer, and it is stated that he quite possibly could have been the Grand Chingon – the title for the head of Four Pi. He had been convicted of the murder of producer Roy Radin and may have been involved in several of the Son of Sam killings as well. (Manson family members even suggested that Manson may have been the Grand Chingon.) In an interview which was broadcast on A&E "Investigative Reports", Berkowitz now asserted his knowledge of the Four P Movement being involved in the drug trade and underage sex soirées which catered to a wealthy clientele who craved depravity. He purported that they also were involved in producing snuff films. It is stated that Manson also recently revealed in a jailhouse interview to have met the heads of The Process in the Spiral Staircase. In the end of the book Terry gives a dire revelation that The Process (or Four P Movement, as I believe he is referring to) is still out there and remains active, but is operating in an underground capacity, concealed behind socially acceptable fronts. Hard to believe that throughout this pack of loose speculation and innuendo, the Four Pi, which Terry would have readers believe, is operating as a malignant evil underlying the very fabric of society and hell-bent on murder and ushering in the Armageddon. However, it is interesting that since the Process first appeared, no member has ever been accused of any crime, nor has Terry's thesis in yellow journalism proved anything to the contrary.

According to author Peter Levenda, members of The Process were often seen in Herman Slater's Magickal Childe store in Manhattan. Allegations have suggested that initially the Process was a front for a German Neo-Fascist group founded by the German Democratic Party and that Mary Ann believed herself to have been the reincarnation of Joseph Goebbels. It was known that she had studied Hitler's ascension to power. Although the Process incorporated Satan into the echelon of gods in the late 60s, The Process Satan symbolism differed greatly from the one depicted in the Church of Satan. Some suggest that the Four Pi group was a continuation of a group that splintered off from the satanic branch of The Process – which rather than disbanding with Mary Ann's strictly Jehovian Process after 1974 merely remained and continued to operate underground. In *Helter Skelter* by Vincent Bugliosi, some speculation was raised that Bruce Davis from the Manson family visited the Process headquarters in 1968 as well as the London Scientology headquarters, but this has never been substantiated. UFO author Whitley Strieber stated that he had also visited the Process headquarters in London in 1968 prior to his alien encounters. In the book *Sinister Forces*, Levenda teeters between just suggesting the possibility of Manson having direct dealings with The Process, and in other places definitively asserting that they had been in contact with one another.

In the early 90s a collective was begun by Genesis P-Orridge, Nivek Ogre and William Morrison, who had all shared a deep and abiding appreciation of and interest in the Process Church of the Final Judgment. It was an open-ended collective and espoused the ideas and theories of The Process. A new order was initiated by Genesis simultaneous to this, which was known as Thee Outer Process International or TOPI (not to be confused with Thee Temple of Psychic Youth or TOPY). The collective was involved with a website at process.org, which offered discourse and dialog regarding The Process. It encourages involvement with writers and artists who wish to share Processean-inspired materials. An online writing attributed to Father Malachi (but very much couched in the G P-O writing style) is called *The Process Is…*, and provides an excellent explanation of the Process philosophy and how the Process techniques can be utilized to regain control in one's life and provide the liberation needed to achieve one's desires. It fully explains the goals and aims of what process.org is serving to achieve: greater understanding of the methods of the Process, and a deeper awareness and purpose in divining one's true will.

In 1996, Skinny Puppy released an album entitled *The Process*. It is a concept album based around the Process. On the Psychic TV CD *Force the Hand of Chance* is a hidden track not mentioned on the track listing which is a short, mind-warping barrage that includes a series of questions similar to ones that may be given to one hooked up to the P-Scope, followed by an unsettling pronouncement: "Welcome to the Process". Music video producer William Morrison of Process Media Labs, in assistance with Genesis P-Orridge, released a video called *The Process is the Product* and, in addition, Morrison made two music videos for The Process release for the songs *Hardset Head* and *Candle* which used elements from the collaborative video. Both are replete with Process Church imagery taken from that initial video collaboration. In 1988, a site sprang up known as the Society of Processeans which appears to be purely an online endeavor that provided information and links to Process publications and other materials. They offered to raise awareness into areas of interest to modern day Processeans and for those desirous to see things through a Processean perspective. It appears to have some connection with process.org. An advertisement for *Love Sex Fear Death* by Timothy Wyllie (published by Feral House) was directed by Morrison and is listed on youtube and includes the secret audio track by Psychic TV, *Welcome to the Process*. A band called Electric Wizard has a Process inspired video on youtube called *The Processean*. Timothy Wyllie has a brief interview on youtube and answers several questions about The Process.

A website called The Neo Church of Final Judgment at 4p2.org was an experiment by Joseph Matheny of Ong's Hat infamy. A recorded interview with Matheny appears at alteri.com/blog/?p=2197, called "Fear and Loathing on the Internet: Redux (Part 1)". The interview is conducted by Nick Pell of Black Sun Gazette and is taken from a podcast from February 23, 2009 on G-Spot. Matheny admits to having been the person who created the 4P2 Project as a social exercise in mythmaking and data collection. He viewed The Process as it was seen publicly as being a "boogeyman" that had a dark, enduring myth that had been exploited and misrepresented through the writings of Ed Sanders and Maury Terry. The fictitious shadowy group responsible in these books was known as the Four P Movement or Four Pi. This was the identity that Matheny chose for his charade because of its ominous and nefarious associations. It was an experiment to see what sorts of response would be received from the conspiracy sites by purporting that the Four Pi Movement was reforming. It was purposely disinformational in its conception and done as an exercise in critical thinking. He simply linked the 4P2 site to The Process Church Wikipedia page to create exposure for the site.

On the page, he included pictures of Berkowitz, Manson, Zodiac, and the Smiley Face Killer to add to the foreboding mystique. The site was organic in its creation in the sense that once Matheny set it up, he left it alone to see what sort of effect it would cause. The site received a lot of traffic and during its peak period, it received over 13,000 visits. The majority of responses came from conspiracy theorists and true crime buffs – particularly those interested in Zodiac/Son of Sam/Manson came to the site. Half of the people that wrote to him sent vitriolic, hostile letters accusing him of horrendous, irresponsible actions. The other half were described by Matheny as disturbed, sociopathic individuals looking to join and/or associate themselves with Four Pi and anxious to be mentored in mayhem. Matheny is a cultural engineer who posits diverse avenues of endeavor such as writing, producing and invention focused on fringe belief systems. He went so far as to identify himself as 'Manson II', the fictional maniacal leader of the Four Pi group who supposedly trained Manson and Berkowitz. Matheny first became acquainted with the Process while hanging out in the same circles as Psychic TV and Skinny Puppy, just as their CD *The Process* was being released. At this period, there was a great upsurge of interest in the ideas and philosophy of the Process. At this point Genesis wanted to usher in a rebirth of The Process and was making inroads in this direction. Matheny was more interested in the methodologies and techniques used in The Process rather than any doctrine associated with it. As Matheny had theorized, only about two percent of the responses to his site got what he was doing. Matheny's inherent approach is to question reality, authority and belief systems, which are blindly adhered to by the vast majority of the population. He views most magical groups as originally having useful techniques designed to break a person out of consensus reality, but once they become institutionalized they devolve into lifeless rituals devoid of their initial power.

For those who were able to be a part of The Process, it represented an initiatory school that allowed for the possibility of spiritual advancement and evolutionary growth to occur. It was a revolutionary system that changed the lives of those involved with it. While some members in the end may have felt themselves to have been financially exploited by the Omega, it gave members a chance to experience life in a spiritual, philosophical mystery school in an environment that couldn't be encountered anywhere else.

TIMOTHY WYLLIE INTERVIEW

Hiram Corso, Frater Robert and Malachi

Hiram: Besides the E-meter, were there any other aspects of Scientology involved in Process teachings, either involving therapeutic methods or covered in the information dealt with in the lectures?

Timothy: I'm not too well-versed in what Scientology does and from Mary Ann's desire to distance The Process from Scientology, I doubt if there was much they wanted to duplicate. I believe that two or three of the exercises in the early Compulsions Analysis were lifted from Scientology. I don't recall the names of the exercises but they generally involved confrontation, insults or direct eye-contact.

Hiram: After getting dramatic results and breakthroughs with the E-meter, were you disappointed that its use was eliminated or did you feel that the evolution of the group's working had superseded its usage?

Timothy: Our ability to "read" other people superseded the need for the meters. Plus, we were intent on separating ourselves from Hubbard's lot and the E-meter (by now the P-Scope) was the most evident connection.

Hiram: Immediately following the Xtul experience, what was the overall message and purpose that defined what those involved in it brought away from it, and what was the mission of The Process?

Timothy: Xtul was a massive shot-in-the-arm for all of us. It confirmed that we were on an authentic spiritual journey. After the failure of London, prior to Xtul, we'd given up on England. Xtul restored our faith that we had something valuable to offer the general public. In terms of the "mission", it really boiled down to spreading The Process message of self-responsibility and getting people to join us.

Hiram: What were the circumstances that precipitated the change from the psycho-analytical group Compulsions Analysis to The Process Church of the Final Judgment? How was this formal change decided upon? At what point was it decided that Robert de Grimston would be the figurehead leader of The Process? It seems in the early period to have been an equal distribution of power between Mary Ann and Robert.

Timothy: The change was a fairly natural progression from Compulsions Analysis to The Process (the Church came later) since the more work we did on the meters, and the business of living in a community, pushed us from a psychological point of view towards a more psychic and then spiritual way of thinking. The formal change to a church was essentially a way of avoiding paying taxes.

Yes, there was a good balance between Robert and Mary Ann, mainly during the Compulsions Analysis period. Gradually Mary Ann's personality took over, people were more drawn to her than him and by Xtul she was clearly the power and ambition. I think it was around the time of becoming a church that Mary Ann pushed Robert out in front. These sorts of decisions were entirely hers – it wasn't a group decision. By that time, only the inner circle ever saw them.

Hiram: What impact do you feel resulted from the unfounded speculations that several authors have theorized about The Process having connections to the Manson family and David Berkowitz – Son of Sam or that they were involved with military intelligence conducting an experiment in mind control? How did The Process react to or change as a result of this?

Timothy: In many ways, the Manson issue was a fulcrul event in The Rake's Progress of The Process. In my book, I suggest that losing the English case was the first time Mary Ann appeared to be fallible. I also feel it was the moment that Mary Ann started sensing she could do without Robert. Settling the American case out-of-court obviously encouraged us in thinking we could make our case – that we'd had nothing to do with Manson – so when we lost in England it was a terrible shock. The news was kept pretty close to the chest so only the senior membership knew we'd lost. It was only much later when I got to look at the court transcripts that I realized how truly idiotic Robert and Mary Ann had been in dealing with the case. Perhaps if the judge hadn't been so obviously biased against us – which he clearly was – we would not have been able to rationalize the loss away so easily. But then again, both Robert and Mary Ann showed themselves over the years incapable of taking any responsibility for their actions, so it wouldn't have made much difference. What the situation should have done was to force us to look at some of the effects our publications were having on people and to take some responsibility for them, but that never really happened.

The Son of Sam alleged connection appears to have been generated by the deluded mind of Maury Terry and based on such flimsy evidence as we liked our German Shepherds, therefore... His book also emerged some time after The Foundation left NYC, so I would imagine it didn't have much effect on them.

I don't recall anyone suggesting the community was a mind-control experiment in the 15 years I was there. And if it was, it doesn't say much for military intelligence! The confrontation at the end of the book in which my questioner demanded to know whether Mary Ann was working with the Intelligence Community was the only time I heard it raised and as far as I remember he had no evidence and was really just stoking the fire. I suppose it is possible she might have been contacted early on, before The Process, but I was as close to her as anyone and I can't help feeling she would have wanted to boast about it if it were true. I just can't see how spooks would have gained anything from the liaison. And if it were true, then they might have been more helpful when we were going through one of our financial meltdowns. And there sure wasn't any sign of that.

Hiram: When it was decided that Robert was to be eliminated in his role of Teacher within the group, were all of his teachings and writings instantly dropped from study and no longer referred to, or outright refuted, or was it gradual change when shifting to the Foundation Faith period?

Timothy: It was a sudden shift, as Robert was kicked out. Most of Robert's books had probably all been sold by then and frankly there wasn't much time for studying or reading. I can't speak for the activities of the lower ranks, but it seems to match Mary Ann's personality that she would ease out Robert's contribution. I'm sure she must have felt by then that she'd never really needed him in the first place.

Hiram: Did any members join Robert when he split from the group?

Timothy: No one from the inner circle or the senior ranks followed him. Only a few peripheral members, disciples and such.

Hiram: What were the origins of The Process use of the salutations As It Is and So Be It? As It Is seems to be derived from the translated meaning of Bhagavad-Gita and So Be It seems a variation on So Mote It Be used in the Wiccan tradition.

Timothy: I believe the salutations emerged organically, rather than as adaptations of previous belief systems.

Hiram: Can you please provide a list of all of the books written by Robert de Grimston (as well as books written by other Process members) and a list of all of the Process magazines that were published?

Timothy: You'll have to get this list elsewhere. *[Process Books and Documents – As It Is, Humanity Is the Devil, A Candle in Hell, The Xtul Dialogues, Exit, Drug Addiction: A Process Statement, The Gods on War, The Gods and Their People, The Seeds of Destruction – A Study of Human Aggression, The Ultimate Sin, Thy Neighbor as Thyself – A Study of Human Contact, Man's Relationship to Man Communication Course, ...And Then There Was Darkness (Father Aaron), For Christ Is Come (Father John), So Be It. Process Magazines – The Common Market (issue one), Freedom of Expression (issue two), Mindbending (issue three), The Process on Sex (issue four), The Process on Fear (issue five), The Process on Death (issue six), The Process on Love (issue seven), The Processeans (monthly newsletter). Process Free Booklets – The Unity of Christ and Satan, How Can I Become a Processean?, The Process – "Fax 'n Figgers", Donating: As You Give So Shall You Receive, The Process – Foundation.]*

Hiram: Were the Omega notified that Timothy Leary was brought to a Process assembly as a potential candidate to join the group? Were they disappointed that he wasn't interested in joining?

Timothy: I didn't tell them, but they probably heard about it. I doubt if they would have had much reaction one way or another – Mary Ann was very much against drugs and I suspect she'd have been very sardonic about Uncle Tim.

Hiram: Which chapters thrived for the longest period and which bore the greatest results? How many chapters were there and what were the membership numbers? How many people were members of The Process in its heyday?

Timothy: The New York HQ of The Foundation Faith was financially the most successful and probably also the most popular. The early Chapters in New Orleans and San Francisco brought people in, and the later Toronto Chapter was also regarded as successful. Chapter numbers changed but at the max there were probably six or eight places functioning at the same time. Actual membership of people within the community probably never exceeded 80-100 distributed through the various Chapters. There were maybe another 200-300 people who were in training – it could take between six months and two years for someone to become an IP (Inner Processean).

Hiram: Can you provide an explanation of the different levels within the Process Church and the requirements for each of the levels?

Timothy: You'll find all that in the book. [The Hierarchy structure in the Process – Acolyte – Disciple – Outside Processean Messenger – Inside Processean Messenger – Prophet – Priest – Master – The Omega (consisted of Robert and Mary Ann de Grimston).]

Hiram: How familiar were you and other members of The Process with the writings and ideas of Aleister Crowley? Did they ever bear any significance to the philosophy of The Process? When did you first become familiar with his ideas?

Timothy: I very much doubt if many of them were aware of Crowley – Robert certainly wasn't, so I doubt if there was any cross-over there. Mary Ann, with her occult leanings must have known about him but I doubt if she'd ever read his work. If there were any similarities, and I can't think of any particular ones, then they would have emerged from a somewhat similar interest in control and manipulation. My visit to the Abbey was a purely personal interest and really didn't reflect the interests of the group.

Hiram: It seems that the book written by William Bainbridge, *Satan's Power*, was the most in-depth analysis of The Process ever written. Was the influence of that book able to further exposure of the group? Was Bainbridge a convert to The Process or just more of an ally?

Timothy: Much of Bainbridge's book was derived from conversations with Robert after he left so it has a bias in that direction. He never got close to the inner circle and what was really happening. I doubt if it had any influence on a broader membership. It was a rather dry and academic exercise.

Malachi: Are any of the ten songs recorded by the Process Version band at Thundersound Studios in Toronto still in existence?

Timothy: I doubt it. Perhaps Best Friends still have a tape in their archives. Apart form the original 2" tape made at Thundersound, I know we duped one or two cassettes, one of which we'd sent to Robert and Mary Ann.

Malachi: What was the usual demeanor of Robert and Mary Ann? Were they open and accessible to Process members or were they wholly removed and aloof?

Timothy: Wholly removed and aloof from all but the dozen or so members of the inner circle.

Malachi: In Malachi McCormick's chapter *Processean Reflections* he states that Robert and Mary Ann thought that L. Ron Hubbard was "a flake". In conversations with Robert and Mary Ann, did they ever elaborate as to why they thought he was a flake? I've read several accounts myself of Hubbard being a debased and slightly off center character – mainly from the biography *L. Ron Hubbard: Messiah or Madman?*

Timothy: Yeah, I know the book. I think he got it mostly right. The fact that Hubbard hadn't got the use of the E-Meter right (well, it was right for him!), plus the bugging incident must have contributed to Robert and Mary Ann's distaste for him. The only thing I recall Mary Ann saying, which she did quite regularly, was that his teeth were falling to pieces and he didn't have the courage to go to the dentist. I can't substantiate this, however, but he did have an awful smile.

Malachi: To what extent did L. Ron Hubbard go to in order to discourage the use of the E-Meter for Compulsion Analysis and subsequent groups run by the de Grimstons? What was Hubbard's and Scientology's perspective on the Process?

Timothy: I believe we were "fair-game" while that lasted. And Scientology always loathed "squirrels" as they called us and others who used their technology. I believe they scapegoated us over the Manson affair (their materials were found at Manson's ranch) and did other acts (in the book) which were simply designed to annoy us.

It's possible, although I don't know this for sure, but our change from E-meter to P-scope (the same mechanism in a different box) might have been driven by Scientology in some way.

Malachi: After reading your new book I was surprised to find out that none of the Process Church or Foundation Faith of the Millennium material was ever registered with the copyright office. Is there any special reasoning behind this or was it just a lack of concern or neglect in doing so?

Timothy: Don't know anything about this but it was probably from a lack of concern. After Robert's books, little written material came out of The Foundation Church or Faith.

Malachi: In the last paragraph of Adam Parfrey's introductory chapter, *Rarely What It Seems*, do you think there's any truth to his statement that today "it's a Process Church world once again, perhaps even more so"? Considering The Process was at its peak years during the anti-establishment hey-days of the late 60s and early 70s, I'm not sure if something like the church would go over in today's environment. How do you feel that the Process would succeed in the present environment? Several organizations (that I won't mention) that are still in existence are nothing more than "lonely hearts clubs" for the emotionally and intellectually disenfranchised. Your thoughts?

Timothy: I believe what Adam meant was that the world was in somewhat the same state as it was in the 60s when catastrophe felt so immediate. I agree with you, The Process couldn't emerge in these days – we all know too much about cults – but it wouldn't surprise me if more and more people are gathering in community settings as the general situation collapses. Perhaps morphogenically they will have learnt naturally from the work of groups like TP (The Process) and other cults who were exploring the limits of community experience. I don't believe TP, for better or worse, would have ever existed without Mary Ann. She created the bonds (and bondage) that held it all together. Best Friends, now without her, essentially functions on the inertia of its earlier iterations. The few groups with a presence on the Web, maintaining links with the old TP, have seemed to me to be without any juice.

Frater Robert: Attorney John Markham (of Boston, Massachusetts) was employed by The Process as their attorney. Some insinuate that he was a member of the group and provided them with several houses for their headquarters. What makes Attorney Markham interesting is that he served as a legal counsel to The Process and then later was appointed as prosecuting attorney for the federal government and was a mover and shaker in the so-called "Satanic Panic" witch hunt of the 1980s. He was also associated with an attorney of the Weld family, a prestigious American family of which Tuesday Weld is related. Jeff Turner claims she was a leader in the Illuminati and others have claimed the Weld family members are Illuminati. Did you know Markham? What can you tell us of his involvement in the Process?

Timothy: Yes, I knew John Markham, although not well and I didn't keep up with him after I left. He was employed by The Process, although I don't know the terms, or quite what he worked on. I don't believe he was ever a member, per se, since we made it so challenging to actually join. He was one of a few people from the outside who also had a sympathy for what we were about – Tommy Baumler was another attorney we employed to incorporate the church.

I can't throw light on the Weld issue or Markham's work as a federal attorney, but I'd have thought they were amongst those unfortunate coincidences so beloved by conspiracy buffs.

Frater Robert: The interim period during which the Foundation left New York and resurfaced many years later as Best Friends at Kanab, Utah (1978-1993) seems little mentioned or chronicled in either your account or the accounts of others concerning them. Could you provide us with a more in-depth chronicle as to what actually transpired during that period?

Timothy: Since I left the group in 1977 I decided not to write about what I didn't know – plus after leaving I wasn't that interested in what they were up to so I'm not the right person to answer this question. I know only that they spent some time on a ranch in the Southwest before moving to Utah. I believe it wasn't an easy time for them.

Frater Robert: The Foundation Church of The Millennium apparently went through a period of "shape-shifting", in which its name was changed firstly to The Foundation Church of the Millennium and later to The Foundation Faith in God. In its later stage it seemed to have become a more orthodox form of Christianity and offer a belief in the Christian trinity, the deity of Christ and salvation from sin – yet it was still firmly focused on End Times issues. It had a healing ministry and psychic consultations listed among its attributes. The address given on the web is: Foundation Faith in God, 3030

Palomino Lane, Las Vegas, Nevada, 89107-4510. I was wondering why none of this later day activity was covered in your book?

Timothy: Again, I didn't cover what I didn't know. Since I'm sure you gathered from the book, much of the belief systems proposed by The Foundation reflected Mary Ann's changing attitudes. From my perspective, we moved from an original psychotherapeutic system, from which emerged an authentic spiritual impulse, which was then steadily distorted and manipulated to become more and more acceptable to the general public as the need for money and prestige took over. By the time The Process became The Foundation, we'd pretty much lost any of the spiritual juice we'd started off with.

Frater Robert: The Black Rose Spiritual Center web site *http:///wwwblackrosespiritualceneter.org/BIfSystms/Chrtsn./FnthOfGod.html* lists Raphael de Peyer as its reverend at the Las Vegas address. Another website lists Michael McManus as the pastor. Michael McManus has a younger sister, Kristi McManus, who plays a large role in conspiratorial theorist Jeff Turner's account. She runs or ran a day care center called Enchanted Child in North Las Vegas. Jeff would have us believe that she literally took over the Foundation Faith In God. Can you shed any light on all of this? The Best Friends Animal Sanctuary in Kanab, Utah (Angel Canyon) was once a film set for Hollywood Western movies (The last film shot there being *The Outlaw Josey Wales*). Rumor has it that the location was purchased from actor Jack Nicholson, or that they stayed at a ranch owned by him before finalizing the purchase of Angel Canyon. Is there any fact in all of this to your knowledge? Who did they purchase or acquire the property from?

Timothy: I couldn't get through to the site above. Raphael de Peyer died recently – either last year or the one before – so the site is evidently out of date. I don't know who Michael McManus is – possibly Michael Mountain, one of the leaders at this point, but where that new surname comes from, I've no idea. We were always changing our names and I doubt if that has changed. Michael Mountain certainly doesn't have a younger sister. I know that since they have become so successful saving animals a lot of people who aren't connected with the original group now work as volunteers, etc. But, again, they would have little to do with the members of the original group and most likely would know nothing of their background. This Kristi person, again as far as I know, never "took over" – if Mary Ann had been alive at the time, as Turner has suggested, she would never have let anyone else anywhere near the inner circle. I've no idea where Turner gets his facts but this one was glaringly wrong. The senior members were always a closed shop and very few from the outside were ever invited into it.

Sorry, there again, I can't answer the details of their acquisition of "Angel Canyon". I simply haven't had any substantial contact with them since I left, apart from two very inconsequential visits there over the years.

Hiram: Are there any topics that were omitted from the book that you wish could have been further explored regarding the Process?

Timothy: Just a few brief incidents that I might have included but overall I feel the book was pretty complete from my point of view. It was never an attempt to tell the complete history of the group and as you can see from my replies here, I didn't know a lot of the things that were going on which I wasn't directly involved with. Another person from the inner circle would likely tell a slightly different story with different accents on the stuff they knew about. It was a very secretive organization, not only occulted from the outside, but also between the levels in the hierarchy. I was in a fairly unique situation in that I was there from the beginning, was generally close to the center of the action, but also was cast down to the bottom every once in a while on Mary Ann's whim.

Plus I might well have been the only one who got to fuck her (although who knows if she wasn't screwing others – I certainly never told anyone else of the incident and no one else would have told anyone either).

Hiram: How did you first become aware of Mary Ann's death in 2005?

Timothy: One of the more human of the inner circle leaked it to one of the ex-members a couple of months after she died. They were clearly trying to keep it a secret and I doubt if they ever wanted the truth out there.

Hiram: How many chapters were there in total and where were they located?

Timothy: This varied over the time as one Chapter opened and another closed. At the peak there were Chapters in New York, Chicago, Miami, Toronto, San Francisco, Los Angeles, New Orleans, Boston, and then at other times, London, Paris, Rome, Amsterdam, Hamburg and Munich. We also had a small Chapter in Kansas City.

Hiram: There have been very few photographic images of Mary Ann that have ever been shown. Considering your background as an artist and the fact that you were intimate with her, how would you describe her both in physical appearance as well as the aura that she emanated?

Timothy: She was around 5' 6", not slim, but with a pleasant rounded figure. Her green eyes were her strongest feature; she kept her hair shoulder length, blondish with highlights. Her face was broad and somewhat brutal, with rather a poor skin. She dressed expensively in loose, mostly silk get-ups. Her face was animated and she was fearless in expressing her opinion. She emanated confidence and an apparently genuine interest in whoever she was talking to. People would tend to lean in to hear her.

She could also express a strong sexual magnetism when she wanted. Her psychic abilities allowed her to probe very effectively into other peoples' needs, shames and compulsions, so her questions invariably went to the core of the person.

She'd clearly worked on her Glasgow accent because her voice was accentless and pitched in low tones and yet, in class-conscious England, it was obvious she'd jumped herself up. It would be anathema to her to be thought "common". She'd read widely, could continue intelligent conversations, yet invariably the contact would move, in a person to person situation, to some form of very personal analysis or perceptive questions that might entrance the other person, or, be far too much for them to cope with. In group situations, she would always become the center of attention. Yet she was clever enough in working a group that by drawing out other people, they were made to feel the center of attention.

Hiram: I'm sure that in The Process there were a number of lower position members who were vying to become a member of the inner circle to wield a greater influence within the group. How was it determined who gained entry into the inner elite? Was it strictly composed of members who joined early on?

Timothy: There were one or two exceptions of people who'd worked their way into the inner circle – my cousin Gregory (Andrew Castle) was one of those. He joined after Xtul and very quickly rose through the ranks. The hardest jump was from Priest to Master – they got harder as you went up. There was a lot of vying for position among those who were working as OPs ("Outer Processeans") and who'd set their sights on joining.

Hiram: If Robert de Grimston was part of the Omega at the top level, how did the Council of Masters have the power to depose him of his position as The Teacher? Wasn't it strictly Mary Ann's doing when he was removed?

Timothy: It was entirely Mary Ann who ousted Robert. The Council of Masters was totally in her pocket. It was largely for PR purposes, mainly for the IPs ("Inner Processeans") who hadn't known what went on at the top. It was a coup d'état, plain and simple.

Hiram: What kind of response have you received with the publication of your book *Love Sex Fear Death*? Have you experienced anyone that wasn't happy to see it in print, such as former Processeans?

Timothy: No, nothing overtly negative from the Best Friends folk. I suspect they are deliberately keeping as quiet as possible about the book. The only comment I've heard, and it was third hand from one of them to a best Friend supporter, was along the lines of "At least we didn't bomb Federal buildings...", which felt to me to be a somewhat lenient bit of self-analysis.

This is pure speculation but it's possible they are resigned to having it all out there and since they are really programmed to not speak about their past except in the most general PR terms, they might even be pleased it came out in this way. Also, with Mary Ann out of the way they might not feel so vituperative about the truth emerging.

Hiram: I saw that you held a lecture in LA that may have included a Sabbath Assembly Ritual. How was it received and do you have any plans to do more lectures like this?

Timothy: It was received remarkably well. We held it in the Silent Movie Theater in LA, sold out the first show, put on a second, and sold out that one as well. I was surprised that the 20-minute segment we did out of the Sabbath Assembly came across as well as it did, people really getting off on the spiritual aspect, the uniting of opposites. In fact, I felt that the audience reacted, if anything, in a more positive way than they did back in the old days. The apocalyptic tone felt more suited to the state of the world today than back in the 60s, when it was only the bomb that concerned everybody.

The musicians involved who had rearranged and played Process hymns and chants were top-rate talents and did a wonderful job with the music.

The Pantheon of Genesis Breyer P-Orridge

Jean-Pierre Turmel, Rouen, 2009

Translated by Sylvie Walder

Because of my manifold origins (Greek, Norman, Breton), I was placed, right from the start, at the crossroads of all mythologies: Celtic, Greek antique and Scandinavian. In comparison to the established religions, ancient mythologies have an advantage: they are, nowadays, freed from any faith. From the lost Gods, nothing remains but a symbol, which is essential food for any mind, for any thought.

Already as a child, I was brought up on the above mentioned legends and mythologies, but also those of Egypt, and later those of the aboriginal peoples, America, Africa or the Pacific... Imperceptibly, I got closer to the present, even if, from a geographical point of view, they still appeared as "distant".

> You may build churches, mark off the roads with chapels and crosses, you will not prevent the gods of Ancient Thessaly from reappearing through the songs of poets and the books of scholars.
>
> – Hawthorne (quoted by Jean Ray in his novel *Malpertuis*, published in 1943)

One of the first texts of the fantastic/Gothic genre I discovered in my teens was *Malpertuis*, a text written in 1943 by the Belgian master Jean Ray (Jean Raymond Marie de Kremer aka John Flanders). I had previously read some of his particularly horrifying tales. A strange novel set in a place, a residence, Malpertuis, which was no less strange. The beings dwelling there are, at the same time, terribly human and monstrous. One of the driving forces of the text is that one eventually understands that they are the ancient Gods of the Olympus, wound up there, close to agony, because no one, or nearly no one, believes in them. This very thought that Gods can be mortal and that they survive only because we believe in them, was a "sulphurous" revelation for the believing child I was (back) then, and for a little while still.

> Gods were born out of Man's belief…
>
> – Voltaire (quoted by Jean Ray in his novel *Malpertuis*, 1943)

But the underlying message of the text was even more interesting. Between the lines one could read that mythologies were, in a way, still alive centuries after we stopped believing in their explanations of the world. As a consequence, they are still carrying out a function; they are still useful to us.

My history with Jean Ray and his *Malpertuis* does not end there. In 1971 Harry Kümel, a Belgian too and a movie director (who directed, among other films, the interesting and malignant one entitled *The red lips/Daugthers of darkness*, inspired by the life of the ill-renowned Countess Bathory) made a film of this book, under the same title: *Malpertuis*. Beyond the film adaptation in itself, which is perfectly mastered, my personal interest lies in the casting, in the choice of the actors.

As time went by, Susan Hampshire, Michel Bouquet, Mathieu Carrière and Jean-Pierre Cassel, became celebrities, "huge" stars. But back then, Orson Welles was already a star, a legend, a living God almost. By his very presence, he gives to the film a superhuman and almost timeless dimension. Stranger still, but this point is essential to my reasoning, is the choice of the singer Sylvie Vartan for one of the roles. By then, she was a queen of the show business, and an idol among the Idols (to quote the relevant term we used back then for the "yé yé stars"). Her presence was, in a way, indispensable in this assembly of Gods and Goddesses, as far as I am concerned, because it established the kinship between the ancient myths and the modern world.

In the 50s and 60s this topic of the continuity but also of the updating of the mythologies was theorized around and illustrated by philosophers like Roland Barthes (one of his books even being called *Mythologies*) and then in the field of the novel by J.G. Ballard. Later on, the works of Andy Warhol on one hand and the ideas of Jung on the other hand, which built bridges between psychoanalysis, alchemy, religions, legends and mythologies, were invaluable for the construction of my way of thinking.

> This [mythical] speech is a message. It can therefore take many forms, not only an oral one. It can consist of writings or representations: written speeches, but also photography, cinema, reports, sports, shows, advertising, all of these forms can serve as a support to mythical speech.

> – Roland Barthes (*Mythologies*, 1957)

Although Barthes often speaks about the Myth in its sociological sense (that is to say, as of something which is not true) he does, homewer, describe the modern world as supporting a mythology nested inside it. Movie stars, an Evangelist moralist-preacher like Billy Graham, striptease, wrestling, but also the extraterrestrials and even an automobile, the DS 19 of Citroën, become mythological under this specific glance. Beyond the modern myth of the automobile, J.G. Ballard grants the status of myth to the accident itself, in his novel *Crash*. An exemplary novel, in which other mythological figures are put, such as Elisabeth Taylor – an immense star of the golden age of cinema, as well as a complex personality.

More than any other modern Rock artist, Genesis Breyer P-Orridge is true to the ancient way of thinking, and in particular to the Greek mythology (we could also in his/

her case draw a parallel to the Scandinavian, Eastern mythologies, etc. because his/her knowledge and his/her capacity to digest it, integrating them into his/her own thinking pattern, are so great)... This personal feeling was strengthened by the very nature of his/her character(s): at once inclined to the most rational, the most abstract thought, and the following moment to the loss of control, to the drunkenness of the senses. One knows that the Socratic way has its counterpart in the Dionysian way (with an in-between, the unstable balance, the median and mazelike way of the Apollonian dimension). On one side the pure Reason, on the other one the unconscious bestiality; here lies one of the fundamental characteristics of the Greek mythology-spirit (as explained to us by Nietzsche). The exploration of these two dimensions (independently of one another), if pushed too far, leads to destruction (whichever the chosen plan might be). Only the middle way, oscillating (alternately), mazelike, between both worlds, allows not only the moving on but also the preservation of the being in its entirety.

> Nietzsche discovers an overlooked principle, inherent in Hellenism, which he identifies in Art: the Dionysian, alongside the Apollonian, underneath the Apollonian. "These names, we take them from the Greeks, who gave a clear voice in the occult and profound teachings of their conception of Art, not in concepts, but in clear and striking forms borrowed from their divine world." (Nietzsche, Kröner edition, Volume I, page 19-20)

> – Angèle Kremer-Marietti (*Man and his Labyrinths*, 1972)

This intuition about Genesis Breyer P-Orridge and the Greek mythology, I finally got to express, not in the form of words but of images, in collages. While the image of (the band) Psychic TV and the Temple Ov Psychick Youth in the 80s was mainly connected to shamanism (which was not false but represented in my eyes only the "visible" part, and thus easily recognizable part, of the movement), I made a collage, in 1984, for the poster of the Rouen concert, which showed, among other things, a statue of a Greek god. The name of the god did not really matter. In my mind, it could be Zeus as well as Dionysos, even Héphaïstos or Arès. The point was to establish the link with Ancient Greece and its mythology. The release of the single *Roman P* on Sordide Sentimental, in the beginning of 1984, had paved the way, by showing, on the cover, the image of a Greek (or Roman) temple in the background... It was meant to stress the indication given by Genesis Breyer P-Orridge him/herself in the naming, "Thee TEMPLE Ov Psychick Youth". We usually do not pay much attention to the word "Temple", although the key might lie in this very word.

I did it again in 1990, in my collaboration (on page 64) in the *Psychic TV* volume, a Vittore Baroni project published by Stampa Alternativa in Italy. This collage showed, in the background, the appearance of the God Pan.

In the 60s, psychedelic and hippy groups got used to writing long "thanks to"-lists, which often included all their cultural references. In that way, they illustrated this sentence, usually ascribed to Newton, and saying something like: "... if I saw further it is because I sat on the shoulders of a giant..." (the giant here representing the inheritance of all the generations that preceded us). Genesis Breyer P-Orridge resumed this tradition, but with a notable difference: the quoted persons are here a part of the work itself. Sometimes positive, sometimes negative figures, but in fact mostly ambiguous and complex ones, just like the ancient gods.

Most often quoted are William Seward Burroughs and Brion Gysin, well known artists of the Beat Generation, and Timothy Leary, the pope of psychedelic culture, but also criminals like Gary Gilmore, Charles Manson, the Moors murderers Ian Brady and Myra Hindley (terrible children murderers), and Jim Jones and the mass suicide of Guyana. By their side, one can also find Aleister Crowley and Austin Osman Spare, masters of The Occult, and Robert De Grimston (seldom quoted, but always present when "The Process", one of TOPY's great references, is involved). And the host of demigods: Brian Jones, the deceased Rolling Stones founder-member, Ian Curtis, the singer of Joy Division who committed suicide, the movie makers Roman Polanski and Derek Jarman, Lou Reed from the Velvet Underground, Syd Barrett from Pink Floyd, the cult exotica musician Martin Denny, the band ? and the Mysterians, the painters Andy Warhol and Pierre Molinier, the psychedelic folk singer Thomas Rapp (of Pearls Before Swine-fame), the experimental garage group The Monks, the musicians of Jajouka, Terence Sellers, author of *The Correct Sadist*, Mr. Sebastian, master of tattoos and piercing, and even Monte Cazazza, one of his/her close friends. Perhaps more surprising, because they are quoted with irony and a certain sense of aggression, are the figures of Queen Elisabeth II, and that of (the pope) Jean-Paul II. But all the gods were not liked though. That is one of the specific features of ancient religions.

As regards Brian Jones, the Psychic TV-track which is dedicated to him, *Godstar*, is of particular relevance to me because of its very title. Composed of the words God and Star, it thoroughly clarifies by this striking shortcut the conceptual approach: Stars of the current times (in cinema, show business, etc.) have the same function as the ancient gods. I do not aspire to exhaustiveness anymore than I shall try to explain the symbolism linked to each figure... I leave this work to more qualified persons than me. My purpose was only to draw attention to the fact that this gods' and demigods' assembly, even if the deities do not dwell in the Olympus, and even if they come from our own times, plays the same role for our mental balance as the one of ancient mythologies.

Those figures are a part of the work of Genesis Breyer P-Orridge, but moreover, he/she integrated them within the assembly of his/her other personalities, at the deepest level (of him/herself). A process of psychic fusion, finding its highlight, and reaching "exemplarity", with his/her concept of "Pandrogeny" which he/she created together, in osmosis, with Lady Jaye Breyer P-Orridge, and which he/she now pursues alone after Lady Jaye's premature death...

Or, to be more exact, with her in him/her, within his/her Pantheon, for all eternity – or at least as long as somebody, somewhere, will find nourishment in his/her work.

The Penis Might Ier Than Thes Word

Kendell Geers, Brussels, 31 December 2009

You let me violate you, you let me desecrate you
You let me penetrate you, you let me complicate you
Help me I broke apart my insides, help me I've got no
Soul to tell
Help me the only thing that works for me, help me get
Away from myself
I want to fuck you like an animal
I want to feel you from the inside
I want to fuck you like an animal
My whole existence is flawed
You get me closer to god
You can have my isolation, you can have the hate that
It brings
You can have my absence of faith, you can have my
Everything
Help me tear down my reason, help me it's your sex I
Can smell
Help me you make me perfect, help me become somebody
Else
I want to fuck you like an animal
I want to feel you from the inside
I want to fuck you like an animal
My whole existence is flawed
You get me closer to god
Through every forest, above the trees
Within my stomach, scraped off my knees
I drink the honey inside your hive
You are the reason I stay alive

Closer, by Nine Inch Nails

In the *Bible* there are two very different stories of the creation. Whereas the first words of the *Old Testament* explain that "In the beginning God created the heavens and the earth", the *New Testament* Gospel of John explains that, "In the beginning was the

Word, and the Word was with God, and the Word was God. He was with God in the beginning." It is not clear, when comparing the two versions, what the essential difference is, what the Word was or whether God was this word or was with a Word. On the other hand, the author of the Gospel of John certainly seems to suggest that there was a divine Word that was either God or with God and somehow contributed to the creation of all things.

Myth has it that the book of *Genesis* was either written or else compiled by Moses. It is difficult to place with any certainty the exact date when Moses was born, but the *Bible* is very clear that he lived in Egypt, where he had been "discovered" on the river Nile and brought up by a Pharaoh's daughter, Bithiah. Given his education in the Pharaoh's household, it seems likely that he might have been influenced by the Egyptian beliefs of the time. It therefore seems relevant to examine these.

Some Egyptian creation myths also mention a sacred word, suggesting that the Supreme Being Atum-Raa uttered the words of creation. But the far more widespread Egyptian belief held that God, Atum, rose from the primordial waters and masturbated him/herself with either his/her "shadow" or his/her hand in order to relieve his loneliness. From the ejaculation, Shu (moisture) and Tefnut (dryness) were created. They, in turn, had sex in order to create Geb (Earth) and Nut (Sky), who were born in a state of permanent copulation so that they could give birth to the Gods and Goddesses that are ultimately responsible for our destinies: Osiris, Isis, Nepthys and Set.

Incest and rape being the sacred rite of the Gods, Osiris and Isis became lovers, inspiring the jealous rage of their brother Set. Set conspired to murder Osiris. Once he had done so, he proceeded to cut him up into 14 parts, which he then scattered across the land. The distraught Isis searched for each of the disembodied pieces, but found only 13 because either Set, or a fish, had eaten his penis. Isis made a substitute penis out of gold and then, singing whilst having sex with her dead brother, fucked him back to life again. Through his resurrection, Osiris became Lord of the Dead and the Afterlife. In the 18th Dynasty, the Pharaoh God Akhenaten ritually celebrated this act of sacred sex (perhaps even Atum's masturbatory act of creation) by annually publically masturbating his seed into the Nile, thus conjuring the floods that life in Egypt so depended upon. In his 1939 book "Moses and Monotheism", Freud argued that Moses was a follower of Akhenaten and therefore an Atenist priest, eventually forced to leave Egypt with his followers after the Pharaoh's death.

Whether or not Moses was directly or even personally connected to Akhenaten remains controversial, but, in my opinion, it certainly could be argued that he shared their obsession with the sexual basis of creation and divinity. Moreover, given the fact the Egyptian creation myth predates that of Moses and the gospel of John, I would like to argue that the "Word" of creation, the word of God, the word suggested in the *New Testament* in the act of creation is in fact none other than "Fuck".

In his 1998 book *Swearing*, Wits University Professor Geoffrey Hughes proposed that the four-letter word predated its more modern euphemisms. The etymological origins of the word "Fuck" are shrouded in mystery, giving rise to numerous urban legends, the most popular of which suggest that it is an acronym that stands for "Fornication Under Consent of King" or "For Unlawful Carnal Knowledge." The acronym is generally thought to be a twentieth century phenomenon, whereas the word "Fuck" was already in use in the 15th century and may even have been used as early as AD 772. Despite many attempts to trace it etymologically, either to Sanskrit, Greek, Latin or Germanic, none have proven conclusive and the word remains a mystery.

Irrespective of its origins or etymology, it could be argued that Fuck is as profane and offensive today as it was a century ago, and its meaning has not changed much, although it has certainly picked up speed. To me, Fuck always seemed to suggest somewhat more than just intercourse or copulation and somehow put a more animal or primal spin on the idea of coitus.

The power and magik of this mere four letter word is best exemplified by the fact that, even to this day, it remains forbidden on MTV, the fortress of everything transient and fashionable.

I have long maintained that if you want to destroy something, make it into a fashion, and that is precisely the function of MTV (or "EMPTY V" as I prefer to call it). Every subversive concept or revolutionary idea from Punk to Ché Guevara gets digested and destroyed into a three-week makeover on MTV, only to then be re-issued as a perfume or T-shirt. And yet you still cannot say "Fuck"!

We call it a "swear" word or a "curse" word and perhaps therein lies the key to its secret identity. We swear an oath or swear on the *Bible* in order "to make a solemn declaration, invoking a deity or a sacred person or thing, in confirmation of and witness to the honesty or truth of such a declaration." Similarly, a curse is also " a prayer or an invocation for harm or injury to come upon one" or "an ecclesiastical censure or anathema."

Whilst "Fuck" wins first prize, hands down, on my profane podium, it is not the only four-letter word in the category of curse words. Curious enough, they all tend to either be sexual in nature, or relate to the excremental or scatological body. Why is it that, even in the atheistic cynical 21st century, it is still considered taboo to use words like "Shit", "Piss", "Cunt", "Dick", "Fart", "Tits" and "Arse" in polite company? Why would they, and especially "Fuck", be so outlawed, almost without exception, well into the golden age of profanity itself?

The key may lie in the nature of language itself. The *Old Testament* tells that an enormous tower was built in the city of Babylon "with its top in the heaven." This tower, which has fascinated artists and writers ever since, was somehow perceived as a threat to God (or the Gods). So much so, that he/she decided to prevent it from being completed through the "Confusion of Languages." It stands to reason that, whatever this tower was or could have been, it would have enabled us mortals to reach up into the domain of the Gods had it been completed. Why else would he/she or they have felt so threatened by it? At the time of its construction, the peoples of the Earth spoke a divine universal "Adamic" language, often referred to as the "Language of the Birds." Many say that, along with the Biblical story of the floods, the Tower of Babel and the origin of language is a universal understanding and belief, common to virtually every ancient culture. From this myth, which I believe to be true, I conclude that language is, at once, both divine and a curse from God (or the Gods).

According to the Greeks, it was the messenger Hermes that gave us language. One of the first things that Hermes did, prior to having being born, was to steal his brother Apollo's cattle, hiding their tracks by having them walk backwards. As a result of his cunning and ingenuity he became the archetypal trickster God and patron saint of thieves, miscreants, harlots, whores and old crones. Until the Middle Ages, many a pagan crossroad was marked by a protective sculpture in honour of Hermes so that travellers could pass protected from thieves and cunning folk. These were simple sculptures, featuring a head and sometimes a torso above a plain, usually squared, lower section, on which erect male genitals were carved at the appropriate height. There is no academic explanation that I know of as to why the phallus should be related to Hermes, but perhaps the answer lies in his role as Psychopomp. Hermes would escort the dead and help them find their way to the afterlife or underworld. He embodied the spirit of crossing-over and was seen to be manifest in any kind of interchange, transfer, transgression, transcendence, transition, transit or traversal (all of which involve some form of crossing in some sense). He was one of the few gods able to enter and leave the Underworld without hindrance. In my opinion, this return from the domain of the dead could be what is symbolized by the erection on his sculptures, as this is a very obvious and visceral change of state in the male member. The return to life of the erection ultimately culminates in the orgasm (which is not coincidentally referred to as a "little-death" in French).

The relation between sexuality and death was by no means the exclusive domain of Hermes. Krishna, Bacchus, Apollo, Mithras, Osiris, Dionysus and Hermes had similar roles and were also all born of virgin mothers in either caves or a stable, protected by shepherds. Nearly all were worshipped by "wise men," fasted for 40 days, changed water into wine (if they did not invent the sacred spirit themselves), only to finally meet a violent death in order to return to life. All of these gods were born on the 25th of December (the Winter Solstice), which is generally thought to signal the eventual rebirth and fecundity of nature. Of course, in the Western world, the most famous of all these resurrected gods is Jesus Christ. The art historian Leo Steinberg explained how, in many of the early representations of the Christ, he was sporting a very proud erection, either traced in the lines of his so-called stomach muscles or in curiously shaped yet unambiguous loin clothes. (*The Sexuality of Christ in Renaissance Art and in Modern Oblivion*, 1983) This sexually charged res-ERECTION of the martyred Christ may have been the representation or embodiment of an underground stream of faith, or simply the bridge between the ancient pagan ways and the newly born patriarchal Catholic Church of Saint Peter. The overlap between the pagan and Christian paths was illustrated by the Emperor Constantine, who declared Christianity to be the official Roman religion in order to cement together the political dissent and threat of civil war, while many believe that he retained his faith in Mithras all the way through. Until his death, he kept the title of "Pontifex Maximus," the title emperors bore as heads of the pagan priesthood. Accordingly, he personally converted to Christianity only on his deathbed. But this testimony, like the confessions by the Cathars and Knights Templar, were reported by the Catholic Patriarchs, so its authenticity remains questionable.

Given the close proximity and overlap between the pagan traditions of Mithras, Osiris or Dionysis and the early Christian church, how did these two streams end up so different and so incompatible? The pagans always maintained a strong relationship between the domain of the gods and their own, believing that "as above, so below," that the seasons and powers of nature existed as much within their own bodies as without. The body was considered sacred in every sense and every bodily function or impulse could be understood as being interconnected to and an embodiment of the divine. The erection thus not only embodied the changing of the seasons and the return to life of all things natural, but also the divine copulation between Shiva and Shakti, Geb and Nut, Isis and Osiris. This directly conflicts with the Christian attitude to the body.

The fundamental difference between the pagan traditions and their Christian offspring is that the Catholic Church finally set itself up as the only gateway to the divine. As Psychopomp and messenger of the Gods, Hermes gave us language and was interlocutor for the divine. He was also the embodiment of our own divine ability to speak the forgotten "Language of the Birds." According to the Tantric tradition, the human body is a divine temple complete in itself, embodying all the divine laws, awaiting only our unlocking of its mysteries. They refer to the physical body as the "Temple of the Nine Holes," the two eyes, two ears, two nostrils, mouth, anus and vagina or penis. I do not think that it is a coincidence that the last two holes are the source of most four letter words, with these words literally describing them or the "stuff" that emanates from them: shit, piss, dick, cunt, clit, cock and Fuck.

The Catholic Church had to destroy the pagan traditions and temples of the nine holes in order to maintain supremacy over their ideology. This was contrived through either building the foundation of their faith directly upon the pagan temples (literally and iconographically) or, when all else failed, through witch-hunts, public executions, the inquisition, exorcisms and auto-da-fé to name but a few examples. Most fundamentally, they taught us to hate our own bodies, to live in a constant state of guilt towards our physical being. Once the body had successfully been separated from its intrinsic divine nature it was not difficult for the Church to then insist that the only access we have to the divine was through their bricks and mortar, via their clergy and cloth. As the power of the Church would later wane, this self-loathing impulse would become the foundation of the new "Church-of-Capitalism". In hating everything about our bodies, it would not be difficult to sell us any snake oil, toothpaste, deodorant, shampoo or holy water as a short term solution.

The fact that Fuck (and its profane cousins) remains to this day a "curse" or a "swear" word is testimony to its intrinsic power. As it was once a threat to the Catholic Church it remains today a threat to the Capitalist hegemony. The threat comes from the fact that in "Fucking" we touch the divine, we experience the "little death" and pass through the domain of Hermes, Dionysus, Osiris and Christ. Through Fucking we literally create life, a mystery that science still cannot even begin to comprehend. Mircea Eliade describes sexuality as "often the first, and sometimes the only, experience of the Transcendent. For that reason, it is important for rediscovering the sacredness of life, a direct experience of the curious organic unpredictable nature of life."

As Hermes gave us his erection to remind us of his divinity and our ability to cross between worlds, he also gave us the divine curse of language. Being a trickster, he hid keys within language that would unlock the secret passages leading us through the profane towards our natural divinity. Despite being taught that, "sticks and stones can break my bones but words will never harm me," the power of words remains unquestionable.

"The 20th century linguistic revolution," says Boston University anthropologist Misia Landau, "is the recognition that language is not merely a device for communicating ideas about the world, but rather a tool for bringing the world into existence in the first place. Reality is not simply "experienced" or "reflected" in language, but instead is actually produced by language."

The magik of the word "Fuck" lies in its contradictory ability to live in multiple words simultaneously. It is both an extremely positive as well as negative word. If I invited you to "Fuck Me", my proposal would embody an entirely different emotional condition than had I shouted "Fuck You!" Besides its strength as an Anglo-Saxon expletive, "Fuck" is also trans-linguistic, for it retains much of it meaning and explosive potential, without translation, in most European languages and used to similar effect for example in French, German, Dutch, Spanish and Portuguese, to name only a few. For me, it remains unquestionably the most evocative and powerful single word in use around the world today. Whether intended as "curse" or insult, or whether spoken of in relation to sex, the connotation remains something excessive or wild. We tend to "make love" to our husbands or wives, speak of intercourse when addressing the doctor, or simply call it sex in general. Fuck is something much more brutal or animal, something darker and more sinister, something "Closer" to the Nine Inch Nails lyrics "I want to Fuck you like an animal, I want to fuck you from the inside". Once again, this distinction between functional physical sex and its divine ritualised darker kin only reaffirms the sacred magikal power of the word. I believe there is no God more closely connected to the bestial Fuck than Pan, running through the Arcadian paradise, lusting after nymphs and unsuspecting virgins with his raging erection, the half man/half goat, the quintessential nature-God. From his name, we not only have the word "Panic" but also the prefix "PAN", which implies ALL THINGS. His own divinity and origin is shrouded in mystery for some myths maintain that he was always there, whilst others suggest that he was the son of the trickster Hermes or even Dionysus and a very close friend of Bacchus. Not coincidentally, according to Greek historian Plutarch, Pan is the only God who is, in fact, dead.

The highly charged moral distinction between the primal four letter "Fuck" and the seemingly cultivated "intercourse" speaks volumes about the Catholic culture that created this division. On the one hand, the expletive nature of the former places it in the traditional domain of the working classes. On the other hand, it could be argued, according to a capitalist cultural Darwinian logic, that intercourse and its euphemisms represent a higher linguistic evolution of the tongue. Many perceive the working classes to have always been closer to the earth, closer to nature, living closer to the beasts. This association may explain the bourgeois fear. Cutting to the chase, this division between the abstract language of the beasts and that of humans could be seen to illustrate the division between the left and right hemispheres of the brain. The right brain controls the left side of the body, the side of the heart, and is said to be the irrational, Dionysiac, chaotic, superstitious, unconscious, the domain of Pan's nature, the Pleasure Principle. The left brain is more related to the liver and is the domain of culture, mathematics, order, logic, language and everything rational. It has been argued that the history and evolution of the Catholic Church was the gradual suppression, by any means necessary, of the Matriarchal pagan faiths in favour of the Patriarchal, a shift from right brain nature-based faith towards the macho, male, homo-phobic, sexist, small-minded faith that eventually gave birth to the soulless EMPTY-V culture we are living in today. I have no doubt that the ecological crisis and epidemic destruction of the planet our generation is currently facing is the direct result of the seeds planted by the Catholic Church more than a thousand years ago.

Returning to the Tower of Babel and the ensuing "Confusion of Tongues", I believe that the languages we know and speak today are the divine curse that God inflicted upon our species to prevent the completion of that tower. These are the languages of our rational left brain. By extension, the Language of the Birds, the true creative/destructive mystical language of the gods themselves remains hidden within our right brain, within our bestial memory, within the PANdemonium of our irrational chaotic other. In ritual magik circles, the term used to described more sexually blatant rites is the "left hand path." In Italian, the word for the left hand is "Sinistra", which literally translates into and gives birth to the English concept of Sinister. It was not until recently that schools stopped forcing left handed children to write and draw using their rational right hand. The Church understood from the very beginning that the male centered left brain was the best censor board to filter our thoughts through the policeman of guilt and security guard of religion to protect us from what they perceived to be the dangerous emancipation of the pagan left hand path.

Since the "Language of the Birds" is obviously hidden deep in the recesses of the right brain, how do we go about opening the doors of perception? In *The Third Mind* (1978), William Burroughs and Brion Gysin illustrate that the key lies in the way we perceive language. If the rational brain is our quotidian censor board and its military machinery the 26 letters of the alphabet, then we literally need to invoke the trickster Hermes in order to disengage that left brain. Once tricked, the left brain opens up to grant access to the Eleusinian Mysteries of the right brain. Over the centuries shamans, priests, witches, druids, pagans, magicians, artists, writers and even scientists like Albert Hofmann have used psychedelics to open the doors of perception. But this has equally been achieved through meditation, starvation, prayer, extreme exertion or stress.

For Burroughs and Gysin, the key is shifting away from the logical lines and control mechanisms of the alphabet towards a hieroglyphic language. Almost all of the ancient languages were written in hieroglyphic pictograms that spoke directly the right brain and vibrated directly through the unconscious. Their method was the cut-up technique, the re-assemblage of text using chance as a divine force not unlike the methods of Tarot or I-Ching, for there is no such thing as coincidence once you accept that we are all mirrors of the divine, as above so below.

Almost half a century before, an English artist called Austin Osman Spare contrived a similar method of moulding the left brain alphabet of logical lines and strokes into a magikal alpha-bête of desire that he called Sigils. The process was one of translating the written Anglo-Saxon text into a hieroglyphic pictogram through the literal folding, twisting and inversion into a charged evocative image. Naturally, he then used his sperm, spit, shit and piss within sexual charged rituals in order to further access the mystical domain of the angels and demons. The Sigil is to the Western tradition what the Mandala is to the East. Personally, I have used it in my work repetitively like a Mantra, in an endless visual loop, a hieroglyphic fractal without limit.

"F" is the sixth letter of the European alphabet, a number associated with the Hexagram, the superimposition of two interlaced triangles. The upward point triangle could be seen to represent the archetypal male force, the elements air and fire, whilst the downward pointing triangle represents the archetypal female force, water and earth. Together they form a "Hieros Gamos" or sacred wedding, the sexual union of the male and female divine, the permanent copulation of Geb and Nut. The Hexagram represents the union of opposites, but not in compromise. Freemason lore says in the *Codex Magica* that "The interlacing triangles or deltas symbolize the union of the two principles or forces, the active and passive, male and female, pervading the universe... The two triangles, one white and the other black, interlacing, typify the mingling of apparent opposites in nature, darkness and light, error and truth, ignorance and wisdom, evil and good, throughout human life."

In medieval Jewish, Christian and Islamic legends, it was called the "Seal of Solomon", for it was engraved into King Solomon's magical signet ring, by which magical force he was granted the power to command demons, genies (or jinni) and to speak with animals in the "Language of the Birds." The *Koran* explains that it was the Djinn, under King Solomon's command, who built the mythical temple without a sound being heard.

The Hexagram, in turn, lends its name to the word "hex," being a "curse," or spell cast by a witch. Using the profound magikal energies of the hexagram, symbolically as well as in ritual, the medieval witch or contemporary magician is able to command the elemental beings to protect, or cause harm, in much the same way that King Solomon was able to use them in building his Temple. The protective strength and magik embodied by this symbol can easily be witnessed around the world by its prolific association with the police or security forces. How many policemen, deputies and sheriffs around the world, for so many generations, protect their public with the hexagram, without even being aware of its magikal properties?

The letter "F" was, in ancient Egyptian, represented by a snake with two horns, being the snake of the Garden of Eden, the snake of Hermes and Moses. In later Hebrew, it became the letter Waw, long connected to the phallus as well as the spinal column in esoteric circles. As the Kabalistic phallus it weaves a connection between the lover and the beloved, the Fucking opposites.

It could also be seen as the only letter of the alphabet that is, in itself, a word and concept, the "F-Word" being synonymous with Fuck. Transformed into a sigil, mirrored and doubled, as above so below, the letter "F" forms a crucifix with three cross beams. More than referring to the Christ or Hermes, the triple cross beam represents the esoteric Hermes Trismegistus, the thrice great author of the *Emerald Tablet* and *Corpus Hermeticum*, said to have kick-started the Renaissance in Florence with its dictum "as above, so below." Within the Patriarchal logic of the church, these beams may be said to represent the Father, the Son and the Holy Ghost, but in the pagan tradition, they are the Virgin, the Whore and the old Crone, but the truth may be much more Hermaphroditic.

Perhaps, dear reader, your patience may by now be finally exhausted, for I may have noted one too many coincidences or concluded once too often that the word "Fuck" is the divine embodiment of the original divine words spoken in *John 1:1*? On the other hand, if you accept, as I do, that language was given to us through the "Confusion of Tongues" and that it is a curse that is also, more significantly, divine, then God (or the Gods) would surely have left hidden messages and keys within his "Gift" (the German for poison). Coincidence, in turn, is simply yet another manifestation or key to that same divine language that ultimately leads us back towards the Garden of Eden and the fucking "Language of the Birds". BUT the only way past the Cherubim guarding the entrance with his Flaming Sword is the union of the left and right brains, the divine fucking Fuck not mentioned in the book of *Genesis* but alluded to in the *Gospel of John*.

If, in the beginning, there was a Word and the Word was with God and the Word was God, then the word must have been charged with everything that God, in his or her infinity, is capable of being and the Word must have been as creative as it is destructive, a Word that stands alone above all other Words, able to invoke love as well as hate, able to command emotion as well as being able to physically create life. From my radically subjective human condition, I cannot imagine any word more divine than FUCK and therefore it is in FUCK that I Trust (God)!

The Calls

Translated from the Solomonic text more commonly known as Ecclesiastes.

Z'EV

The present material includes the first two chapters of *Ecclesiastes*. However, the common arrangement of chapters and verses has been replaced with a continuous sequence, so whereas *Ecclesiastes* has two chapters with a total of 44 verses, the calls have 86 stanzas.

one

the creation of the calls out the love through the letters' perfection
arise arranged through breath of breathing
of-and-from the whole breath enveiling the waters of time and cycle
joined in the words spoken strong in the calls

two

the liquid blood of life weeps
its tears a sacred treasure within the all
the all works through the calls as the light waves without and within

three

the whorls out the words call the generations of travelers
in the worlds to come the travelers rise fore the east as the three names
alef – lamed – hay, forward and back
setting off on the quest for the yod and mem
their counterparting fulfilling the name
alef – lamed – hay – yod – mem

four

behold the gates and the entrances of the paths:
all and around
the paths of all and around are a brightness within
the lights that in their flux and flow are the gates of cleaving and leaving

five

the sun of the spirit and the soul of the moon are one
their winds winding through possession, embrace and dimension
they pass through these depths as a stillness
they unite in the signs of respose
they unite as the moon moans as one with the sun
reflecting the breath of the sun on the moon

six

all the gates, all the 50 gates descend
from out the susurration and the mensuration beheld in the no-thing
they extend in the no-thing as time in its cycles
they shaken, awaken drawn out toward that face where their gaze
dwells astonished
soft and sweet and covered with skin

seven

there are names that empower the 7 lower spheres
in their hands these names bring to bear splendorous whirls in the real world
these whorls burst forth
first, low and roaring with noesis
and secondly in and within the questing afire in woman and man

eight

the travelers are as words empty, open and entire
beholding the 7 invocations and 9 evocations of their quest
first with their eyes, guideposts at the crossroads
next with their hands in reflection, a refraction drawn out from within
and then with their ears hear the strong songs enkindle obeisance

nine

they gesture as the living names, she-he and it-is
and then too the names the 4 quarters encompass
the ritual names of the yod and the hay
are the infinite actions of she-he and it-is

ten

beheld in the sun and the moon

beneath the sun the moon reflects the repetition of its cycles
enlightening the letters bearing the burdens prophetic
upon the backs of those conjoined in the unions of love

eleven

all this the travelers seer
all this is seen in the cyclical moon, as the moon that becomes,
that becomes to occur to the partners in sacrifice
the moon of two partners, a fullness, a darkness throughout time
as partners becoming the myriad memories of the presence of no-thing

twelve

the partners are the beginning of two dreams
dreams outflowing into being this beginning commixing sleep and the sleeper
in dreams that unveil the inner layers of inspiration
these are dreams that veil the luminous memory
the memories redolent of the gathering of allegory and offering
united in chant and in song

thirteen

they call to gather the living chaos
they gather and draw from among, inner, and above the guardians
of animus and
the guardians of anima offering into being the signs of breath and speech
below the innermost heart spirals in their harmonizing calls
calls as a knife which cuts with no pressure culls as it carves
the neck of the dove
turtle dove

fourteen

they call from their wisdom and knowledge all the guardian fires
guardians refracted as coals glow from the heavens hermaphroditic
these lowest of heavens low

fifteen

they begin with speech to sing in chorus in call and response

sixteen

they summon the seering clouds
they augur from them through their love they are placed
on the altar of the elohiem
for this is the altar of the consecrated times, of the waves upon waters,
and the emanations of their hearts

seventeen
for they are they that will in all and always render their offerings to
the vaporous clouds of breath to the spirit and to the word

for it is they that extend the phrasing of the inspired response,
to the lucid so divine repose, in coition

eighteen

they are they, their offerings transport into and through two selves
embraced in the true self
they are they that offer reverence through the firmaments
they are they that symbolize all the actions of the cycles of time
for they are the intentions of the performance of the names

nineteen

these are the names sharp to sharpen the actions balanced beneath the stars
the fires in suspension beneath the waters,
these are the names which calls cry from the tears
of the twined lights of the sun and of the moon

twenty

call the breath of all
the lovers find their pleasures in the solar soul
before the pleasure, the abilities and the powers
of arrangement and preparation
they speak saying: 'forebearance' and 'release'

twenty one

they conceive of these potencies and potentials
they speak the words that encode
'thou-shalt-be' and 'be-thou' and 'tremble'
they call to themselves as a wolf baying over and over again

twenty two

over and over again the wolf acquires speech to speak of the crossroads
with speech bound by and joined in the flaming heart of speech
for the tongues of speech are licking thick and strong and as white as flame

twenty three

call the majesty that shall be
call yod – hay – vav – hay

twenty four

to embody the elemental fire of the flames of wisdom
a'flame rising over all
over all the living lights of the spirit before the presence
as its delight descends to adore the heart of the flame adorned

twenty five

take then delight in the flavor of the chosen
well met in the reflection that comes from the fiery union
of the partners beloved
in recognition and understanding and in their numerical values

twenty six

they call the essence of repetition, they call the essence a'fire within the heart
as within uncoil the scrolling laws of life as they rise as the lotus to light
and within uncoils the brightness of the locus within

twenty seven

they understand their understanding which is joined
as the angel of the sighs geometric
this is the she-he, this is the it-is in the eyes of the lovers,
dove eyes of the lovers enfocus the light of their souls
throwing sparks to breed their ingathering flames
a'flaming their fiery wisdom, their fiery wisdom is hot, dark and numinous

twenty eight

vav – yod – vav
in mirroring image these are the 2 double swords

the sword of wisdom and the sword of knowledge

twenty nine

the heart speaks
'be thou the speech of the noesis that shall alloy the powers of the all'
for two are the names of nous that reflects and refracts: vav and hay

thirty

they call, they array
with their image they exclaim the breath: hay – vav – alef

thirty one

they call the heart within its chambers
their chambers begin as circles
these circles are drawn first to begin a circle and then to encircle
and hearken to the speech which says: call
they call that which coils lustrous through the names: hay – hay

thirty two

'be thou' is pronounced and arranged as:
the words of flame, the flame colored heart, the burning bush
which enlightens,
the wings of the dove, the blood reddened face and the songs of the flesh
sweet and pleasant
these are the signs of the abiding, the obeisance, and the postures
these are the signs that lead into a circle to spiral into the leadened waters

thirty three

they recall the wisdoms beheld by the eye
they call the hosts established in turn and by turns over influence
and consequence

thirty four

alef – yod – zayin – hay
these are letters that adorn the loins in heat, the salted liquids,
and the vaporous veils

thirty five

they call out the source of the ten spheres of the tree of life: yod and hay
for theirs are the names all hallowed out
for theirs are the names spoken in the swearing in of the likes of:
chet – yod – yod – hay

thirty six

they tread the great path of mercy
they call the practiced actions to recall the positions that came
come to pass within
the postures and their signs in time that come to pass within
their stance and their signs that sigh and sing and seal

thirty seven

their calls engrave that which bursts forth through their rituals
their rites begets and becomes the twilight becoming to pass as
the garments of freedom
the garments are white, that which is ash having burned
the garments are worn to break through and set free to burn
as or as if as the circular signs

thirty eight

they behold their patterns coming to pass through
the winged ones and things, the serpentine ones and things
wandering through the spheres of wonder scaling the world tree

thirty nine

they call forth the firmaments and the spheres
blessing the ways of the whispering charms they let loose the leaden water
they name the signs that mark the spheric circumference

forty

behold the circles and their conjurations, their circumference the ritual silence,
behold the auspex whose oracles combine and unravel through hay – yod – hay
who calls the vows of creation and their conjunctions?

forty one

whose light once loosened breaks forth as the morning breaks forth as their verbal will strops the swords of hay – hay – yod

forty two

behold their countenance
atraxic yet salivating before the presence
they call with the voice that is drawn out from the waters
before yod – hay – hay

forty three

they call the fundament forward, gathered in turn to turn
and to turn to their own true way
they call the conjunctions of the locus of creation silver and gold
the sun and the moon
forty four

king and queen of the east, behold their songs and their singing
behold their pleasure beheld within their liquid strengths
strong the daemon above and strong the daemon below
their calls beheld by 2 great eyes of mercy

forty five
they call forth connection and consumption
both coupled and both uncovered in space as the crowned queen and king
as the yod within the hay

forty six

behold the presence of the ways, the marks upon the spirit breath breathes
the marks upon the spirit of the face which calls sapience
which calls forth the waves of existence

forty seven

call the all
the queen and the king who themselves beheld the crowns of creation in sighs
the world whirls inside, inside the queen and the king themselves
in song inside

forty eight

so call them that coo, both in love and in longing
and in lamentations in love and in longing for the measuring rhymes

beheld in their innermost hearts and it beats

forty nine

for the beats are crowned by the laying of hands on hands
the hands that open and close the hands, open and closed,
are laid on their crowns dealing out all the works of vav – hay – yod
fifty

they call on their symbols, on their crowns, on the works of
vav – yod – hav

fifty one

behold their faces shining with oil or is it saliva?
they call forth the actions of their hands strong in their strength
and their fullness and the fullness of the works of
hay – yod – vav

fifty two

call the veils of the solar soul, throne of no-thing beneath the sun
call the no-thing to presence in the works of
hay – vav – yod

fifty three

they appear as wisdom dancing in the circle in the locus
they appear as knowledge saltating and dancing naming three names:
the 100 stars gathering, the 7 strong veils, the ancient of days

fifty four

behold through these 3 names yod – vav – hay
the ravenous queen can be called to transform

fifty five

the rapacious king sighs 'no-thing', sets his sights on the stones of pure marble like
water
called to transmute these three names yod – hay – vav

fifty six

together they feast on the treasures of wisdom and the pleasures of knowledge
their sighs of understanding call the crowns of the light and of the dark
behold there their 2 double crowns
yod – hay and vav – hay

fifty seven

behold their eyes focus, the foci: their hearts, their first fire and their blood
in correct combination the foci enlighten the darkness and its dancers both

fifty eight

the behold the hands of their time of understanding

fifty nine

calling awe to the presence of the no-thing
they claim the name which calls the name which calls and restrains
the whole of the assembling spheres

sixty

hearken, the convocation of the calls of she-he, of it-is
behold, are they, they are the 2 angles of the crossed ends of the road

sixty one

hearken to the calls
that guard the beholding of the vision of the no-thing so strong
at the cross-roads

sixty two

call all the words of creation, call the words of the ways, call the vaporous veils

sixty three

no-thing arises, a gathering fullness, redolent memories;
the eternal secret, the infernal secret a furnace smelting of sulfur and lead
for no-thing is the source of the waters, the mother prophetic, her 50 gates

sixty four

unveil the kiss of death, unearth the inhabited earth, call forth the firm serpent
yea, call forth the serpent strength, oh yea, call forth the serpent power

sixty five

inhale the perfumes of change, exhale their actions maintaining the balance
calling forth the veils
they bequeath the name of the solar serpent

sixty six

behold the practice of the breath scales the solar serpent

sixty seven

call the changes in-and-for and in-and-of the no-thing
call the songs of the all gathering change
call the fruits of fruition

sixty eight

hark, their calls minister to the change
they are they that change and they are themselves exchanged
through grace and with flavor

sixty nine

they bow to the strong light of yod – hay – yod – hay
consumed in their compounding union

seventy

beheld the hand of understanding a mudra of yod – hay – hay – yod

seventy one

they call the ancient of days via alef and vav

seventy two

they behold their reflection in the substance, in the locus
that focus their reflection in outward expression

seventy three

behold their beauty yielding invisible light
beheld in their dark red hearts, the hearth of both wisdom and knowledge
their ritual names conjoined as shadow and light

seventy four

their ritual names the foundation, the no-thing, the fire of the whole heart
and the ascension their union allows

seventy five

their calls focus of the locus
he serpent she lotus

seventy six

possessed they call the strong odor
beholding a vision of wisdom and knowledge
beheld as a page of the book of formation forming they whorl

seventy seven

their interpenetration manifest as the flesh of wisdom
and the knowledge of flesh
their manifestation interweaving the veils of pleasure and the pleasured veils
for conjoined they are mistress and master of the will

seventy eight

they call their blood to boil like a wine infernal
nethermost they lay below the powers of the hand
the hand whose mudra stirs the passion in their flesh
that passion whose highest peak is named 'the traveller'

seventy nine

on their travels they remember to remember themselves as time
as smoke rising in a column
bears witness to their offering at the gates of great love
of the great lovers alef and tav rising to and into the beginning and end

eighty

the repetition of these movements sing the signs of life
behold the shaking fingers, the beating heart and
hay – vav – hay
the call initiating the descent of the names mistress and master
of the waters both leaden and light

eighty one

the ancient of days alters the stars fanning the flames of the dark sparks
dark as aged blood, dark as the lissom threnodies sung in the chorus of the alter lilith
before dawn before sleep before the skeletal songs sung
at the hearth in the heart of the breath
hay – vav – alef

eighty two

the vision of no-thing comes to light the lovers illumined they lie
in their union
gifting each to the other a spirit perfervid, a passionate soul

eighty three

behold the songs of no-thing
in silence they gather the letters and shape and form the full name of
hay – yod – alef
they call the alter lilith and poised in her embrace beheld within the crossing waters

eighty four

giving life to the lovers
whose limbs entwined their blood to flame
whose limbs entwined to enthrone upon their faces prophetic desire
how longing of wisdom, how yearning of knowledge
as much as understanding closes their eyes
whose limbs entwined pronounced the calls
their calls to love
love closes their eyes

eighty five

they cross the waters

circular waves, spherical webs, currents that flow within and without
his wisdom her knowledge, understandings rhythmic contractions
their sferics strengthened in song and in chorus reflecting the emanations
evoking invoking their end

eighty six

envision the calls of their end
that sparks to enkindle their call
to the locus, of this presence
the numerical value of elohiem

Dreamachine
– The Alchemy of Light

Frater Robert

For decades, I have encountered references to the Dreamachine in books, films, and interviews with Beat author William Burroughs and others. Most of the things I have read go little beyond the platitudes from author/artist Brion Gysin, Burroughs, and the late mathematician Ian Sommerville. In this sense, the Dreamachine has acquired and assumed a place in the mythos of the second half of the last century.

One can easily find instructions and plans for fabricating your own Dreamachine. There are discussion boards and blogs on the Internet as well as books describing various innovations and alternative designs based on the original prototype.

Aside from Burroughs' fame as an author, other lesser luminaries have in some way become a part of the larger mythos of the Dreamachine: Marianne Faithful, Genesis P-Orridge, Kenneth Anger, Iggy Pop and Kurt Cobain, to name the most prominent. This has further popularized and kept the Dreamachine a subject still in the popular imagination.

Sorely lacking, however, have been accounts of its actual efficacy in doing what it is claimed to do (namely, creating alpha-wave brain activity and inducing visual phenomena and dreamscapes in the mind's eye).

As I mentioned, there are endless effusions of praise for the originators as well as the Dreamachine itself, but few statements concerning its actual practical effects. This led me to speculate that it may be that we are being beguiled by a contemporary rendition of "The Emperor's New Clothes," yet my own natural curiosity led me to studying flicker technology in many different modes – the Dreamachine included.

The first step in my quest was, of course, to construct a Dreamachine. I had a number of old record players collecting dust in the attic. Using the template from the book *Flickers*, I spent an afternoon meticulously cutting out the calibrated shaped openings on a bendable sheet of poster board with an Exacto knife. I attached a bottom cylindrical piece of silver mirrored cardboard in hope of increasing the luminosity of the light, as well as to have a base for a hole at the center to place over the record player spindle.

Undoubtedly, the very first flicker effect emanated from fire and/or the sun itself. It may well be that Neolithic man watched the simulated movements of deer, bison and mastodons on their cave walls before a nearby flickering fire. Humans may have sat enthralled before such a moving display as they listened to saga-singers relating the history and heroic lore of their respective tribe.

John Michell, author of many popular accounts of geomancy, ley lines, prehistoric sites and sacred geometry, speculates in his seminal work *A View Over Atlantis* on possible ancient practices that incorporated flicker light as a vehicle for inducing heightened or altered states of consciousness by way of utilizing trees planted evenly along a ridge top which at a particular time of day would create a flicker effect for an individual walking or running at the proper pace along a preconceived pathway paralleling the ridge for purposes of shamanic initiation.

Michell also goes on to mention the flicker effects generated by way of stained glass windows in Gothic cathedrals (the light being broken by the division of the glass by the leaded framing of sections). Light, itself, was thought of at that time as the province of Lucifer, the light bearer, and so the light was filtered through the images of saints and deities of Christianity. Such cathedral light effect is similar to the sun as it shines through the fractal patterns of tree branches in a forest.

Use of flicker effect in one way or another has a history that pre-dates the Dreamachine. It has been claimed that Nostradamus developed his technique of scrying the future by the use of his splayed hand passing rapidly before the closed lids of his eyes facing the sun.

Flicker effects were also employed in many visual devices intended to create a motion picture of sorts: various devices such as the phenakistiscope and the zoetrope. Eventually, such devices served to bring about the motion picture, or movie, that we know of today. Perhaps the most primitive employment of flickering images is the stack of paper with each page denoting the sequential movement of a figure, which is held in the hand and flipped through with the thumb. A most recent employment of this basic technique was utilized for advertisement along subway walls in New York City. As the train goes by, the passengers abroad can see a moving advertisement along the walls of the tunnel.

Among the major precursors of the Dreamachine concept was British novelist and man of letters Aldous Huxley. He deals with stroboscopic light effects in several of the appendixes to his seminal work on psychedelics: *Doors of Perception* and *Heaven and Hell*. In a certain sense, both in this work as well as his opus futuristic novel *Brave New World*, Huxley describes what are, in effect, light shows for the citizens ("Feelies") of his dubious utopia in which the drugged out citizens attend projected light shows on the ceiling of the theatre for entertainment. Huxley took these concepts little further than this. He spoke of seeing patterns and colors as a result of flickering strobes.

Two other early researchers into the neurological effects of stroboscopic flicker were Grey Walters and Cambridge Professor John R. Smythies. Walters is best known for his book *The Living Brain*, which was, in part, the inspiration for the Dreamachine. Both Brion Gysin and Beat novelist William Burroughs were aware of his theories. He also wrote numerous articles and books dealing in some way with his experiments and concepts. Chiefly, he figured out the timing sequences for getting various effects with strobes in inducing various brainwave states. Smythies and an associate philosopher, C. D. Broad, were very methodical in their experiments and studies and went so far as to record the various patterns: spirals, checkerboards, grids, parabolas and such that they experienced with stroboscopic effects.

Gysin's own introduction to the flicker phenomena was his now legendary bus trip through the French countryside in which he was resting in his seat, eyes closed as they drove through a tree-lined road with the sun flickering through the trees. The effect of the flickers of sunlight on his eye lids induced a visionary dreamscape of sorts. He was very impressed by the experience, and the Dreamachine he and Ian Sommerville later developed was the axiomatic outcome of this experience.

What Gysin experienced was not altogether unknown previously. There have been certain stretches of roads, lined by trees which have had an undo number of auto accidents believed to have been the result of flicker effects. Some bicycle riders attested to going into a sort of trance while riding through certain stretches of road with trees along the side inducing a flickering sun effect. Fortunate for bicycle riders is the fact that as they began to feel such effects, they invariably slowed their pedaling down and the spell was broken. Conversely, such has not usually been the case with auto drivers.

So it came to pass that Ian Somerville innovated the circular drum with cut-outs for the light rays to flicker through (suspended on an overhead aperture that was situated into the center top of the cylinder), creating the first Dreamachine prototype that utilized a record player at 78 rpm speed to create a flicker effect of between 8 and 12 flickers per minute (which was theorized to induce an alpha brainwave in the viewer). Later cylinders were modified to accompany a 45 rpm record player since the available number of players that included a 78 rpm speed became more and more scarce and thereby difficult to acquire.

William Burroughs, who was a close protégé of Gysin, became one of its primary advocates and promoters. Burroughs seems to have had something of a penchant for pseudo-scientific devices such as scientology e-meters, wish machines, orgone boxes and so forth. The Dreamachine plays a part in his cut-up novel *The Ticket That Exploded*. He also mentions the Dreamachine frequently in interviews and essays.

Through the connections of New York socialite Leila Hadley, who had taken an interest in the Dreamachine, Columbia Records Corporation had an initial interest in the Dreamachine as a manufactured product to be marketed. Allegedly, they decided against it with the possibility of its inducing epileptic fits in some of its less stable potential users (or so the story goes). Perhaps they were actually unable to see what real effects the Dreamachine had as a practical device. There have been a number of similar devices marketed over the years (such as the Nova Pro glasses, Proteus Mind Machine and David Pal Mind Machine) that create a similar effect and have the added virtue of changing speeds to induce different and varied brainwave patterns, as well as making a compact and easily portable device for the same purpose. I have heard of no lawsuits or epileptic seizures reported from such devices to date.

There was the news item from Japan detailing the great Pokemon cartoon panic of 1997 when episode #38 allegedly induced epileptic seizures in 12,000 Japanese children who claimed various disorienting illness while watching the segment. When news programs replayed the flashing segment in question, it inadvertently stimulated a second wave of contagion and even more children fell ill, some requiring medical attention. Of course shortly afterwards, videos of the notorious segment became a hot item for collectors, and pirated copies cropped up worldwide. The veracity of this was never proven, to the best of my knowledge. Television does work on a flicker mode. The FCC in the USA does have rules and guidelines concerning the pulsation rate of flickers for public viewing. In fact, the flicker effect of television may be responsible for the almost hypnotic effect it has on some children viewing it.

It is estimated that approximately one person in 10,000 has photosensitive epilepsy, which can be triggered by a number of visual phenomena, including, in most cases, lights flashing at rates between 15 and 20 Hz.

It was recently reported in the press that NASA was considering a device built around a pair of electronic shutters, which they claim have demonstrated to be effective as a prototype of stroboscopic goggles or eyeglasses for preventing or reducing motion sickness. The momentary opening of the shutters helps to suppress a phenomenon that is known as retinal slip. The shutters would open at a standard stroboscopic flash rate of 4Hz, and the flash rate would be adjusted according to the sense rates of rotation. The maximum flash rate would be 40Hz.

The preceding brief chronicle on the history of the Dreamachine in no way covers the many facets and details of the flicker phenomena due to obvious space considerations of this publication, and also because this has all been detailed in books, most particularly John Geiger's *Chapel of Extreme Experience: A Short History of Stroboscopic Light and the Dreamachine*, which more than adequately covers the basic history and personalities connected with the subject. It is a book I highly recommend. An equally interesting documentary film is on DVD, which was an outgrowth of Geiger's book and is simply titled *Flickers*.

Theoretically speaking, the Dreamachine is intended as a device to induce alpha brainwave activity. This is the brainwave that the human mind needs for visionary dreams and creative thought. Hatha Yoga, by way of mild hyperventilation, attempts to achieve this clear state of creative mental activity by way of prana (breath) and controlled breathing activity. A similar employment of hyperventilation is the primary component in the Kundalini experience itself: a visionary mystical experience of great force.

The various basic brainwave patterns are as follows:

Delta: (4Hz)
Delta waves are only present in the deepest stages of dreamless sleep.

Theta: (4Hz – 7Hz)
Theta waves are present when in light sleep and drowsiness.

Alpha: (7Hz – 13Hz)
Alpha waves are generated in the thalamus when in wakefulness (with closed eyes), where there is a relaxed and effortless alertness, and while meditating.

Beta (13Hz – 40Hz)
Beta waves are the normal rhythm of the brain when a person is awake and active.

Likewise, hypnagogic states attempt to induce the same goal. Hypnagogia is that mental state that exists between waking and sleeping. It is a sort of twilight zone between the two. It is achieved largely by lying down with eyes closed and maintaining a modicum of wakefulness right at the edge of deep sleep. It is the mental state at which most visions and mystical visitations occur. There is nothing new about this technique. Peter Kingsley, in his highly interesting and well written book *Reality*, describes such techniques used by the early Greek Philosophers who usually laid on their backs in caves for days on end, drifting in and out of sleep and wakefulness, and when in a hypnagogic state, visiting the realms of Gods and other dimensions of reality. There is an interesting section of Gary Lauchman's book *Secret History of Consciousness* which deals with this subject at length, and also in another book exclusively devoted to the subject: *Hypnagogia: The Unique State of Consciousness Between Wakefulness and Sleep* by Andrea Mavromantis. The isolation or floatation tank exercises and experiments of Dr. John C. Lilly are simply a new innovation on this very ancient practice utilized by shamans, mystics and philosophers of the past. A whole school of Tibetan Buddhist practices also deals with isolation.

So basically, all of these practices aim pretty much for the same goal of lucid or cognitive dreaming, alpha wave inducing exercises and the visionary experience of mystics: all separate pathways to the same destination or dimension.

I have, for better or worse, often been accused of pursuing any given interest I have to an exhaustive degree, so when I approached my self-built Dreamachine, I spared very little in modes of approach, experimentation and innovation.

Initially experimenting with the Dreamachine, I covered the same ground of experiences that I had read about. I saw colors, first in the red and later the blue range. The same could be achieved with a single strobe light just as easily. The dreamachine had little, if any, advantage over the use of common strobe lights.

Next, through more prolonged sittings before the machine, I became aware of patterns (spirals, checkerboards, etc.). Once again, this was little more then what you can achieve by rubbing your eyeballs with your knuckles, which is something we all have at one time or another done as children. I started with a 100-watt bulb and then changed it to 150, which really brought up the luminosity factor.

I recall avantgarde film maker Kenneth Anger being asked in an interview segment of the documentary *Flicker* what he had experienced with the Dreamachine. He was honest in saying, "I don't think it really works unless you smoke a pipe of hash. I think it's too dangerous taking acid because you could flip out."

The fact of the matter is that with the use of Hashish, LSD or any number of psychedelics, you are prone to have visions with closed eyes without any outside inducements. The question for me was not whether or not one would have visions with drugs plus the Dreamachine, but rather, whether those visionary experiences would in anyway be enhanced by the utilization of the Dreamachine.

I began my experiments with Melatonin 3, several pills of it. It does, in the sleeping state, seem to generate wild and crazy dreams, so why not in conjunction with the Dreamachine? It seemed to add nothing to the experience.

Next in line was Cannabis. The Dreamachine combined seemed no better than if each were experienced independently. In fact, it seemed to induce the usual grogginess that Cannabis induces. A second time, I drank some Ephedrine tea, a Caffeine-laden plant sometimes referred to as "Mormon Tea" since it grows profusely in Utah and other desert regions. Apparently, it grows in abundance in the region of the Euro-Asian Steppes.

Many of the tattooed Scythian mummies found frozen intact in the permafrost of southern Russia have leather stash bags respectively of Cannabis and also of Ephedrine. It could be that these two herbs were used in conjunction. The use of Ephedrine with Cannabis would nullify the lazy and groggy effects of Cannabis by itself, thereby keeping the imbiber not just "high" but hyper-awake at the same time. Unfortunately, no noticeable differences occurred for me in relation to the Dreamachine.

Next on my list of herbs to try in conjunction with the Dreamachine was Calea Zacatechichi, also known as "Dream Tea" or "Bitter Grass." It is a plant indigenous to the state of Oaxaca region in southern Mexico and is used by Mexican diviners and shamans for oneiromancy (a form of divination based upon dreams). The problem with Calea is that it is a very horrible, bitter-tasting tea that leaves a very bad aftertaste. Generally, it is ingested as a tea, and then to fortify the effects, several joints are rolled and smoked. Smoking it was not bad. Drinking it, I was only able to take about three sips and could not face up to more. I decided to make a tincture of it. I had some Ouzo and used it employing an infusion method. After a week or so, I clarified and drained off the liquid and, thus, had a very concentrated form of it. I ingested this by taking several spoonfuls separately and holding them under my tongue as long as I was able. It was not tasty in any sense, but it was far more tolerable using this method.

I was to read somewhere online that composer and Dreamachine maker David Woodward (who had a brief friendship with Burroughs shortly before he died) had also employed Calea with his Dreamachine. Living in sunny California, he was able to cultivate the plant himself. It is a difficult plant to cultivate from seeds and is usually done from cuttings. Woodward also fabricated what is called a wish machine for Burroughs. One of his Dreamachines was on display in galleries for a while and supposedly sold for a substantial amount of money.

After the Calea was taken, I spent about an hour in front of the Dreamachine. It seemed to induce the very best visual patterns I had not until this time experienced. I also began to experience the so-called wagon wheel effect where you have a sense of the direction that the cylinder is moving, and at some point it seems to change direction and alternates back and forth from one direction to the other periodically.

Later, adding Cannabis to the equation, the patterns became even more pronounced and active.

Moving on from this use of herbal allies, I decided to move the Dreamachine and set it up next to a futon on the floor. I positioned it so that the flickers would play upon my eyelids, as I would lie on my side facing the Dreamachine and induce a hypnagogic trance. I am someone who can sleep with the lights on overhead with no lack of ability to fall asleep under such conditions.

I had been practicing such hypnagogic states for about a year, lying back for an hour or two every afternoon and pursuing various visionary dreams. With practice, one becomes proficient in doing so. Initially, it is difficult not to slip into a deeper sleep at some point.

The hypnagogic experience occurs in the nether region, or period between sleep and

The author's set-up with one central Dreamachine and three reflecting mirrors.

waking (or vice versa). Certain individuals suffer from hypnagogia as a sleep disorder. It is the state of consciousness in which people often have hallucinatory experiences of visions, ghosts, celestial visitations and such. It is also a state in which the subconscious rises to the surface and offers thoughts and insights otherwise not experienced in our normal waking state.

My hypnagogic state began as it usually does with a jumble of images, words, and a mostly incoherent collage of things. Sometimes I begin to compose poetry or songs or art. After 15 minutes or so things become more coherent and sensible and seem to plane out and maintain coherency.

On one particular occasion, I found myself looking at a book. It was a Chinese book, or so I instinctually knew or assumed it to be. The book was the first treatise ever written on the subject of rain. It dealt with the subject from every conceivable angle: scientifically, poetically, botanically, etc. It was one of the most coherent visions I have ever had in a hypnagogic state, and all the while, the Dreamachine spun out its flickering effects.

Oftentimes after using the Dreamachine, even if nothing very noteworthy occurred, I would feel creative and afterwards have many innovative ideas in various realms of thought. It always seemed to enhance my creative quotient after its use. Generally, an alpha wave state of mind is inductive to such creativity. Often I have taken advantage of this state of mind after waking from normal sleep. Before that first cup of coffee and before the demands of the day, I would sit at my computer and go over a collection of poems for the purpose of revision. Seldom would I ever leave without having affected some change or revision. I would sometimes do this for a month straight going over the same material, and always, each and every time, find cause for revising or transposing lines.

Several weeks after this experiment, I did the "dread experiment" that Kenneth Anger had spoken of: the Dreamachine plus LSD. The effects were not all that amazing. I did see vortexes on their side spinning away into the infinite vanishing point and such, but it was nothing like I had expected, and I did not flip out in any way. I simply got bored with the patterns and went on to other activities.

Shortly after the LSD experiment was my major breakthrough in using the Dreamachine. I began to ignore the patterns created on my eyelids in favor of focusing my attention instead within my mind. One of the things Dreamachine aficionados never seem to discuss, at least to my knowledge, is the difference between lucid dreams as opposed to visual patterns created while watching the movie screen on their eye lids. They are different approaches altogether. The majority of people, when they first get close to the Dreamachine in motion, expect to see some psychedelic lightshow burst forth on their eyelids. You don't. You may see squiggly patterns or cross hatchings, but like I noted previously, you can do that by rubbing your eyes. To really see anything worthwhile, you must look within your "mind's eye" or imagination like any other dream or vision - it is not to be found on your eyelids. When we dream in normal sleep our dreams are not projected on our eyelids. They are a part of a neurological process within the brain itself.

Using this approach, the visions became lucid; the colors, vibrant with sunlight; the landscapes, paradisiacal; female figures, luscious and bodacious when I slipped into salacious imagery. This was the breakthrough for me in using the Dreamachine.

Despite this breakthrough, I continued to experiment in different ways. I tried blue/red 3-D glasses. Nothing special occurred with that. I had thought of gluing small Fresnel lenses to the cut out openings of the cylinder to intensify the flashes but never got around to that tedious approach.

One small innovation that seemed to enhance it was by backing up the cylinder with three one-foot square mirrored wall tiles. This, in effect, created three dream machines going at once (the fourth being hidden behind the actual device). It was like a crystal chandelier with moving light. One technique that worked well for visionary experience was to place my head to one side of the three mirrors, between the actual Dreamachine cylinder and the mirrored one to the right. In this way, the flickers from one played upon one eye lid while the flickers from the other played upon the second eye lid. The mirrored flickers were of course in perfect sequence with the actual one, but they were both moving in opposite directions since all is reversed in a mirror.

So in the end, the fabrication of a Dreamachine and the journey toward learning its uses has been a fun adventure. For anyone interested in such mind altering and expanded consciousness, I highly recommend building and experimenting with your own.

Terence McKenna: Mushrooms, Sex and Society

Philip H. Farber

In the early 90s, I was asked by the *Future Sex* magazine to interview Terence Mc-Kenna on the subject of sex and psychedelics. At the time, TM was just breaking out into the mainstream. A confused *New York Times Magazine* piece had plastered his face and some of his wilder ideas before millions and smaller, hipper publications were scrambling to get on board. Unfortunately, this interview wasn't quite pornographic enough for *Future Sex* and they decided not to run it. The piece was eventually published in my own *Paradigm Shift* web zine, in 1998, which is the version you will find below. Now, yet another decade (and then some) down the pike, Terence's ideas are as intriguing than ever. – *PHF*

The mainstream media hasn't quite got it figured out whether Terence McKenna is putting them on or not. His theories about the origins of contemporary culture in the psychedelic trips of the distant past seem startling to those who have overdosed on Reagan/Bush/Larouche-style propaganda, but they are not without precedent if the names Aldous Huxley, John Allegro or R. Gordon Wasson mean anything to you (if they don't, check out the 'authors' section of the card catalog). McKenna's ideas have hit the media in the form of several books, most notably *The Archaic Revival* (HarperCollins), *Food of the Gods* (Bantam), and *True Hallucinations* (Harper San Francisco). He has also maintained a close connection to the burgeoning rave scene, lending spoken-word performances to concerts by the Shamen and recordings by Space Time Continuum. Major publications from coast to coast have lined up to give him press, generally favorable, if confused.

PHF: Can you briefly explain the theory you put forth in *Food of the Gods*?

Terence McKenna: The primate tendency to form dominance hierarchies was temporarily interrupted for about 100,000 years by the psilocybin in the Paleolithic diet. This behavioral style of male dominance was chemically interrupted by psilocybin in the diet, so it allowed the style of social organization called partnership to emerge, and that that occurred during the period when language, altruism, planning, moral values, esthetics, music and so forth – everything associated with humanness – emerged during that period. About 12,000 years ago, the mushrooms left the human diet because they were no longer available, due to climatological change and the previous tendency to form dominance hierarchies re-emerged. So, this is what the historic dilemma is: we have all these qualities that were evolved during the suppression of male dominance that are now somewhat at loggerheads with the tendency of society in a situation of re-established male dominance. The Paleolithic situation was orgiastic and this made it impossible for men to trace lines of male paternity, consequently there was no concept of 'my children' for men. It was 'our children' meaning 'we, the group.' This orgiastic style worked into the effects of higher doses of psilocybin to create a situation of frequent boundary dissolution. That's what sexuality is, on one level, about and it's what psychedelics, on another level, are about. With the termination of this orgiastic, mushroom using style of existence, a very neurotic and repressive social style emerged which is now worldwide and typical of western civilization.

PHF: In what sense did the mushroom influence or create an orgiastic state?

Terence McKenna: All central nervous system stimulants create what's called 'arousal', which means restlessness. In highly sexed animals like primates, it also means sexual arousal. So, psilocybin was a stimulant to sexual activity. In an evolutionary context, the more sex you have, the more outbreeding you have of those members of the population that are not experiencing this stimulation. So, on one level, at the lowest dose, psilocybin increases visual acuity, which means better success at hunting. Then, at the middle dose level, it creates this hypersexual activity. Then, at still higher doses it creates the full-blown psychedelic experience, about which we are as uninformed and as easily amazed as our remote ancestors were. So, it was a three step process. It was basically a chemical that had been allowed into the diet that boosted us toward boundary dissolution, language acquisition, sexuality without boundaries, and so on. With those behaviors in place, humanness emerged. Then, as the mushroom faded from climatological reasons, in a sense we became schizophrenic. The bestial nature, the animal nature, that had been suppressed by the psilocybin in the diet, re-emerged, so you get male dominance, standing armies, kingship, walled cities, the whole bit that leads to western civilization.

PHF: What is the place of set and setting in the arousal response?

Terence McKenna: In the primitive context, I think, probably, there were orgies which were regulated by the lunar phases. In other words, orgies at the new and full moon. Basically, I think of the ego like a tumor or a calcarious growth in the psyche that will form unless there is the presence of psilocybin. For a hundred thousand years, nobody went longer than a month without having this boundary-dissolving experience. After the psilocybin faded, the ego was able to get hold and then eventually redefine the whole personality around it. It's a maladaptive response, I think, because it leads to the consequences we see all around us.

PHF: At what age would the psilocybin be introduced to prevent the ego from forming?

Terence McKenna: We're just speculating here – nobody knows – but I imagine that it could well have an initiatory rite at puberty, or it could have come even earlier. Also, we're talking a long period of time, as much, perhaps, as half a million years, that this was happening. So it may have started out that psilocybin mushrooms were just edible mushrooms, an item in the diet, and only when you ate a lot did you discover that they were also stimulants and psychoactive. Then, as you approach more recent times, they were obviously institutionalized into a kind of goddess worshiping, cattle worshiping, orgiastic religion.

PHF: Are you suggesting that Paleolithic shrooms were less potent than those that present-day psychedelic users consume?

Terence McKenna: No, I'm just suggesting that as human intellectual capacities evolved, people went from unconsciously getting loaded and being stimulated by these things, to actually realizing that the mushroom was what was behind it, and then to consciously seek them out for those kinds of experiences.

PHF: Do you see a resurgence in the psychedelic orgiastic consciousness?

Terence McKenna: Certainly psilocybin is a very important factor in the English rave and house music scene and psychedelics, though not psilocybin, were certainly a part of the 60s scene, which was then also associated with an orgiastic versus a monogamous style of sexuality.

I'm not advocating that we return to orgies. After all, these African populations that I'm talking about were small groups of people between 70 and 125 people, roughly, and with the global pandemic of sexually transmitted diseases, you can't exactly advocate orgy, but I do think that, in social circles where psilocybin and psychedelics are being used, monogamy erodes and people tend to have more than one sexual partner, without the subterfuge and secretiveness that attends that in the ordinary dominator context. I guess I would say that the lesson from psilocybin is not that we should return to orgy, but that we should take a look at the modification of monogamy to permit people to have more than one sexual partner at a time, without having to be socially stigmatized.

PHF: Do you think that there's an ideal recreational drug that may be created?

Terence McKenna: Many psychedelics have the effect that I've mentioned here. The reason I fasten in on the mushroom is because we evolved in the African grasslands, so if you're looking for a psychedelic stimulant to sexuality and consciousness in the context of early human evolution, it's going to be a grassland plant that requires no preparation and no combination with some other plant, because this all happened before that level of culture. Psilocybin emerges as the obvious candidate and I would say psilocybin is probably the best suited for this even today, because it's the one that we co-evolved with.

PHF: What would you recommend in the way of a psychedelic, romantic experience?

Terence McKenna: I think if they take 3-1/2 to 4 grams of [dried] psilocybin mushrooms, in comfortable, dimly lit surroundings, that they'll discover a dimension to sex that you're just not going to approximate any other way. I mean, this is a pretty well-kept secret – or maybe it's not so well-kept – but it's certainly true that psychedelics have a tremendously enhancing effect on sex. It's not exactly that they're aphrodisiacs, because they don't have an effect on performance, particularly, but whatever goes down is experienced much more intensely and vividly.

McKenna, Ramachandran and the Orgy at the Dawn of Time

Philip H. Farber

I have long been fascinated with the ideas that Terence McKenna put forth in *Food of the Gods*, paramount among them the thought that psilocybin in the diet of early humans was instrumental in the development language, music, and culture. It's one of those mentally stimulating speculations that Terence was so good at producing. Alas, short of a time machine, we have little way to prove his hypothesis.

Most scientists do agree, however, that something happened about 40,000 years ago that turned a pack of savannah-wandering apes into language-wielding, society-building humans. Fossil records show that our brains were already their present size about 250,000 years ago, but somehow we took our time figuring out how to activate the functions that produced cultural phenomena.

Those functions, it seems, lie in what neuroscientists call the mirror neuron system, a discovery that came out of a fortuitous accident in a lab in the 1980s. Three researchers at the University of Parma in Italy, Giacomo Rizzolatti, Leonardo Fogassi and Vittorio Gallese, were studying hand movements in macaque monkeys. They had a monkey wired up with electrodes to measure brain activity in the inferior frontal cortex, paying close attention to an area of motor neurons that became active when the monkey was grabbing, pushing, picking things up, and so forth. When researcher Fogassi reached toward a bowl of fruit and picked up a banana, that area of monkey brain cells lit up, just as if the little fellow had reached for the fruit himself – but the monkey hadn't actually moved a muscle! That is, just by observing someone reaching for a banana, the monkey was experiencing, for himself, what that would be like.

The experiment was repeated by the original researchers and by many others, with similar results. More recently, experiments in humans confirmed that we, too, have a "mirror neuron system" that is activated in our brains when we observe other people. Which means that, to some extent, ego boundaries dissolve and it is possible to feel someone else's pain (or joy or dyspepsia or satisfaction), walk a mile in their moccasins, or, literally, share a laugh. It also explains why we enjoy watching actors in movies and athletes in games – as we watch, our own brains are experiencing almost as if we were the character on the screen or the player on the field and we get to share in the emotion or exhilaration. Mirror neurons offer a clue to the phenomena of the contact high, why the designated driver giggles like an idiot along with everyone else, and why yawns are contagious. And perhaps we've also solved the mystery of why air guitar is so much fun.

Neuroscientist V.S. Ramachandran has hypothesized that the "great leap forward" in human society came in part as a result of the activation of the mirror neuron system in our proto-human ancestors. The mirror neurons enable imitative learning and also allow memes to spread very rapidly. Ramachandran suggests that it is possible that isolated tribes or individuals had, in fact, developed language, music, art, tools and culture, but that, without a sophisticated, active mirror neuron system, the ideas quickly "dropped from the meme pool." Instead, once fortuitous circumstances brought about an innovation, the mirror neurons of the early humans – which had evolved for some other reason, perhaps – allowed the cultural tools and information to spread quickly.

Ramachandran offers the idea that some of our vocalization ability, music, and, indeed, the rudiments of language, developed as part of our courtship rituals. A gestural language and vocalization allowed early humans to express and share emotions and to woo a mate. "Croonin a toon," as Ramachandran says, rose in sophistication as our mirror neurons likewise developed. When one of our ancestors had an idea that went beyond emotions or gonadic gratification, it had the opportunity to be transmitted quickly throughout the tribe and to neighboring tribes. Once we were able to express these ideas in real language, they spread even faster and had a snowball effect.

So was the great leap forward largely internal and neurological, as Ramachandran suggests, or was our neurology influenced by a psychedelic diet, as McKenna says? I would happily propose that these two ideas are not mutually exclusive. Indeed, they could be highly compatible.

The development of mirror neurons began with sex, so that's as good a place as any to begin to push the speculation. Let's say that these brain areas developed in part through natural selection. That is, they tended to aid the survival of the species. Apart from fleeing hungry carnivores, survival generally means reproducing, courtship, nesting, and providing the means to feed offspring. In short, these are the fundaments of a cultural code – all pretty much based in sex. The appearance of mirror neurons, for whatever reason, really made sex more complex, interesting, and raised it to eros, to the level of art. The human who could best express his or her emotions and urgency of rutting, would get laid the most and pass on the linguistic, croonin, mirror neuron genes.

So there we were, bipedal primates wandering the plains. We had all this great neuro-circuitry in our brains, but we were only using it to get laid. Let's jump forward to the present day for just a moment. Neuroscientists, Ramachandran among them, have come to believe that there are some people who have not "switched on" their mirror neuron system. These folks are generally categorized as "on the spectrum of autism." Now many of these people function fairly well in society anyway, though they may seem socially awkward, they are able to work, have families and so on. Genomic research has demonstrated that all of these people, including severely autistic children, have the genes and probably the neural circuitry for a functioning mirror neuron system, however, for reasons unknown, those particular genes are not activated. In a Scientific American piece on mirror neurons and autism, Ramachandran suggested that chemical agents might be identified that would switch on the mirror neurons for autistic people. One candidate for a possible mirror neuron-activating drug, he offered, was MDMA, the empathogenic phenethylamine more commonly known as Ecstasy.

Now just imagine if some ritual or chemical circumstances would fire up mirror neurons for a whole proto-human tribe at once. The result would be a big, boundary-dissolving group experience. Hell, it would probably be a big orgy. As I write this piece, brain scan studies involving psilocybin are underway, so we soon may know if McKenna's fungal friends also activate the parts of our brains that allow us to share experience and dissolve the ego boundaries that, in part, define our present culture. I think it's a fair bet, with an additional bonus, perhaps. Recent genomic studies of LSD demonstrate that acid very specifically targets genes that are involved with neuroplasticity, with the brain's ability to rewire itself and learn on a deep level. I would be surprised if psilocybin didn't also express the same genes. If both these speculations prove true, then we have a substance that not only can aid in the dissolution of ego boundaries, but also encode this experience in the brain as a fundamental way of experiencing the world.

So, without being able to send the MRI machine back into pre-history, the closest way we might have to test these theories would be to perform the experiment for ourselves, to test psilocybin in orgiastic, ritual conditions. It might be a tough a job, but someone ought to do it. Brain scans are optional. Who's with me?

THE TWILIGHT OF PSYCHEDELIC AMERICA?

Thomas Bey William Bailey

Whatever point we designate as the departure point for modern psychedelic culture (say, for example, the synthesis of LSD by Albert Hofmann, or the mass psychedelic rite at the Woodstock festival where an estimated 100,000 "trips" took place) it's clear that this psychedelic ethos is – when compared with a normal human lifespan – in its "twilight" years. Dr. Hofmann himself lived to be a remarkably spry 102 years of age, but that's besides the point. With psychedelic counterculture in its late stages as such, it seems like a good enough time to ask some pressing questions: will the energy animating this movement dissipate to the point where it becomes powerless as a cultural force? Will the psychedelic ethos simply find a new "host body" in emerging "post-American" cultures that, owing to oppressive regimes in the past, missed out on the original mid-20th century flourishes of this culture? Has it already died on the vine, with its death as of yet unannounced?

PSYCHEDELIC SACRIFICE

Well, let's make one thing perfectly clear at the outset: America's love affair with drugs (if not necessarily psychedelic ones) is going nowhere anytime soon. With a source as august as the Wall Street Journal recently reporting that the net effect of the "War On Drugs" has been absolutely nil (indeed, Americans' drug consumption has increased in the decades since the "war's" inception), it's safe to assume that this nation of self-styled moralists still moonlights as a nation of chemical eccentrics. Within this apparent paradox, though, lies the key to the American public's ongoing dalliance with recreational pharmaceuticals: righteous, square-jawed American morality has always been a by-product of religious fervor, but the same can be said for Americans' chemically-assisted attempts to merge with the celestial and the ineffable. As modern U.S. church ritual strips itself of its remaining vestiges of pagan grandeur, opting instead for bland mega-church services featuring PowerPoint presentations and "prosperity gospel" sermons (merely financial self-help sessions with a smattering of scriptural reference tacked on at the end), it seems only natural that those thirsting for a taste of the ineffable will begin looking for it in less officially sanctioned places. If nothing else, the continuing decline in weekend church attendance – now down to some 19% of the population on any given Sunday – gives one pause to think, when also considering that the number of Americans identifying themselves as "spiritual" people easily dwarfs that percentage.

The unwitting leaders of the American counterculture have certainly not gone too great lengths to deny this connection between drug-based spirituality and waning commitment to institutional religion; with Dr. Timothy Leary in particular admitting "I am a religious leader and I must behave like one." Dr. Albert Hofmann, who first synthesized the LSD-25 that would be Leary's springboard to fame, also saw it as a "sacrament for modern age: the antidote to the ennui caused by consumerism, industrialization, and the vanishing of the divine from human life." It's impossible to tell how much the drug underworld is securing converts from the ranks of those disillusioned by the Christian church (let alone from the technocratic 'straight' society mentioned above.) One thing we can surmise, though, is that the popular appeal of the "religiosity" conferred by psychedelics is due to its hearkening back to a much older model of divine epiphany, one in which spiritual rebirth occurs within the present life rather than at its conclusion. The mythologies of old are rife with stories of mortals traveling to and returning from the underworld, or the faerie world, or to any number of variations on a realm populated by beings with previously untapped reservoirs of knowledge – whatever small sampling of knowledge was brought back, and at whatever great price, it was still meant to benefit those still dwelling in the here-and-now (more properly referred to as "waking consciousness"). Outside of dream states, deep meditative states and less common forms of threshold state, there remain few options besides drug-taking for stealing glimpses of another possible existence.

What modern psychedelic culture has managed to achieve, even in identikit suburban homes in the U.S., has been to reinstate self-sacrifice as a means towards reaching more sublime states of being. This is not 'self-sacrifice' in the sense of offering one's earthly wealth up to a higher deity, or even committing altruistic actions toward one's fellow man (although such behavior might follow as a result of the "self-sacrifice" in question). This old pagan notion, in contrast to the sacrifices demanded by the now-dominant monotheisms, involves sacrificing oneself to oneself – undergoing an intense psychic ritual that is largely irreversible, a shedding of psychic skin, as it were. The Eddic legend of Odin's self-hanging from the World Tree, Yggdrasil, betrays a motivation that runs parallel with the more adventurous imbibers of hard psychedelics. As per esoteric researcher Michael Moynihan, "...his "lower" or "unevolved self" – that is, his initial state of being – has been sacrificed and immolated in order to reconfigure itself in, or "receive", a "higher self". By doing so the "lower self" is destroyed and left behind, so there can be no ongoing demand of "bribery" from the higher self." This was far from an easy transaction, as the god hung "wounded by his own weapon, tormented by pain, hunger and thirst" until the runes revealed themselves and "the god throve and grew in wisdom, [becoming] the god of rune-lore and magic as well as of eloquence and poetry." It's also worth adding, as a mythical side note, that Odin's companion ravens "Thought" and "Memory" fed themselves on a form of psychedelic mushroom now commonly known as Rabenbrot, while his steed Sleipnir fertilized fly agaric mushrooms [Amanita Muscaria] with the foam of his nostrils. Going further East, we can also look to the Tibetan ritual of chöd for another parallel to the psychedelic journeyman's willful and risky opening of the psyche: this is the terrifying graveyard ritual in which practicioners invoke demons and invite them to consume their bodies, after which these demons (and, consequently, the fear of death) are conquered by realizing them as emanations of one's own consciousness.

RISE OF THE SUBURBAN SHAMAN

We must remember, though, that drug culture in the U.S. has never been monolithic in its sense of purpose – there have always been, at the very least, two separate cultures dedicated to the polarities of either spiritual questing or more hedonistic self-affirmation, with temporary alliances between the two sprouting unexpectedly and vanishing just as unexpectedly. The underground supply lines and distribution networks for illegal drugs have relied on people with a variety of motivations to keep them smoothly running, from those with a missionary zeal for enlightenment to those guided by little more than a profit motive. To complicate matters more, the counterculture has never spoken as one entity when it comes to drug matters: when the aforementioned Dr. Leary was at the dazzling peak of his powers, the other grand magus of American counterculture, William Burroughs, remained highly skeptical of Leary's campaign to "turn on" the populace at large. Burroughs' interest at the time was in non-chemical means of enhancement such as biofeedback, and at any rate he did not share Leary's absolute optimism when it came to self-actualization through drug use: "95 percent of these people have no idea of what their "own thing" is," he said of the nascent hippie movement and their clarion call to "do your own thing." Writing in *The Job*, he also claimed that anything achieved chemically could be done with other means, encouraging the breakdown of verbal association lines through the application of his "cut-up" technique to tape recording. All the same, it seems that the sensory assault and anarchic aspirations of the late 1960s would have been unfathomable without psychedelics to seal the deal. For American youth to change overnight into adherents of Vedanta, Buddhism and Gaia-loving paganism, some kind of spanner had to be abruptly thrown into the works. Psychedelics did, as Burroughs fretted, provide such a "quick fix" that irresponsible use of them was likely to send people scurrying back for the shelter of their pre-"turned on" states of mind. All the same, true shamans – those who could properly "handle" and decode the oncoming rush of irrational information – had been a distinct minority ever since the first usage of "plant allies." This minority (maybe even less than 5% who "knew what their own thing was") was all that it took to perpetuate the culture, and to secure a small army of hangers-on and curious dabblers.

The "culture war" of the 1960s effectively ended in a stalemate, with both psychedelic proselytizers and skeptics claiming enough victories for said war to continue on to the present day. Despite its loving re-packaging by those who lived through it, and who went on to found bastions of "cool capitalism" like Ben & Jerry's or Tower Records, the Haight-Ashbury scene of flower power and LSD dreams was never the only game in town: the "straights" still counted as the solid cultural majority in any age group (just look at the blockbuster popularity of country music in the music charts of those days), and other segments of American Bohemia took "drop out!" as their cue to engage in nihilistic behavior rather than any kind of mass consciousness-raising through ahimsa [passive resistance]. As hinted above, though, the interaction among different cliques was never a cut-and-dry adversarial one. Even in a supposedly decadent speed-freak set like Andy Warhol's Factory crowd (and Norman Billiardballs' amphetamine-fed splinter group of thrill seekers, the Mole People), they were only one person removed from a deep Eastern spiritualist like the composer LaMonte Young, who Warhol acolyte Billy Linich crowned "the highest-quality dope dealer in the avant-garde movement" and who acted as a mediator between different strains of counterculture.

Ego Tripping, 'Straight Edge', And Other Backlashes

For a while, though, it looked like the psychedelic upheaval was ready to be completely nullified, as the pendulum swung back towards pure materialism: prior to the 1987 stock market crash, the nation's "Reaganomic" prosperity spawned an elite class of cash-rich kids who knew they could easily get what they wanted without having to consult any ancient oracles of hallucinogenic wisdom. And so, the decade's popular culture was partially lorded over by people content to live in a "perpetual present", or a state where the future arrived before any thought had been given to it, and the past was a state confined to brief media clips. Their attitudes were best described by "ontological anarchist" Hakim Bey as such:

> Each "lifestyle" group buys the simulation of rivalry and enmity with other such groups of consumers [...] assured of its ungulfable, existential alienation from all other classes and races (as in Lifestyles of the Rich and Famous.)

The metropolitan youth of the 1980s seemed to be racing against each other to see who could most quickly leave the "furry freaks" of the 60s in the dust: with the music video clip becoming one of the prime forces in youth cultural development, organic living was decidedly "out", and antiseptic, prosthetic, android cool was the ideal to be emulated. Chopping up the ego and visualizing Bardo states was the kind of thing that just got in the way of "keeping up appearances" and getting on the guest list at the club (where, as fate would have it, people were dancing not to live bands or even DJs, but to music videos projected on huge screens). The pop demigods of the day were not elemental figures like Hendrix, but carefully synthesized creatures like Madonna and Michael Jackson. The former was bitterly characterized by theorist Jean Baudrillard as "product of a glacial aesthetic, devoid of all charm and sensuality," while the latter was also dubbed by him as "better than a child god because he is child prosthesis – an embryo of all those dreamt-of mutations that will deliver us from race and sex." As the visual (or tele-visual) culture goes in America, so goes the drug culture – and so arch-synthetic, hyper-materialist prototypes of humanity were replicated through narcotics that would heighten focus and sociability instead of heightening any vague notion of "consciousness". You didn't need to read Bret Easton Ellis novels to see that the scene-makers in this era were far more concerned with lifestyle than life, with projecting a sculpted surface image that concealed... well, more layers of "surface." The rise of the market for anabolic steroids during this period was no accident, either: the man-mountains of the pro wrestling circuit, for example, provided a larger-than-life athletic counterpart to the lab-assembled idols of the pop music world.

Now, the archetypal hippies were so roundly dismissed as a symbol of misplaced ambition, so derided for their monumental failure to get the lion lying down with the lamb, that new youth subcultures even formed with abstinence as their ideal: the "straight edge" faction of hardcore punk kids, notable for their visible and audible uniformity, penned tunes like "Lost In Space" and "DeadHead" chastising their counter-cultural forebears for their detachment from street-level reality. Mind you, they reserved plenty of bile for the cocaine fantasies of their 80s rivals, but the psychedelic "flower child" still loomed large as the epitome of the "living dead", the specter of a defeated belief in "free love" and the universal goodness of human nature. This was all fine and good, but the hardcore punks' decision to call bullshit on the hippies for such a belief also meant they themselves were standing on shaky ideological ground: contemporary watchwords like "scene unity" meant little when the punks had already concluded that people joined together in communities only for ultimately selfish reasons.

IF 6 WERE 9… OR, IF THE 60S WERE THE 90S

The North American 1990s, as you'd expect from the final decade in the Gregorian calendar's millennium, presented a much different picture: it was a time for hasty "spiritual accounting" and also (more prevalently) a time of profound and often crippling anxiety – thanks to the latter, those born in the decades preceding the 90s were able to marvel at a hitherto unseen proliferation of suicidal cults, survivalist militias, blood-and-circuses mass diversions, and cyber-age snake oil salesmen. Practically the only people who seemed to be celebrating the acceleration into the next millennium, rather than bracing themselves for a stormy Götterdämmerung, were the members of a resurgent psychedelicized counterculture that vaporized its pre-millennial fears with the empathy-producing panacea known as MDMA, or "Ecstasy" in the vernacular. Although Ecstasy was the most desirable among the counterculture potions of the 1990s, it hardly stood alone: everything from the animal tranquilizer ketamine to the brief but apocalyptic "businessman's highs" of DMT and salvina divinorum were circulating throughout the amped-up underworld, with a predictably wide range of heavenly and hellish effects. Such "old school" concoctions as LSD came out of hiding, as well: the "acid" in the dance music genre "acid house" clearly referred to more than just the fizzy, caustic sounds generated by the genre's musical workhorse (the Roland TB-303 bass sequencer.) From the mid-90s onward, online information clearing houses like hyper-real.org also provided in-depth dossiers on exotic chemicals that most people had never even heard of, let alone imbibed – in many cases, the drugs were too obscure to have yet been classified as illegal, prompting mad dashes to find them before the secret was out. Meanwhile, that site's hosting of space for numerous audio and visual artists made it clear that these chemicals did not exist in a cultural vacuum.

The Internet, of course, would become the bonding cement for many a tribe of intrepid ravers and ecstatic trance-dancers, but it wasn't the only line of communication available. There were chroniclers of the scene in "proper" print media such as the *Mondo 2000* magazine, a West Coast publication whose "Guide To the New Edge" still serves as a fitting document of the greatest psychedelic upsurge in America since the high 60s. Looking back through this volume, what is surprising is the culture's apparent fearlessness of cultural fusion: old grandmasters like Burroughs and Leary resolve their enmities and solidify their role as avuncular chaperones to the cosmic dance. Elsewhere, the ecological horror of the Industrial performance troupe Skinny Puppy is recommended as a good listen in the same breath as "sample-a-delic" kitsch like Deee-Lite. The harsh film imagery of David Cronenberg and the dystopian writings of the cyberpunk genre sidled up next to curious reportage on "smart drinks" and "tele-dildonics". It seemed like a hybridized counterculture had finally arrived in which the psychedelic ethic superceded the psychedelic aesthetic: that is to say, one could go around in nostalgic tie-dye clothing and "consciousness beads", or a modest Adidas tracksuit, or even carry themselves with a gentlemanly Burroughsian mien, and not have to worry so much about whether any of these looks was the "correct" one. You could mix violent electronic sounds and bio-mechanical sci-fi imagery with "shoegazer" ambience and slow-morphing Mandelbrot fractals, without tremendous fear of reprisal from your scene peers. In theory, what mattered was – whether one was aware of Aleister Crowley or not – using his "the method of science, the aim of religion" as a template for interfacing with all levels of lived experience. As could be expected, a culture with such a tolerance for all creative raw materials, and a downplaying of "genre" allegiance, had its share of "misses" as well as "hits": oversized, floppy velvet top hats and glowsticks on the dance floor were like the kind of disposable trinkets sold in New Orleans during Mardi Gras. But little of this was harmful, even if it failed to remain the pop-culture currency for more than a few years.

The only thing was, it seemed that not many people were looking in on all of this from the outside. Excepting the occasional effervescent P.R. junkies like promoter Michael Alig and his Club Kids, media attention was not something that most electro-psychedelic youth hungered after anyway: media attention was just a precursor to the attention of police and other organs of the State, and therefore more trouble than it was worth to have one's goofy, MDMA-enhanced smile broadcast on television for a few brief moments. The mass media's bias was, in that benighted age of daytime talk shows and their prurient displays of social dysfunction, towards locating and shaming the "dark side" of any social phenomenon that had even a scintilla of popular acceptance. Perhaps more media coverage was given to the corporate-sponsored Woodstock revivals in 1994 and 1999 (the latter ending in a fin de siècle death spiral of looting, rape, and noxious plastic-bottle bonfires) than was ever given to the watershed events of the fluid culture built around electronic dance music and psychedelics. Techno-pagan rites like Burning Man remained intellectual curiosities to be reported in the pages of *Mondo 2000* and *Wired*, and of course recounted all over the Internet (another radical cultural development which only seemed to garner television reportage when there was something gravely "wrong" with it.)

And so, it was not exactly surprising that this giddy mixture of chemicals, circuitry, and spirituality was given a pass in favor of the more enduring image of 1990s youth: that of the "slacker." The rave lifestyle, while perhaps the one 90s counterculture that relied most heavily on pharmaceutically-aided socialization and introspection, was overshadowed by a number of other less ecstatic counter-cultural variants arising in the same period. It was not the hedonistic, youthfully exuberant, and pluralistic surge of rave culture which became the soundtrack of youth during this period, but rather the alienated, threadbare "grunge" music of Nirvana and their numerous progeny (to be fair, the "grunge" term was largely disavowed by these groups themselves). The heroin-infused personal trauma of Kurt Cobain is more talked about and memorialized these days than any period flirtation with, say, "smart drugs", while the advertising campaigns of the day betrayed a similar attitude among the more well-attired heirs of the 80s cultural elite: the "heroin chic" ads of Calvin Klein and others shone a blaring spotlight onto a negative playground where careful styling, cynical disaffection, and death drive effortlessly mixed. The easier availability of heroin for middle class kids, and the added attraction coming from its newfound purity (and subsequent ability to be smoked rather than injected) should probably be seen as the "chicken" preceding the "egg" of its pop culture renaissance.

In the 90s interregnum between the Cold War and the Global War on Terror, the cachet of the "disillusioned artist" also experienced a resurgence, however co-opted, within American popular culture. The mid-1990s were yet another period of unrivaled economic prosperity and relative peace in which young, affluent Americans became acquainted with an aesthetic of self-denial and voluntary alienation. If such a stance sounds all too familiar to students of counterculture, it's for good reason – merely track down the 1959 issue of Life magazine in which Paul O'Neil bemoans the contemporary youth culture as being "...some of the hairiest, scrawniest and most disconcerted specimens of all time [...] who not only refuse to sample the seeping juices of American plenty and American social advance, but scrape their feelers in discordant scorn of all who do." O'Neil is, of course, talking about the Beat Generation, from whom the 1990s "slackers" borrowed some choice mannerisms – although it can hardly be said that the slacker culture innovated on the same level as the Beats, given their contentedness to bask in self-reference, un-constructive sarcasm, and non sequiturs. Slackers tended to document, through 'zine culture and other routes, only that which could be appreciated on an ironic level, and were remarkably intimidated by the expression of genuine, un-ironic love for anyone or anything. In fact, their major cultural contribution was probably to highlight the difficulty of creating a purely "new" movement without first borrowing from previous cultures – and also to highlight how little some people were capable of accomplishing even with a great deal of personal freedom. Their schtick wore out its welcome quickly, and one of the most enduring quotes from The Simpsons – a slacker favorite, no less – remains Bart Simpson's wish for "another Vietnam to thin out their ranks."

As the largely white, middle-class slacker phenomenon spread throughout the areas defined by that demographic, the predominantly black, urban culture of hip-hop was beginning to make major inroads into mainstream popularity with its own defiantly drug-soaked product. Thanks in part to the efforts of "gangsta" hip-hop megastars like Dr. Dre and Cypress Hill, you could walk into any shopping mall in the country and walk out with a t-shirt or baseball cap emblazoned with a huge marijuana leaf and the imperative to "LEGALIZE IT" on the front (you could also score a tacky pot-leaf medallion if you had a little more spending money.) Eventually, this public airing of psychedelic iconography – quite often being deployed by people who had never even tried psychedelics, but liked the t-shirt design – would begin to raise some troubling questions. For one, in a nation still so adamant about prosecuting its War On Some Drugs, in which the sitting president had to launch a straight-faced P.R. offensive claiming he "never inhaled" the joint that once fell into his hands, why was such commercialization of drugs being tolerated? Could it be that the authorities saw this new twinning of drugs and corporate culture as a way to blunt the former's power as a tool for deep psychic investigation? Did they maybe encourage a situation where, upon seeing hordes of boorish, adolescent stumble-bums decked out in pot-leaf merchandise, the real "seekers" would lose heart and begin viewing their own conquests of inner space as an elaborate sham? All of this is very speculative, but, considering that the spearhead of the U.S. drug movement has always been college-educated progressives casting a disapproving eye on consumer culture, it doesn't seem all that far-fetched. What better way to defang this movement than by putting forth the dumbest of the dumb as its emissaries, and by insisting that its cultural value was no greater than that of high-fructose corn syrup? Psychedelic critics like Robert Anton Wilson certainly suspected foul play on the authorities' behalf, but in a broader context of encouraging generalized idiocy (not only drug-fueled idiocy):

> Despite all the people using "smart drugs" […] the majority, at least in the U.S., has grown steadily stupider. I attribute this to a deliberate policy of "dumbing down" the population, instigated by our ruling Elite after the donnybrooks and Katzenjammerei of the 60s taught them that too many educated people represented a real danger to the status quo.

Even in the 60s, though, the seeds of this dumbing down were in place, and when not coming from "The Man" himself, they were coming from the psychedelic rank-and-file, who thought that their electrical surges of right-brain power were more than enough to help them coast through life. Needless to say, Wilson was in disagreement, bemoaning the fact that people who "…can throw an I Ching hexagram and know its meaning, [and] know all about Hedonic Engineering and staying high" weren't quite so knowledgeable about "…how the mysterious Stereo works, or what keeps planes from falling out of the sky." For all the best efforts of Wilson, Mondo 2000, hyperreal.org and the select priesthood of "neuro-politicians", there was still going to remain a kind of psychedelic Lumpen proletariat whose arrogance led them to believe that only a meager amount of "straight" research had to be done in order to get through life. The drugs would then, abracadabra, pick up the slack and teach them the rest.

PSYCHEDELICS IN THE "POST-AMERICAN WORLD"

So, here we are on the cusp of the millennium's second decade already, and it doesn't seem like attitudes have changed much since the 1990s – only the intensity of the old pro-drug and anti-drug positions has really changed, with the Internet bringing new players into either camp daily (or, at the very least, turning up the volume on the voices of those who joined the fray long ago.) Members of the American "traditionalist" brigade, with their perpetual terror of displacement at the hands of an expansive immigrant population, are more active than ever at embodying H.L. Mencken's definition of Puritanism ("the haunting fear that somebody, somewhere, must be having a good time"). They are also busy resurrecting the claim that recreational drug use is the alien cultures' strategy to weaken the defensive resolve of the Anglo-Saxon Protestant male (Mexico's marijuana trade, as the target of the 1969 "Operation Intercept", was one of the first objectives of the expansive War On Some Drugs.). However, as they raise a tremendous hue and cry over illegal Mexican migrants using national parks to grow marijuana plants, they reveal themselves as ignorant of their own heritage: if they were real "traditionalists" espousing "European" values, they would know that the use of psychedelic plants dated back to the Neolithic period even in Europe. Those same self-appointed arbiters of morality might also be surprised to know that the use of visionary plants in pre-Christian Europe was done out of respect for three of their most closely guarded values: self-restraint, respect for hierarchy, and personal responsibility. As confirmed by researcher Christian Rätsch, the administration of psychedelic plants in the "old country" was reserved to prophets, seeresses, Druids and so on, while their administration was also limited to communal rites and festivals. The usage of hemp for the eroticized Hochzeit ["high time"] of the love goddess Freya not only took place in the land that is presently Germany, but such use of the plant – dating back more than 7,500 years – was its earliest recorded use. Anyway, keeping in mind the restrictive use of drugs in antiquity, perhaps Dr. Leary was onto something when he recommended not using powerful drugs like LSD without the proper "set and setting" – it was not something to be taken "anywhere, by anyone" even in the late 20th century with all its technological amenities, and definitely not something to be used with the base intention of filling up blocks of empty free time ("empty" free time in itself being a very recent development in the story of Homo Sapiens).

The puritanical traditionalists mentioned above are polytheistic followers, in a sense: where these people are concerned, the Christian god and the god of post-Enlightenment, rational scientific progress seem to be on equal footing with each other. This contradiction has never been satisfactorily explained, but this is where we stand: the United States as a "shining beacon on the hill" which has beaten back the heathens through its marriage of logical positivist/rationalist know-how and its divinely ordained, Christianized drive to convert and conquer. So, because of the revered status we still confer upon lab technicians of any stripe, psychedelic spirituality is once again having to sneak in through the "back door" of official, institutional approval – even as I compose this essay, a friend has linked me to an article claiming that hallucinogens are again being considered as a "legitimate subject of research," with a group known as the Multidisciplinary Association for Psychedelic Studies lobbying for hard scientific inquiry into their curative properties. Never mind the fact that the results of such research have been made clear decades ago, unless the chemical composition of LSD itself has changed since that time. Anyway, the M.A.P.S. is here to assure us that, this time, the course of study will be different, since it will focus on "pressing health needs" and "pressing treatments other than curiosity." More importantly, though, they warn prospective guinea pigs that "this isn't fun. There's no Grateful Dead music playing. This is serious business."

On this last count, the M.A.P.S. is correct, but for the wrong reasons: psychedelics are serious business, but serious insofar as they are respected as highly variable tools for individual advancement and for personal Socratic inquiry. They are not tools for helping to maintain any kind of socio-economic status quo or for helping society to stay on its present course. For, after all, what is the present course of that society? It is one divorced from natural law, and basing its prosperity on, quite literally, nothing: the creation of fiat currency, backed by nothing of solid value, drives the engines of the nation's expansionist militarism and its clumsy foreign adventures. While ostensibly fought for the establishment of a global democratic Pax Americana, these foreign wars end up being little more than battles for raw materials and natural resources, which themselves are fed back into the war machine to perpetuate this deadly loop anew. If this is what all of "society" is struggling to uphold, then this is a society that is in need of a massive re-think.

At any rate, recent developments suggest that psychedelic culture is far from dead in this country, and that the life cycle of the 1960s is just beginning again: first comes institutional experimentation, then comes the "leak" into popular acceptance, then comes the anarchic climax of that popular acceptance that mobilizes police and military forces into action and pushes the movement deeper underground. Unfortunately, there is no reason to believe that "this time" intelligence and empathy will increase across the board with help from another psychedelic revival: most likely, the stupid will continue to inflate their stupidity as more distractions and conveniences spring up around them. Meanwhile, the smart will also gather up knowledge at an unprecedented rate, while also maintaining a reverence for true mystery and inexplicable phenomena. You could easily compare this distribution of intellect to the way in which the country's wealth distribution is skewed: a tiny sliver of the population controlling 80% of the wealth, while the middle class vanishes and the impoverished plumb new depths of uncertainty. However, immaterial intelligence and material wealth do not spread in the same manner, and the former, once it has spread, is not as subject to quick burnout. It can survive even through the deep night of official pogroms – the psychedelic culture as a whole has outlived millennia of such repressive hysteria. With the current generation being the most transient and well-traveled of the modern age, as well as one which is finally avoiding the dangerous polarities of techno-phobia and techno-philia, keeping any kind of information under wraps is difficult – the electronic communication tools created to globalize the labor force have been impossible to keep out of the hands of more insurrectionary elements, including ones with a clear psychedelic agenda.

It's probably safe to say that the next major wave of psychedelic activity, much like everything else that was once exclusively associated with the North American cultural scene, will be enacted simultaneously on a number of different stages worldwide – not just within the West. Just one case in point: at the moment, the growing middle class of China is equal in number to the entire population of the U.S. In the American experience, the middle classes are constantly reviled as being the wellspring of cultural mediocrity, but they have also bred the skeptical individuals most likely to confront the influence of the military-industrial complex, and to occasionally extend the habit of personal inquiry to psychedelic practice. It's not that impossible that, among the expanding middle classes of Asia, a new psychedelic underground is already hungering for a break from lockstep conformity, disillusioned by the unprecedented pollution and desertification of their lands, and dissatisfied by the paltry gains that are given them in return for all of this. If "passing of the torch" to another nation or people means that American-style psychedelia has really sounded its death rattle, then so be it – it was never really "ours" to begin with. Our humble culture of psychedelic sacrifice was an attempt to temporarily revive the ancestral memories of incredibly divergent cultures within the dominant world power of the day, and to isolate the moments of those spiritual histories still worth preserving. In the final reckoning, only the language used to relate these experiences, and the cosmetic trappings that they came packaged in, were distinctly "American". Otherwise, the organic and elusive nature of psychedelia shrugs at the continual shifts in geopolitical power, and lies in wait for anyone brave enough to once again seek it out.

LSD Again

Ernst Jünger

Translation and introduction by Annabel Lee

This short essay appears in the book *Annäherungen: Drogen und Rausch*, Ernst Jünger's collection of his writings about drugs and alcohol.[1] The essays range from poetic musings and historical overviews of intoxication, to descriptions of his adventures with wine, beer, cannabis, cocaine, opium, tobacco, mescaline, mushrooms, ether, speed, chloroform, and LSD.

In 1943 the Swiss chemist Albert Hofmann inadvertently discovered the hallucinogenic effects of lysergic acid diethylamide (LSD), which he had synthesized in his Sandoz laboratory in Basel. He shared the new substance with Ernst Jünger in 1951. The essay below recounts a further trip that the two "psychonauts" took together in 1970 at Jünger's home.

A highly observant author such as Jünger chooses his words carefully and I have tried to render the text as faithfully as possible, but must admit to the inevitable infidelities of translation. Beginning with the title of Jünger's book itself, the general inadequacy of translation is revealed. *Annäherungen* means "approaches, approximations, or convergences." *Drogen* is easily translated as "drugs," but *Rausch* is a word with many meanings, most of them related to inebriation. *Rausch* can indicate a state of euphoria, ecstasy, rapture, passion, or a thrill – it is akin to English "rush," but has a different semantic range. Another word lost in translation into English is *Sie*, the formal "you," with which Ernst Jünger and Albert Hofmann respectfully address one another. – *A.L.*

LSD Again

At the right time and at the right place I can add ergot as the "missing link."[2] For a long time I had kept three ampules of the "extract of its lethally delicious juices" next to the Mexican rarities that Guido had brought back for me from his travels. Last Friday, Albert Hofmann came over from Switzerland to correct my assessment of his synthesis.[3]

---

1. In the recent edition (Stuttgart: Klett-Cotta, 2008), it appears as section 295 on pp. 396–99. My thanks to Michael Moynihan, and to Viktor Szukitsch at Clett-Kotta, for helpful suggestions regarding aspects of the present translation. All footnotes are those of the translator.

2. English in the original.

3. After his first LSD trip, Jünger's assessment to Hofmann was that LSD "is nothing but a house cat compared with the Bengal tiger mescaline; at best it's a leopard." See "Chinesischen Gärten" in *Annäherungen*, 355.

A "synthesis" – thus should an operation, which cannot be sharply defined as a discovery or as an invention, probably be described. Everything is revealed; we lift away a veil from nature and its forces, the interior of which we do not penetrate. That is dangerous, as it was in this case, too. Then from the abundance we trim what suits us. The Great Mother's riches are tapped. The technical world is not only mill, it is also milking parlor. This is visible in the retorts and all the way to the form. In this landscape things are not only ground down finely and split apart, they are also drawn from millions of boreholes and taps, and distilled. We milk even the light-beams and the air.

Today, we were not to concern ourselves with this; right after breakfast we took a different trip that ended with nightfall. Contrary to my expectations, it was possible for me to take notes – which shows, incidentally, that I have already become a more seasoned traveler in these latitudes. Here is the logbook, without commentary:

Wilflingen, the 7th of February, 1970

> 10:25 No file to open the ampules; it had to be gotten in the village.
> LSD   E. J. 150 gamma or 0.15 mg
>   A. H. 100 gamma or 0.10 mg
> Dissolved in a small glass of water, slightly fluorescent.
> "It tastes like nothing."
> "Nothing is a dangerous thing."
> "Have a good flight!"

Conversation about synthetic substances. Just building blocks which we arrange and rearrange. Formed bricks come from the clay pit; findings, not inventions. Even the grower of highly cultivated flowers can't do without seeds.

10:45 A. H. feels the first effects. A tightness in the shoulders, sleepiness. "Rather somatic." Record-player: Mozart.

10:55 Concerto for Flute and Harp in C major. A bluetit pecks at the window. Does it hear anything? You overhear everything if you descend deeply enough into the Undifferentiated.

The titmice pick at seeds from little pouches, the yellow of which is now becoming more intense. The piece of limestone with the fossilized fish also takes on an intense orange which I had not observed until now, even in sunlight. The bricks on one of the Stauffenberg towers become more brightly red, like at sunset.[4] In places where they are covered in moss, the green is more vivid. The color blue, by contrast, is still completely dead. We are dead, industry colored, lying fallow.

I'm sitting in the study, A. H. is in the library. It begins to snow.

11:15 Now the blue is also getting stronger. Black is still dead. Should I go over there? That could startle him, though.

He feels the need to lie down. For him, Mozart was "like the turning of porcelain figures." In other words, still dead.

"Could we still make it? It would be a test, at any rate."

---

4. Jünger's house is owned by the Stauffenbergs and stands directly across the street from their residence in Wilflingen. Today it is the Jünger-Haus Museum, dedicated to his life and work.

"Ah, that comes of its own accord."

11:40 "Would you like to sleep?"

"It would not be sleep."

"It shouldn't be, at any rate."

11:50 Outside world still disturbing. Tractors. But now this murmur – – – as if two were whispering in one of the universe's private booths.

"Those are jesters."[5]

The bells ring. "Better than the machines."

Are our senses keener? Or is matter itself becoming offensive? We will never be able to plumb these depths.

12:10 Our boat rocks violently. Also into the prosaic.

12:45 For a moment I was with myself – with Himself – alone. Then to A. H. "Now somewhat better. Better, yes, better – even if not entirely."

For a moment, identity.

13:00 Comparisons with eagles.

A. H. "In our language there's nothing comparable. It does come from another world."

We now enter different rooms where it's peaceful. Only someone acquainted with war knows what peace means.

A. H. "The blue is becoming transparent now."

E. J. "The name Hofmann, too."

13:15 It becomes quite pleasant. As if it were streaming richly into the manifestation.

13:16 I make another attempt with eagle flight. Not only the edges – the linen is violet.

13:30 E. J. "I don't need any more intensification now."

A. H. "I think it suffices."

13:50 Again: the eagle position – eagle flight. Three times: the wings!

14:00 The last, most delicate approach – the finch, his, who wishes to sacrifice himself.

14:35 "Long" absence.

15:00 Eagle flight. Identity.

15:23 Three wings.

15:30 Spring comes. That was the most charming, most tender agreement with the return.

16:35 Blue, radiant.

A. H. "I experience the beauty of these rooms – – – well, it does have a source.

17:15 Strokes of the eagle's wings, three.

With the break of night we began conversing with one another: we were alighting. The flight had been a success – only the machines had been bothersome; their tempo is the main enemy of both meditation and artistic impulses. A mechanized, brutal will; you are either run over or galvanized by it.

One ought to choose places amidst remote gardens, with simple, tasteful décor. Little metal, bronze is best, much wood of the sorts used for violinmaking, straw mats, thatched roofs. No splendid view, neither to the sea nor mountains – a pond would suffice, a small wall with a lizard resting on it.

We took another walk around the village, each of us for himself, before we sat down at

---

5. *Schalknarren*: classic jester figures; they still appear in costumed carnivals.

the table. A thaw had set in, but then there was frost once more; the emanations were still vivid; the snow glowed like the freshly discharged slag of a blast furnace.

Nochmals LSD

Ernst Jünger

Zur rechten Zeit und am rechten Ort kann ich das Mutterkorn als missing link nachtragen. Ich bewahrte vom „Auszug seiner tödlich feinen Säfte" seit langem drei Ampullen neben den mexikanischen Raritäten, die mir Guido von seinen Ausflügen ins Haus brachte. Am letzten Freitag kam Albert Hoffmann aus der Schweiz herüber, um mein Urteil über seine Darstellung zu berichtigen. Darstellung – so muß man wohl eine Operation bezeichnen, die weder als Entdeckung noch als Erfindung scharf zu umreißen ist. Entdeckt wird alles; wir heben einen Schleier von der Natur und ihren Kräften, in deres Inneres wir nicht eindringen. Das ist gefährlich und war es auch in diesem Fall. Dann schneiden wir aus dem Überfluß für uns zurecht. Der Reichtum der Großen Mutter wird angezapft. Die technische Welt ist nicht nur Mühle, sie ist auch Melkstube. Das wird schon an den Retorten sichtbar, bis in die Form. In dieser Landschaft wird nicht nur raffiniert gemahlen und aufgespalten, es wird an Millionen Bohr- und Zapfstellen auch angesogen und destilliert. Wir melken selbst den Lichtstrahl und die Luft.

Das sollte uns heut nicht kümmern; wir machten uns gleich nach dem Früstück auf eine andere Reise, die mit Einbruch der Dunkelheit endete. Wider Erwarten war es mir möglich, Notizen zu machen – das zeigt übrigens, daß ich in diesen Breiten schon befahrener geworden bin. Anbei das Logbuch, ohne Kommentar:

Wilflingen, den 7. Februar 1970

10.25 Keine Feile zum Öffnen der Ampullen; Sie mußte im Dorf besorgt werden.
LSD E. J. 150 gamma oder 0,15 mg
       A. H. 100 gamma oder 0,10 mg
Aufgelöst in einem Gläschen Wasser, leichte Fluoreszenz.
„Schmeckt nach Nichts."
„Das Nichts ist eine gefährliche Sache."
„Auf gute Fahrt!"
Gespräch über synthetische Stoffe. Auch nur Bausteine, die wir hin- und herschieben. Geformte Ziegel kommen aus der Tongrube, Findungen, nicht Erfindungen. Auch der Züchter hochkultivierter Blumen kommt ohne Samenkorn nicht aus.

10.45 A. H. Spürt die erste Wirkung. Ziehen in den Schultern, Müdigkeit. „Noch mehr somatisch." Plattenspieler: Mozart.

10.55 Konzert für Flöte und Harfe in C-Dur. Eine Blaumeise pickt am Fenster. Ob sie wohl etwas hört? Man hört alles mit, wenn man tief genug in das Ungesonderte steigt. Die Meisen picken Sämereien aus Beutelchen, deren Gelb jetzt intensiv wird. Ebenso gewinnt die Kalkplatte mit dem versteinerten Fisch ein intensives Orange, das ich selbst im Sonnenlicht bislang nicht an ihr beobachtete. Die Ziegel auf einem der Stauffenbergschen Türme werden kräftiger rot, wie bei Sonnenuntergang. Dort, wo sie bemoost sind, wird auch ihr Grün lebhafter. Die blaue Farbe dagegen noch ganz tot. Wir sind überhaupt tot, industriefarben, brachliegend.

Ich sitze im Arbeitszimmer, A. H. in der Bibliothek. Es beginnt zu schneien.

11.15 Auch das Blau wird jetzt kräftiger. Schwarz immer noch tot. Ob ich hinübergehe? Das könnte ihn aber erschrecken.

Hat Bedürfnis, zu liegen. Mozart war ihm „wie das Drehen von Porzellanfiguren". Also noch tot.

„Ob wir das noch schaffen können? Wäre immerhin ein Test."

„Ach, wissen Sie, das schafft sich von selbst"

11.40 „Wollen Sie schlafen?"

„Schlaf ist das nicht."

„Wäre auch schlimm."

11.50 Außenwelt immer noch störend. Traktoren. Aber schon dieses Raunen – – – als tuschelten in einem der Séparées des Universums zwei.

„Das sind Schalkschnarren."

Die Glocken läuten. „Besser als die Maschinen."

Verschärft sich unsere Wahrnehmung? Oder wird die Materie offensiv? Das werden wir nie ausloten.

12.10 Unser Boot schlenkert gewaltig. Auch in das Nüchterne.

12.45 War einen Augenblick mit mir – mit ihm selbst – allein. Dann zu A. H.: „Jetzt etwas besser. Besser, ja besser – wenn auch noch nicht ganz."

Für einen Augenblick Identität.

13.00 Adler-Abgleichungen.

A. H.: „In unserer Sprache nichts Vergleichbares. Kommt doch aus einer anderen Welt."

Wir treten jetzt in andere Räume ein, in denen es friedlich wird. Nur wer den Krieg kennt, weiß, was Frieden heißt.

A. H.: „Das Blau wird jetzt transparent."

E. J.: „Der Name Hoffman auch."

13.15 Es wird durchaus angenehm. Als quölle es reich in die Erscheinung hinein.

13.16 Versuche es wieder mit dem Adlerflug. Nicht nur die Ränder – das Leinen violett.

13.30 E. J.: „Ich brauche jetzt keine Verstärkung mehr."

A.H.: „Ich glaube, es genügt."

13.50 Wieder: die Adlerstellung – der Adlerflug. Drei Mal: Die Schwingen!

14.00 Die letzte, zarteste Annäherung – der Fittich, dessen, der sich opfern will.

14.35 „Lange" Abwesenheit.

15.00 Adlerflug. Identität.

15.23 Drei Schwingen.

15.30 Der Frühling kommt. Das war das charmanteste, zarteste Einverständnis mit der Wiederkehr.

16.35 Blau, strahlend.

A. H.: „Ich erlebe die Schönheit dieser Räume – – – nun, sie kommt schon wo her."

17.15 Adlerschwünge, drei.

Mit Einbruch der Dunkelheit begannen wir uns zu unterhalten: wir stiegen aus. Der Flug war gelungen – störend waren nur die Maschinen gewesen; ihr Takt ist der Hauptfeind sowohl der Meditation wie der musischen Einschwingung. Mechanisierter, brutaler Wille; entweder wird man überfahren oder galvanisiert.

Man müßte Orte inmitten entlegener Gärten wählen, mit einfacher, gediegener Ausstattung. Wenig Metall, am besten Bronze, viel Holz von Sorten, wie man sie zum Geigenbau verwendet, Strohmatten, Schilfdächer. Kein großer Ausblick, weder auf Meer noch Gebirge – ein Wasserbecken würde genügen, ein Mäuerchen, auf dem eine Eidechse ruht.

Wir machten noch einen Gang um das Dorf, jeder für sich, bevor wir uns zu Tisch setzten. Es hatte getaut und begann wieder anzufrieren; immer noch waren die Emanationen lebhaft; der Schnee glühte wie die frisch ausgestoßene Schlacke eines Hochofens.

THE EDGE OF INDIAN SPIRITUALITY – THE ORAL TRADITION OF NAKED YOGIS

A Speech at the World Psychedelic Forum, Basel, March, 2008

Baba Rampuri

Magic happens anywhere worlds meet: at a crossroads, the seashore, graveyards, airports, hospitals, mountain tops, and temples. But those places where the Ordinary World meets the Extraordinary World require pilgrimage, whether internal or external. The act of making a pilgrimage is that of suspending oneself between worlds. Those locations to which one makes a pilgrimage, are called tirthas, crossing over places. They are spaces containing the meeting of worlds, and standing on those intersections, one may be at once in both worlds. Tirthas mark hidden entrances to the Extraordinary World.

They resemble a fold in the page, a hinge between the macro- and the microcosms. A reflection of the inner journey onto the external world or a reflection of the heavens onto the Earth. Those who go on a pilgrimage become witnesses of mirrors.

The main reason for pilgrimage is for darshan, The Beholding, and the resulting blessings. Darshan derives from drsh, "to see", and is The Beholding, not "the looking", as a tourist might do, but The Seeing. And, as the mirrors continue to reflect images deeper and deeper within, Analogy operates reflecting the macrocosm and the microcosm.

The World must benefit from his pilgrimage, so having had darshan, the pilgrim brings something back to his village. Pilgrims return with more than memories, something auspicious, that brings magic and prosperity home.

Pilgrimage is also story, each pilgrim a hero, and every hero has a quest. That quest may take the pilgrim outside the realm of society and into the extraordinary world, where the rules have all changed. And it is here that the pilgrim connects with …

The stars.

The pilgrim reflects a story on the surface of the Earth that is told in the night sky and connects with its great chain of resemblances and its reflections. It means achieving a body-less state, a kind of immortality – becoming a ghost, as the pilgrim's spirit may be absorbed knowingly or unknowingly by so many other humans over time. And those humans may lend hands and tongues to that spirit.

I feel extremely honoured, pleased, and humbled to be here speaking to you this evening. The presence of so many great thinkers, magi, shamans, and alchemists here in Basel, sharing their very considerable experience, knowledge, and commentary with us, makes me feel the Spirit of the Earth, Herself, Her eternal Renewal and Her blessings.

And it's exciting for me to have an audience like you, from all over the planet, here to explore our consciousness, and take this experience back into the world.

The organizers of this incredible conference deserve the highest praise, and I want to thank you all, especially Lucius Werthmüller and Dieter Hagenbach… but most of all, Dr. Albert Hofmann, a truly great man, who by his dedication and work, by his mastery of his art, made it possible for many of us to acquire greater knowledge of ourselves and the world, and to have access to the extraordinary worlds many of us have spent our lives exploring. To me, he is a living deity.

Dr. Hofmann is the greatest living alchemist, and perhaps the greatest for a very long time. The tradition of Agrippa, Paracelsus, and others, many of whom practised right here in Basel, regarded the alchemist as ultimately constituting the only real subject and object of his own experiment. So when Dr. Hofmann became both the subject and the object of his experiment, on that day in 1943 when he unwittingly had that first trip, he successfully invoked a spirit that has lived amongst us ever since, opening doors of perception and experience, giving us the possibility of impossible thoughts, and taking us where we never thought it was really possible to go.

Many think of alchemy as the art of turning base metal into gold by use of a philosopher's stone or magic elixir. Using this analogy, the ultimate purpose of the alchemist is the transformation of the ordinary human life into the extraordinary by means of the knowledge of the self. Paracelsus taught here in Basel that the whole universe is reflected in man, and the keys of knowledge are the same.

In 1527, the alchemist Agrippa stressed in a letter that there is a secret interpretation and understanding which cannot be conveyed through the printed word alone, but must be transmitted from the master to the disciple, echoing Pythagoras and Plato.

And he wrote, "Whosoever therefore shall know himself, shall know all things in himself; especially he shall know God… and how all things may be fitted for all things in their time, place, order, measure, proportion and harmony…"

Agrippa was very suspicious of faith. He insisted on direct knowledge of the sacred by its experience.

I think it's fair to say that experiences with LSD and other perception altering substances created a diaspora of trippers on various quests for knowledge in the 60s. A number of signposts pointed increasingly to India. Many who I later met in India, from all over the world, would say, in effect, "LSD sent me."

We had a glimpse of something and wanted more access to the Extraordinary World in which it lived. It compelled us to take the psychedelic experience further, and make some sense out of it.

A dear friend, Uma Giri, a Swedish model in the 60s, who became one of the rare foreign female Naga Babas wrote, "LSD parted the veil and made an opening into something else, into more than we had ever been able to see in and around ourselves. Its atmosphere was magical and mystical, but for me, these qualities were just not reflected in the English surroundings. The music, Timothy Leary, the Beatles meeting the Maharishi Mahesh Yogi: all this said to us that India was where the magic, the mystic, and that something else, might be found. People had smoked dope. But that didn't do it. It was LSD that carried the idea of India to us all."

A few years ago, I was visiting a collective of psychedelic young people in the States, and I couldn't help but notice their posters of Indian Gods, mainly the God Shiva, on their walls along with other psychedelic art. Since none of them had been to India, nor seemed into an Indian spiritual thing, I was curious what they saw in the poster of Shiva. "I dunno," said one, "it's just cool." At that moment, I saw myself in that young man, and realized that I had gone to India searching vocabulary.

And many of us combed the world and its religious, philosophical, and shamanic traditions, searching for a vocabulary with which we could begin to make knowledge out of perception – which we could use to start creating those categories of thinking that were so obscure in our modern consumer society.

I could only sense in my youth that those enigmatic posters of the Indian gods and goddesses were not merely decorative, but magic talismans, offering protection, capable of invoking cosmic energies, as well as a conduit to an extraordinary world. And even that magus himself, Jimi Hendrix, appeared in one. The *Axis Bold as Love* album cover.

The *Bhagavad Gita*, *The Tibetan Book of the Dead*, and various works of *Vedanta*, and mythology, philosophy, started giving us words that we didn't have before: karma, dharma, guru, nirvana, kundalini, maya, bardos, even yoga and yogi. And then the discourse of India: "All this that you see? With your eyes? Well, there's a lot more happening. Let Aristotle be damned. This is all illusion. Who is it that's doing the seeing, anyway?"

It was not nearly enough for me and others to read the philosophy of India, or assign meanings to the mysterious posters, which were indeed talismans of protection and guidance.

The psychedelic experience drew a line in the sand, a preliminary standard by which we could measure other mystical experience.

We watched the Earth breathe and come alive. We saw the interconnectedness of the things of nature. It was as if our consciousness itself was painting this world, or indeed, reflecting it.

The title of my talk this evening is *The Edge of Indian Spirituality*, and I want to explain this just a bit.

I see the mainstream representation of India in much the same way as I see the mainstream news media. Our understanding of India is an imperial culture's construction of its colony. I clearly saw this in my own thinking, and continue to discover its artefacts in my thoughts. I felt blocked in my own attempt to penetrate below the surface of things even after a number of years in India. I discovered that I was limited by my own imagination, that my search for meaning kept turning inward upon itself. I found that the meaning I assigned to things was not new insight into an esoteric culture, but old meanings that I used new Indian words to represent. I felt like someone who was colour blind trying to correct the overwhelming blue or red dominating a photo in Photoshop.

Like a detective searching for the motive of the accused, or an archeologist digging for potsherds in his attempt to understand something that ceased to exist hundreds or thousands of years ago, I was compelled to find out who I was, what made me see the world in the way that I did, what made me organize my perceptions in a way that was consistent with the discourse of the land of my birth. For this was the only way I could truly gain entrance into the extraordinary world.

I found that the vocabulary and language of Comparative Religion, basically Christianity, and that of Psychology, only constructed an idea of India, which was different from was under my feet. It was like reading a description and analysis of an acid trip by someone who had never experienced it. All the rational thinking in the world would not take one any closer to the experience and its articulation.

I am going to travel back, past the 20th century a couple hundred years, then back past the so-called "enlightenment," and even past the renaissance to hermetic times to find a European vocabulary to articulate the Oral Tradition in India.

As I look around our wonderful symposium here, I see a number of others, who have to do similar things to be able to articulate a knowledge largely revealed by Plant Deities and other Gods.

I was enchanted by the yogi-shamans, the Naga Babas of India – naked in ashes, long dreadlocks twisted with Marigolds piled on their heads like crowns, proudly austere, sitting with straight backs in some yoga asana, giving blessings to wide eyed pilgrims, seekers, and the poor, shouting out mantras and spells that charm or curse peoples' lives. That was the public image. I couldn't interpret, then, the hip arrogance I saw, in their sometimes bloodshot eyes.

They seemed about as far from the ordinary world one could wander, sort of my story as well, having traveled about as far from the land of my birth as one could go. They were naked, they wore ashes from their sacred fires instead of clothes. They had few possessions other than the few magical instruments like tridents, tongs, and water pots, that adorned their sacred fires. And lest I forget, chillams filled with cannabis sacrament.

It wasn't that they were mad – it was theater, there was a narrative, something arcane from another age. If it was theater, it was also ritual, and where those two worlds met, one being the mirror image of the other, the narrative of self-knowledge is performed.

According to Indian storytelling, some 2500 years ago appeared a man who became known as Adi Shankaracharya, India's greatest philosopher, prolific commentator of ancient texts, poet, and for our purpose here, the greatest organizer of the ancient tradition of Yogis, the founder of the monastic order known as Sannyasis. About 1500 years later, a number of lineages of Naked Yogis, or Naga Babas from among Shankaracharya's order of Sannyasis, formalized even more ancient bonds into an association called The Akhara.

In India, today, an akhara is usually a club where traditional wrestling takes place, more often than not, in the back of a Hanuman temple. The Naked Yogis, however, in The Akhara of old (and still today), performed a different kind of wrestling – outwardly intellectual, rhetorical, and political, but below the surface of their theater, operated a "human machine" called tradition, that carried knowledge down through time. When Alexander the Great's ambassador to the court of Patliputra (now Patna in the Indian state of Bihar), Megasthenes, observed the Naked Yogis in the fourth century B.C., he described them as gymnosophists, "naked philosophers." There were also the so-called naked philosophers in Greece at the time, who would hang out at a gymnasium, and wrestle, naked.

The Akhara's collected lineages look back for their origins to the Age of Treta, countless thousands of years ago, the age of the epic poem, The Ramayana, and to the Three Headed Guru of Yogis, Dattatreya, their ultimate founder. Guru Dattatreya is naked, his dreadlocks touch the earth.

He is the son of one of progenitors of the human race, Atreya, and his wife, the personification of female shakti, Anasuya. His three heads are those of the Indian trinity, Brahma, Vishnu, and Shiva, his four dogs are thought of as the most ancient and sacred texts of the Indians, the *Vedas*, the Cow of all Desires follows him around, and the Mother Goddess, Herself, sits on his lap. After all, he is the incarnation of her husband, Vishnu.

Dattatreya is the original Guru of yogi shamans: He who has crossed over and shows The Path. Even being an avatar (literally, "the descending one"), he is mostly known as the avadhut, a "messenger descending [from the Gods]". He is always pursued, for he is the Knower of the Self. As much the Herald as the Mentor, he makes the narrative known to those who join in his theater. The Guru provides the means of knowing the self, which reflects the entire universe.

Even today in The Akhara of Dattatreya (which is now called the "Old Akhara"), each yogi sees Dattatreya as his guru. Our physical gurus, for we start out with five, are called "witness" gurus. They give initiation to the disciple into the "oral tradition," which is called the Tradition of Knowledge.

"Hinduism" is a recent word constructed in the West by India's colonizers to represent a set of beliefs thought to be held by most Indians, thus a religion. But traditionally, those thought of as Hindus (originally referring to people who lived on the "other" side of the Indus River), have no concept of "Hinduism," but speak of the sum of knowledge among their diverse traditions as the "Sanatan Dharma." In the oral tradition of the Naga Yogis, we think of the Sanatan Dharma as the Book of the World.

The world is the container of all things and The Book of the World is its articulation. Its language is Primary Language, not Sanskrit, but a language of signatures: marks, signs, flags, and cyphers, that call our attention to outer resemblances which indicate inner, hidden relationships. The world and the sky are awash in Language, they reflect each other, as man reflects the earth and the sky.

The reader of The Book of the World becomes its commentator, and its commentary is called Shastra, the Oral Tradition. But Shastra means scripture, no? The *Vedas*, *Puranas*, *Bhagavad Gita*, etc., the Authority of all Indian Tradition. Scriptural authority is always invoked in religious and philosophical debate, discussion, and sermon in India, not usually sufficient proof in itself, but certainly a strong component part of a convincing argument.

And, indeed it is as well within the oral tradition. In fact, the oral tradition is always quoting "scripture." But which one(s)? I would question my gurus and fellow disciples, guru-bhais, when they would sing their shlokas to make a point. "Where does that come from?" I would ask, implying an assumed linear order to the universe.

But my gurus didn't memorize shlokas from books, even "Holy Books," and they didn't use my linearity. They would "pull from the sky" the Primary Language, or pull from "what is heard", the mantras, or pull from "what is remembered", the songs and the ironies, and then perform the commentary.

An oral tradition, being pre-literate, does not mean that its members are illiterate or don't read books. The leadership, the hierarchy, among Naga Yogis is Brahmin, normally well educated, quite literate, often keeping volumes of notebooks. The difference between a preliterate and a literate tradition has largely to do with where authority of a source of knowledge lies. A literate tradition relies on books for its authority while the pre-literate tradition relies on the spoken word. For the Naga Yogi, member of an oral tradition, the source is the tradition itself, what is said, what is heard. Not just by one's guru or gurus, but echoed among all the lineages throughout the order.

An oral tradition is much more than the fact of oral transmission from guru to disciple. One man's idea or system, however good or enlightened, does not make a tradition. A tradition is a living thing, the embodiment of living story, which spills past the beginning and the end. A comprehensive narrative emerges, encompassing archetypical heroes, nemeses, mentors, allies, and others whose plot elements are driven by the rhythm of the moon against the background of stars and planets, beginnings, middles, and ends, and in that story content we find all the knowledge of the natural world. This narrative is repeated and acted out tens of thousands of times every day by its cast of characters. Living Theater for Living Story.

I will be the first to admit to you that when I was first initiated into the oral tradition of the Naga Sannyasis in 1970, I imagined the tradition to be a contained philosophy and practice, something finite, like a package, or a book. I had to climb this mountain, and it was there, on top, what I wanted – a pot of knowledge. And I did climb. But when I arrived in that place I had imagined as the top, I discovered that this was only the first small preparatory climb, the rambling foothills of a great mountain range, the true peaks of which remained shrouded in mist. Suddenly, its glorious majesty would reveal itself for a moment – and then back to obscurity.

I had no handles, no maps, no landmarks to determine where I was or where I was going. The only of my mentors who spoke English died within two years of my initiation into the ancient order. My first several years of discipleship focused on the rules and customs of the new Extraordinary World in which I somehow arrived.

I wanted to know why we did things in a particular way. I wanted to know how all the rules and rituals connected together to mean something or make something. I really wanted books, I wanted to study about what I was immersed in. But there were no books as there were no classes nor examinations. I had to find the authority for knowledge from the voices of the tradition itself.

My first secret sacred knowledge was that of removing ghee-grease from pots and pans using cold water and vibhuti, sacred ash. I mastered that quickly, but went on to practice it for several years. This was a small knowledge that I gained.

The mantras, practices, and other forms of respecting nature were not so easy. I didn't know what the mantras meant, but did my best to mimic what I heard, and I tried my best to imitate how others performed the rituals and pujas.

I vainly attempted to construct the world of Naga Yogis in my imagination, but I found that my castles crumbled with each new insight I stumbled over. Obscurity is the agent's biggest problem. It took me many years to understand anything, and many more years to be able to articulate what I understood.

Becoming a baba starts out as an exercise in copying and mimicking. This is to prepare the soil for a great spirit to enter. Many great spirits live in the world of babas, some benign, some horrific. Some spirits pass through whole lineages of yogis, while some might possess individuals. And in some, passes the spirit of Guru Dattatreya, himself.

The Akhara of Dattatreya, located in Ujjain, Central India, is one of the monastic homes of the spirit of Guru Dattatreya for many millennia. His spirit passes into the body of the spiritual leader of The Akhara, called the Pir, during a vedic rite of abhishekh. "Pir" is actually a Persian word, used largely by Muslim Sufis to refer to a spiritual leader, and this demonstrates Dattatreya's iconoclasm. The Pir will never leave the Akhara, and we he dies, his body is buried inside the compound – Dattatreya Akhara is also a mausoleum of all the Pirs possessed by Guru Dattatreya, going back thousands of years.

As my guru, Hari Puri Ji Maharaj, instructed me at the time of my initiation, my entrance into this world, that he was only a shakshi, "witness" guru, as were the other four Naga Babas that completed my "Five Gurus." The Guru is Dattatreya, Himself. But He is obscure. Manifested, but very removed, hard to know.

"There are bodies we must choose," said Hari Puri Baba just before he left his body for the last time, "that have certain minds, certain dispositions. These become suitable for passing the Tradition down through time."

These aren't the only spirits floating through space possessing bodies. There are various spirits of love, hatred, aesthetic perfection, patriotism, violence, and benevolence among the vast world of spirit beings that inhabit humans. Humans become possessed by the spirits of deities, rivers, planets, and celestial dancers as well.

The process of becoming a yogi, a commentator of The Book of the World, is a process of absorption rather than study as we know it. In the course of one's life living inside of the Tradition, one may hear the same story told many times by one's guru, and each time there might be some additions and anecdotes, giving one the impression that somewhere there is a huge living story, which is simply too big and complicated to tell or sing, and the stories from the mouths of its tellers are only small portions of it. And one hears the story told by others in the tradition, some articulate and intellectual, some mystical, and some just plain entertaining. The "real" story" is not in the language of commentary, but that primal language of The Book of the World, itself. If one could put together all the recitations of the story, by all members of the tradition, now and forever, then one would have the whole text.

There's a lot of information, and there's a lot of illusion and falsehood in the world. We search for authority. The Tradition provides handles – the "playing field" and the rules of the extraordinary world, and the Guru is the mark of authority, of knowledge.

The Guru is no longer a human being of the ordinary world. He has completed his worldly obligations to family and caste, marked it by a ritual funeral, and joined a mythological world. He has crossed over to the other side.

He becomes the point of contact with The Tradition, his disciple's patron, protector, witness, and mentor. To the disciple, he is The Tradition, itself, the living commentary of the Book of the World.

According to the oral tradition of the Naga yogis, the main role of the yogi in his relationship with the world is to give blessings. He is not a preacher, and only a teacher in a very general sense of making people aware of the importance and direction of knowing oneself, and therefore bringing more balance and happiness into one's life. The "world" comes to the yogi for his blessings, that magic touch, which makes the impossible happen and charms one's life – bringing health and prosperity.

But, the Yogi doesn't have the blessings to give in the first place. Blessings – Prosperity, Health, and Well-being, are the nature and substance of the Earth Mother. We know Her, by Her fertility which resembles a rich blanket of vegetation growing on Her surface, the fields of grain, Her mango trees heavy with ripe fruit, and her herds with udders full of milk. She is often pictured with sugar cane stalks, for Her taste is sweet. The Yogi, having an uncluttered mind resembling that of a still mirror-like lake, is connected (yoga) with Her, and acts like a conduit through which HER blessings flow.

The practice of the Naga Yogi consists of identifying all Her personalities, whether benevolent or catastrophic, and to each one, offering respect. Having put all the petty illusions of his ego in their proper places Her benevolence may flow unimpeded.

With one's mortal gurus and guru-bhais as witnesses, one calls on Guru Dattatreya for teachings. And he comes and sings his song through the mouths of his yogis and other devotees. His words, on the surface, in translation, tickle us with their irony and iconoclasm. He tells us:

> Birth and death, freedom and bondage, false and true
> Belong to mind, not to you.
> Why do you weep my son,
> Nor you nor I have name or form?
>
> If everything is one, being freedom itself,
> Why become absorbed in the self?
> Why become absorbed in the non-self?
> Why become absorbed in being
> or absorbed in non-being?
>
> The Pure is not found by yoga's eight limbs
> nor found by quashing mind's whims,
> not by initiation from a guru, until
> awakening on its own, it's bright self shown.
>
> I am not a guru, I give no rite
> I have no work to which I'm tied.
> My true nature unembodied and clear
> is like the starry hemisphere.

All this is on the surface and is meant to be attractive and entertaining. It is very translatable and makes for interesting listening or reading. The translation appeals to our rational thinking, it makes good sense and is articulate in English and other languages, which has little to do with how it may sound in Sanskrit.

For in Sanskrit, in the bursting out in song that lives beneath the voices of its singers, in its hypnotic meter and rhyme, in the nuances and duplicities of words and sounds and their meanings that could never be anything but what they are, portals open up again.

He sings through us:

jnanamrtam samarasam gaganopamoham

We sing it forty times. Do you think he's trying to make a point?

It is Guru Dattatreya's refrain, punctuating all of Alice's rabbit holes; a line that has never left me alone since the moment I first heard it. It echoed through my head. It made me chant it. It is a line which is at the very foundation of the Tradition of Knowledge. And, one finds curious resemblances with the Hermetic traditions as well.

Being a Westerner, my nature is to first consider the grammatical subject of the line, and sure enough the subject is "I," "aham..." and then the verb, an implied, "to be." How do I translate the implications of having the subject so far away from the action, at the tail end of an articulation, as much for meter as for clarity, a final "aham."

I am "the immortality of knowledge" – jnanaamritam, a mere lifting of "a" to "aa", by fusion, takes us from death to immortality, "a mrita," is literally, "no death." Amrita is also nectar or elixir, and we will call it the Elixir of Immortality.

"We got the juice," says the Pir of Dattatreya Akhara. Well, he used the word, "rasa." Rasa has many meanings, the most common is juice, and it's often used as "essence" as well. But there is also a transformative element in this essence, as rasa can also be Mercury, Quicksilver, a shape-shifter, capable of transforming other things. Rasayana is alchemy as it is the rejuvenation of the body.

Mercury-Hermes was the "Messenger of the Gods" in the ancient Mediterranean. Translated into Sanskrit that would be, "Avadhuta," the common name of Guru Datta-treya, and the name of his song. "Thrice Great" Hermes Trismegistus bears an uncanny resemblance to the "Avadhut," whose three heads are those of the Indian Trinity.

The Pir had been an alchemist. He vehemently denied he had ever turned base metal into gold, but nevertheless had been attacked in his youth by robbers, looking for his loot. They couldn't find his formulae, they were in his head. And he had no books.

Sama is one of those expansive words that finds articulation in countless languages around the world. "Same" in English, for example. In almost any bazaar in the world, traders and shoppers understand the expression, "sama-sama," "same-same." Two things that in some way are the same. Sama suggests similarity, equivalence, things that are in balance, using man as the fulcrum of all proportions.

Our surprise and delight in seeing identical twins is based on the irony of "same but different." It's not their "equality" that attracts us, it's the fact that there's an essential similarity that the two people share, and we want to know what that similitude is. Sa-marasa speaks to us of essential sameness, of similitude.

The key is the concluding statement "gagana upama aham". Gagana is the firmament, the night sky. There are many words for sky, such as akash, which means "where the light comes from." So let's think of gagana as the firmament, which is a dome housing stars and planets. Upama is a word indicating comparison, resemblance, simile, analogue. Aham is not simply, "I am," but also is the "a" and "ha", the "alpha" and "omega", the beginning and the end, and everything in between. Appreciating the approximation involved, Dattatreya says,

> I am the Analogue,
> reflecting the firmament,
> the immortal Elixir of Knowledge.

Hidden samarasa-similitude is indicated on the surface of things – a visible mark for an invisible analogy – to make it known. The dome of the sky reflects of the dome of our speech, from our throat to our lips. The stations of articulation and their operations in Speech mark the vocal apparatus as the heavenly bodies mark the firmament. The domes are analogues of each other. For, as the stars are the witnesses and therefore the storytellers, crisscrossing all lives and all events, now and forever, Speech makes those stories known and establishes the possibilities of all knowledge. Knowledge is transported in the boat of storytelling on the Ocean of Story. The "speech" of the sky contains within it the language of The Book of the World, whose syllables reside in the sacred geography of our mouths.

The operations of the vocal chords and the breath (such as its retention, exhalation through the mouth, and through the nose) taking place at five stations of articulation, ranging from our throat to our lips, give rise to the 50 syllables (from "a" to "ha") which are the elements forming the foundation of Speaking and therefore, Knowledge. These syllables create the world, and at the same time contain all the possibilities of knowing that world. We worship these collective syllables as the Mother Goddess, and individually as Matrikas, Little Mothers.

We make pilgrimages to those shrines, crossing over places, of sacred geography of the mouth, beat the drums and ring the bells, there, for worship, and use each one of the holy places to erect mirrors of Her sacred syllables, which then reflect all of Her creation.

It is said that before there was Speaking, Shiva one day played his double headed drum, and the sound of each beat produced a Little Mother, who is known by her syllable.

The striking of the drum resembles the striking of the vocal apparatus to produce syllables. The syllables that rolled off Shiva's drum, known as Maheshwara Sutra, emerged in such an arrangement as to give Speaking its greatest possibilities.

I once asked Hari Puri Maharaj why it seemed that all the greatest yogis were also grammarians. "It's the same thing," he explained to me and continued, "the Yoga Sutra sprang from the mouth of Patanjali, spontaneously, but it took him eighty years to compose his Mahabhashya, his shastra on Grammar." The most "famous" grammar in the three worlds was composed by Ravan, the arch demon, himself. And then there is a long list of gods, rishis, and yogis who composed their grammars up until the time of

Panini, who is thought of as the last of the great grammarians, about 2500 years ago.

> "There are seven million two hundred seventy two thousand three hundred eleven nadis, subtle tubes of energy, in the human body, the yogi is he who counts them all! And how do you count them? First you have to distinguish them from each other by their vibration, their sound. Then you have to make a great chain, a garland of all the sounds, and here's the trick: you have to know how sounds fit together, link up, and then maintain the integrity of the chain. You don't want it to break on you. That's why yogis are grammarians and vice versa."

> "The arrangement of Nature might appear chaotic but it is not accidental. When I saw that Nature placed two things next to each other, I realized this to be an interior connection between them and that they share a similarity. And in this bond, properties, movements, and influences are exchanged. Syllables and sounds are linked together as they touch and change each other. Everything in the world is adjacent to something else, and so is linked into a great chain of the things of the world."

The Mother of Creation is known as Saraswati. Her onomatopoeic name reflects that primal contact of earth and water, the Striking. One can almost hear that name if one listens to water running over stones in a stream, sarsarasara.... And She has many other names as well. One of them is Speech. She is the power, the shakti of articulation, of Speaking, and Knowledge. She creates the world with the Primordial Word. A striking of the string on her Vina.

In fact She is that primordial word. Before there was the world, there was pure consciousness the tradition calls Shiva. One may think of Shiva as the simple syllable "a," an articulation that is yet to manifest anything.

Pronounce it, "a." It's a sound we produce when our thought has not yet crystallized, when we don't remember something... "aaaaa.... what is his name?" It's the foundational sound to our speaking.

"A" is the world in potential, but as yet, without differentiation. Our first beholding of Saraswati is in the stress which arises from the divine desire of the One to be Many; for the undifferentiated One to know Itself... First creating Two, subject and object. The first movement which takes place both in the Dome of Speaking, and in the World is from "a" to "i."

Feel it, pronounce it. "aaa – iii." "I" is called the seed syllable of Desire, Kama Bija.

The narrative of creation thus becomes an analogue of Speech. As the story unfolds, so does movement take place in the Dome of Speech. The syllables unfold in the Dome of Speech as so many Little Mothers giving birth to the world, combusting in that first movement from "a" to "i."

According to that narrative, primordial consciousness, the potential subject of knowledge, the syllable "a," and primordial matter, nature, as yet unmanifest, the potential object of knowledge, the syllable "i," appear through Cosmic Mind Stuff – reflected in an unruffled mirror-lake of Intellect, into a separation between a subject and an object of knowledge.

A discrimination arises between the Same and the Other, which are identical reflections of one another. The world's existence requires a drop in the mirror-lake, causing a ripple, a desire for identity, for separation. That first rippled reflection of I-dentity, ahamkara, Ego, appears as Movement, itself, and three qualities, excite this drop into its full manifestation of the world.

With The Active pulling, The Passive resisting, and The Balanced balancing, the world comes into existence with a thunderous "a-ham". The syllables all join together in a chain of the world. And according to how those sounds of the syllable coalesce in our dome of speech, how they join together, now determines how we know that world.

Where the "la" syllable is produced, the tongue points to the teeth, which perform the function of eating resembling the Earth, its produce and the breaking up the solid matter. "La" is density – the earth is to subsistence of all, like the teeth are to the human body. And teeth are adjacent to tongue as earth is adjacent to water.

Where the "wa" syllable is produced, the lips come together, thought is externalized through the lips as the flow of expression, an analogue of the flow (sara) of water giving expression of the world from cosmic thought. The "Wa" syllable corresponds to Wa-ter and is the name of the Creatrix, Saraswati, as Wak, Speech.

In the direction of less density, the friction of the tongue on the roof of the mouth producing the "ra" syllable, is hot, reflecting Fire. The tongue points upwards towards the intellect, where the data gathered from the organs of knowledge is digested, and towards the Sun, whose light will reveal the world.

The "ya" syllable, which you can experience arising out of "i" (i-ya), is produced as the tongue moves towards and slides towards our seed syllable of desire, "i" – pointing and moving towards Feeling, hence Touch and its objectification, the element Air, which is also its density.

The "ha" syllable requires the least effort and corresponds to the element of least density, Ether, which reflects space and time, which is perceived by Hearing. It arises out of the formless "a". "Ham" is thought of as the effortless roar which accompanies the full manifestation of the World.

These syllables, Little Mothers, along with their 45 sisters, constitute (sacred articulation of) the World and its knowledge.

The garland of these syllables, the varna mala, Kali's necklace of skulls, is a chain of convenience, in which all things of the world are proximate to each other. Convenience is an upama, a resemblance, connected with space in the form of a graduated scale of proximity. In the adjacency of syllables an upama of "place" appears, marking a site upon which nature has placed two things, and between those two things, movement, influences, passions, and properties are communicated. Even among syllables. This relationship is the "hidden" reason for their adjacency, upon which is superimposed the visible mark.

Upama-resemblance, however, is not limited to place, and is able to function without motion, from a distance, like the reflection from a mirror, a duplication of the world. Reflection enables things to imitate one another from one end of the universe to the other without connection or proximity. Distance does not exist between things reflecting each other through space, any more so than the distance can be measured between your reflected face and the surface of the mirror.

Upama as Analogy joins together Proximity and Reflection, and through it, all the marks and signs of the universe can be drawn together. We can see that analogy in the *Brhadaranyaka Upanisad*:

> Truly, the dawn is the head of the sacrificial horse;
> the sun his eye; the wind his breath; the universal fire his open mouth.
> The year is the body of the sacrificial horse;
> the sky his back; the atmosphere his stomach...
> the stars his bones; the clouds his flesh...

Things resemble each other. Signatures of the world tell us where the upama-analogy lies, how one sees it, or by what mark it may be recognized.

Adi Shankaracharya established his main monastery, Sringeri Math, where he witnessed a pregnant frog trying to cross the deadly hot sands in the noon day sun, trying to reach the river. Then he saw a cobra, whose favourite food is frog, slithering up to the poor animal, and upon reaching her, spread his hood, revealing his fangs, but to Shankara's great surprise, the cobra used his spread hood as an umbrella to protect the mother-to-be, and provide shade, so she could safely reach the river. He thus found the "signature" of Sarada Devi, Goddess of articulation and knowledge, and it was there that he built her temple.

The story being played out in the ashram or the circle of the lineage is always an analogue of the story told by the sky, a reflection of the firmament. The activity on any particular day is consistent with the phase of the moon, the position of the sun in the ecliptic, the relationships of planets and stars, and the day of the week. The sky determines feasting and fasting, honouring and invoking different personalities of nature, times of gatherings, initiations, and empowerments, meetings, travel, pilgrimage, times of silence, times of giving, times of receiving, and many other things.

One day, out of morbid curiosity, I opened a Hari Krishna newsletter, spam, that was in my email. In it, Lord Krishna was described in such a pathetic monotheistic manner, that he appeared to me as the plastic Jesus of shopping mall born-again Christians. So I dashed them off an email protesting their demeaning and insulting of Lord Krishna. The editor was surprised, as he probably receives reams of mail challenging their claims of the supremacy of Krishna, and here I was saying the opposite. I accused them of being Orientalists, of superimposing Western Culture, in this case Christianity, on the East and its culture. So he sent me three pages of quotes translated into English from the *Shrimad Bhagavatam* that supported what they wrote. I thanked him for the beautiful verses, and I truly appreciated them, but I wanted to know one thing. I wanted to know where Authority was located. In the ink on the page or from the mouth of the guru? He correctly explained that the guru articulates and interprets what is written in Scripture. But suppose, just SUPPOSE, for a moment, that there was some contradiction between your guru and the *Srimad Bhagavatam*, that on a particular point guru and scripture disagree. What do you take to be the ultimate authority? I will admit it was a trap, shamelessly I set him up. Scripture, he answered.

The monotheist religions require a central doctrine, and a central text, which is the basis for that doctrine, that's why they have been called the Religions of the Book. "The Book" was originally manuscripts, and eventually printed texts. Their authority lies within the "book."

When the colonizers of the 18th-19th centuries and their scribes in the human sciences wanted to map Indian thinking, they had the daunting task of defining indigenous Indian religion in such a way that it could fit in the categories laid out for it and put it on the grid of all things. They had to construct, as it were, an Indian religion, so that it also would have a central definitive doctrine and a central text. A printed text.

The printed text has been indispensable to knowledge in our modern world until the advent of the video screen and internet.

We have critical editions of Indian texts, which scholars have created by comparing several different manuscripts of the same text. Scholars then edited out obvious errors, and used their academically honed deductive logic to determine other mistakes, omissions and additions, and determined originality and genesis. And these "original" manuscripts were often commissioned by the aristocracy, so that someone listened to an oral rendition of a text or its commentary and wrote it down. And of course, when word got out that Europeans were looking for manuscripts, the frauds and forgeries also appeared, by the truckload. One of the most famous being the *Ezourvedam*, a fraudulent text composed by Jesuit missionaries in Pondicherry (French colony in India), to demonstrate the inferiority of the idolatrous Indians compared to Christianity. Voltaire, God bless his soul, used this text, believing its authenticity, to demonstrate the subtlety and superiority of Indian thought to a decadent Christianity.

You have a yogi in the oral tradition, who is reading the Book of the World and commenting on it daily, and someone comes along and writes down what he says or sings. And then his words, or at least what are recorded as his words, are removed from his body, from his lips. This is the manuscript. It's as if a snapshot of a day in the life of the oral tradition.

I'm reminded of Magritte's painting of a pipe that has the words prominently written across the canvas, "Ceci n'est pas une pipe". Well, can you smoke it?

The words require a voice, and that particular voice of authority in the oral tradition provides the context and the exegesis. Once removed from its source the text may now take on a life of its own. Interpretations may be read into it, it may be edited, updated, made more clear, translated. The words may undergo some sort of transformation, according to the needs of the academy, not according to the dynamic of tradition. And, they are forbidden from leaving their pages, imprisoned by the front and end covers of the book.

Gutenberg and his printing press started the modern process of taming the wild profusion of knowledge, "civilizing" vast overgrown tracts of wilderness. Knowledge started migrating into the printed page, where it could be safe, and where it could be safely displayed like the wild animals in the cages of a zoo. The more it migrated, the more it became information and the more it lost its context. But in the process, it gained a much larger audience than that only within the reach of a voice, and as such, usurped the authority of that voice.

Books demand literacy, which was rare when they first started showing their covers. A modern education, culture and discursive reasoning were necessary if they were to be useful, even if one could find access to the product, itself. Amazon was a big woman in those days. But most important of all, the culture of literacy demanded a change in the way language was used.

Language and the World became disconnected. Language began to express man's ideas about the world rather than being an articulation of the world itself. A new mapping process began. Words got lost, they no longer marked anything and were condemned to live only on the pages of books, from which they were borrowed to colonize people's speech.

Indian Tradition has it that in each day in the life of Brahma resides a full cycle of time for the world, divided into four ages. Everything begins perfect, everyone's enlightened, and it's all downhill from there, until we reach the bottom of the fourth age, the Kali Yuga, in which we are now, and that culminates in a great dissolution, "pralaya." Then, after a very long timeless moment, a new cycle arise out of the same pralaya. There's no New Age in the Sanatan Dharma.

So it is with the Oral Tradition and Readers of the World. A process takes place, not unlike the children's game of Post Office, in which someone whispers a statement in another's ear, and that statement is passed in a circle from whispering lips to waiting ears. The further down the line it goes, the more the statement degrades from the original. In the case of the Oral Tradition, the Primary Language remains the same, it's written in the sky, after all; the commentary must change. This is supposed to happen. If an oral tradition is not dynamic, it dies of stasis. The articulation of the commentary must have a relationship with the world's current discourse, and its here we discover its contraction.

One day in Varanasi, I asked Kapil Puri Maharaj, one of my gurus, the date of Adi Shankaracharya. He replied that Adi Shankaracharya, son of Shivaguru and Aryamba, was born on Vaisaka Shukla Pancami (the fifth day of the bright half of the moon in the month of April-May), under Purnavasu (a star in Gemini), in Kaliyuga 2593 (corresponding to 509 B.C.).

One of Guru Ji's disciples was sitting there, a young baba, who had risen to the top of Sampurnanand's Sanskrit College there (many babas also receive a high level education), raised a question. He said that now we have extensive libraries and can compare many texts, and we have scholars who do research in these texts to find out many interesting things, such as the time of Adi Shankaracharya.

He went on to explain that by finding dates that can be confirmed by historical methodology, scholars can assign dates with reasonable accuracy. From references in his texts, his style, references or lack of references to him, his guru's texts, and their connections, scholars have dated Adi Shankaracharya as having lived in the 8th century A.D.

I thought Guru Ji was going to have him wash out his mouth with Chandrika Soap.

Isn't this amazing? Adi Shankaracharya is arguably India's greatest ever philosopher, prolific composer of many of India's greatest texts, as well as India's greatest religious reformer, and yet we have a dispute of 1300 years as to the period of his lifetime.

Kapil Puri spent the rest of the afternoon narrating the lineages of Adi Shankaracharya, the numbers of years each one occupied the Seat of Authority, until he covered the 2500 years the Oral Tradition articulates as the time that has passed since his lifetime.

It seemed like a big crack going right down the middle of the bell-metal of this ancient tradition; a flag marking a collision taking place beneath the surface of the world.

Years later I would see that my young guru-bhai, who is now one of the spiritual leaders among Naga Yogis, had absorbed the tradition of our gurus, but uses his knowledge of yet another world, that of the academy, to increase his scope of commentary, in which he can distinguish the oral tradition.

But where does it leave the vast majority of seekers? Where may one seek authority, now that Speaking and Writing are no longer the prose of the world but spring from the fickle ideas of man, pumped up by media, and now the all-knowing video screen. Google and Wikipedia have taken over, and with their overlordship, things are frozen in their ironic identity. Things can be nothing more than what they appear to be. Those hidden relationships between things of the world and between words and things have become deceptive as upama-resemblance has lost communication with its own surface marks.

Content-less words, without reflection or resemblance to fill their emptiness, unattached to anything, float off on their own, like balloons randomly drifting through space. They are no longer the mark of things, but sleep between the pages of books that gather dust.

The Yogi who once read nature and books alike as part of a single text, who put mirrors to the world revealing the secret upamas beneath its signs and marks, is now the rare laboratory animal of the researcher in the human sciences. The New Age places him in the same category as fantastic gods and demons, to be discovered among piles of lonely words in the cages of books and on the TV or computer screen.

What has become important is identities and differences, no longer resemblances. The consumer age is built on marketing. The age of resemblance has been left behind, and it leaves in its wake, games, whose enchantment grows out of the new kinship between resemblance and illusion, and the distorted memory of an oral tradition in which all the things in the world could be linked indiscriminately to man's experiences, theatre, or credulities.

The noble, rigorous, and restrictive figure of the Yogi is to be forgotten. The signs that mark him are to be thought of as the fantasies and charms of a knowledge that had not yet attained marketability.

The new yogi stands on his head and marvels us with his contortions and acrobatics. His body is perfect, he's vegan, eats egg-less egg salad, and drives a nice car, for the world rewards him for his teachings.

But, magic happens where worlds meet. Where the world of the Oral Tradition of the Naked Yogis from India meets the Symposium of Consciousness in Basel. Let's not buy and sell for the moment, nor shop or advertise. I am not for a moment suggesting that any of you renounce the world and go live in a cave. I'm not suggesting you go find yourself a guru, nor study the Indian scriptures, or philosophy.

I'm holding a mirror up to you this evening, a mirror I found in some cave in India. Yes, the mirror is Indian, it's handcrafted by the lineages of the oral tradition. Take a look in it. You see yourself… and your land, and your culture. Your Mother Ganges is your Mother Rhine, here in Basel, she gave birth to Basel. And look, she points North in a bended knee, as does the Ganges in Shiva's city, Varanasi. The Mother Rhine is not H2O, she is a great Goddess of Articulation, who brought prosperity and high culture to a vast tract of Europe. Just 400 kilometres downstream, on her banks, Gutenberg invented the printing press. But she is known for her most dense attribute, her water, which in my mirror appears as holy water. It's powerful and it's free.

I believe a time has come for us all to become true yogis, "connected ones." Yoga comes from yuj, meaning to connect. Connected with the Earth Mother, connected with Her Earth Spirits, Her Plant Deities, and each other. The Earth Spirits are sad, not because they are languishing beneath countless tons of cement, but because we have forgotten them. It is my hope and prayer that, nourished by the sacred work of Dr. Hofmann, and a number of others in this wonderful congress, we may connect once more with all the forces and personalities of nature to protect our earthly home.

Last year while sitting at my sacred fire on the banks of the Ganges, a young baba, who I've known for a number of years had something on his mind. "Baba," he asked me, "What is this… drop?" The question delighted me, yet I feigned ignorance. To which drop are you referring, I asked him. He thought about it for a moment before bursting out, "the drop that contains the whole world!"

As I questioned him further, he told me that he had tried one, and then went on to narrate his experience. I noticed a profound difference between his first trip and mine. For me, that first trip opened up worlds that I didn't know existed, whereas for him, it made more clear and articulate a world that he was already familiar with.

"I had to pee," he said, and explained that he went over to a wall, but the wall told him not to do it here. Then he went over to some bushes, but the bushes also forbid him, and wherever he went the spirit of that place communicated with him preventing him from peeing. Finally he left the compound of the ashram, and found a lonely spot in a desolate field. For him, the silent language of the world became spoken, and the whole world beckoned his attention with their comments, prohibitions, and jokes.

But when he returned to his two tripping companions, other babas, he found that as the world's silence became chatter, he no longer needed to speak with his friends, as they could now communicate inside of each other's heads. In fact, they discovered they could visit each other's bodies.

They went over to the temple in the far end of the compound. There, the deities were no longer confined by the carved stone in which they were housed, but emerged in all their slendour, dazzling the three young babas. "Their shapes kept changing, and then they took the three of us for a quick tour of the heavens."

The acid had served to make their mythological realities that much more lucid. They had no hallucinations, there was no confusion, everything seemed to become crystal clear.

When I asked him if he would every try it again, he smiled. "Why? You got any?", he asked.

Goddess bless you all!

May The Earth Mother bless all of you with
health, happiness, prosperity, and knowledge!

Worship a plant deity!
Hug an Earth Spirit!
And love each other!

Thank you!

In Search of Magic Mirrors
Journeys in India and Nepal 2005–2010

Aki Cederberg

Introduction

As far back as I can remember, I have been drawn to and felt a strong resonance with certain things, sights and signs, not exactly knowing why, and perhaps more intensely than many of those around me. Some of these things have been found in the waking world, while others have revealed themselves in visions and dreams. Many are far enough in the distant past to be in the realm where memory, dream and waking reality all meld together in one indefinable mass of consciousness. As a result, through the whole of my life, I have been guided by some indefinable force that has propelled me toward these things and their manifestation, revealing and realization.

Some of these dreams have been of such majesty that they have never left me, becoming mental talismans or maps of inner landscapes I have sought to find, even if I don't remember exactly when I have seen them. In one such childhood dream, I wake up in a bed in the middle of strange temple, whose pillars rise up monolithically against the roof somewhere beyond sight. There is primal music echoing in the large circular hall, perhaps played by some kind of organ, that creates a surreal sonic harmony. As I scale its walls I discover it has neither doors nor windows, and one cannot exit or enter – one simply is there. Nevertheless, I feel as I have arrived at the source of all, and feel at home in this strange place.

In another later dream, I descend through the sea in a spherical vessel, and arrive at a cave-like underworld shrine to primal, undivided truth and knowledge. There is an altar on the main wall, on which shines a sign that I understand to be a synthesis of a mark for fire and a mark for ice combined. Surrounding the sign are innumerable small black-and-white framed pictures of people who have grasped and expressed this knowledge in their life and work.

Ever since realizing these and other dreams and visions, I have sought their equivalent in the waking world. It has been as if my soul or spirit had been imprinted with images, and consequently my life has been a search for those images in the outside world, applying the hermetic axiom "as above, so below" to "as within, so without". Rather than looking for "truths" or "meanings" stemming from outside of oneself, it has been a inward quest to find and to make manifest deep inner truths – truths perhaps not found in books, ideas, theories, ideologies, religions or "isms", but in living reality. In essence, I have been in search of magic mirrors.

I have also always had a strong Wanderlust, a great thirst for journey, for travel, for quest and adventure. I have sat on the shores of the great, vast ocean, and felt the waves bring with them a sense of restlessness, of faraway places, of grand discoveries – a calling and a longing for some distant land beyond the horizon. Perhaps it is in my blood, my line of ancestral seamen and sea gods beckoning me, calling me out into their realms.

All of this in turn has taken me on journeys across the earth, on pilgrimages to worlds above and below, and needless to say, to some very strange alleyways. The story to follow is of one such pilgrimage, consisting of a series of journeys to an extraordinary world where – in the face of our ever-more secular and modernized modern world in which ancient living lines of knowledge and magic are broken and severed forever – an ancient line of knowledge and magic is still alive.

I: Pilgrimage

Some years ago, I travelled across India and Nepal for several months. I was on a magical mystery tour, ranging from North India to the South and back again, all the way to Nepal, crossing the lands from one sacred site to another. In retrospect I can see how little books resembled the reality of things, and as a consequence, how lost I was momentarily. However, there are few things as edifying as direct experience, and the journey, in all its uneasy glory and magical momentum, certainly was that for me. As I look into this time and place in the past, it all comes back to me in a whirlwind of moments, a surreal mixture of deep depths and great heights.

To travel in India can sometimes in itself be an overwhelming, even psychedelic, experience. Everything in that ancient land, where modernity is still at pains in the shadows of old gods, is multiplied and manifold – people and things, sights and sounds, joy and suffering. To be confronted directly with the wide spectrum and reality of life and death, of both sublime, majestic beauty and power, as well as horrific suffering and ugliness (sometimes hand in hand), is not something we as Westerners are necessarily used to. One quickly becomes aware of one's cultural biases and how much they shape, limit and inform our view of the world, whether we like it or not. Yet over time, things start to unfold in a different manner. Beyond the apparent confusion and chaos, a strange, subtle and almost comical order begins to reveal itself, where things, despite contrary appearances, somehow happen.

And so there were strange, turbulent times. Life out of balance in hellish, overcrowded, methane-smelling metropolises, and in shitty, underdeveloped, surreally poor villages. The never-ending slums, the shacks and huts in the dirt, the bolted doors of the temples. People literally living in public toilets. The constant screams, screeches and car-horns. The everyday explosions of bombs made to either destroy or delight. Terrorist attacks in crowded markets and buses. In the evening news, angry, despairing faces and blood on the streets. The endless barking dogs under gray, polluted skies where no stars are visible. The hecklers, beggars, thieves, amputees, the bereaved children with deeply set, dark eyes. The legless, leprosy-ridden human creatures shuffling around in carts made of cardboard boxes. I remember one of them in particular, who some American travellers called the "sucking ass-wound boy".

In Delhi, deranged with dengue, I was having fever-dreams mixed with images of

Kali. Later, as I sat in a hospital, I watched actual birds fly inside the main hall. The doctor told me that my blood values were all over the place, but finished with an overly happy smile, and the mandatory Indian mantra of *"Don't worry sir, everything is alright"* – even when it clearly was not.

During the festival of Navratri ("Nine nights"), celebrating the goddess in her various forms, the streets were lined with statues of the fierce goddess Durga. Concluding the festival is Dusshera, to celebrate the victory of the god Rama over the demon Ravana. In a field in Faridabad, a slum of Delhi, three gigantic statues of demons filled with explosives were shot at with burning arrows by guys dressed as gods. The statues exploded and crashed to the ground with a force suitable to that of demons. The air filled with smoke and screams, the sky rained with burning bits and ash. The gathered masses ran madly around the blazing, crumbling fire-statues, the scene reminiscent of some dreamlike drunken war. Pushing through the multitudes, I felt the stare of thousands of eyes, while the police were exercising crowd-control with unmerciful blows of their canes.

At the insistence of an Indian friend, and out of morbid curiosity, I visited the local centre of the International Society for Krishna Consciousness (ISKCON), commonly referred to as the Hare Krishna movement. This movement, so popular in the West, is a watered-down, Christianized modern Hindu sect that has made Krishna into its Jesus. Consequently, it has very little to do with ancient lines of knowledge. At the centre the statues of the mighty Indian gods were made out of cheap-looking materials. My ears hurt as the loudspeakers were turned up way beyond their capacity and blared out the distorted mantra central to the Hare Krishna followers. Despite their claims, the repetition of this mantra was not the answer to everything.

And then later on, travelling in Nepal with my friend and artistic partner, there was the young girl somewhere between Kathmandu and Pokhara, with a seriously scarred-up face, blind in one eye, but clearly beautiful beneath all the scars. She was collecting signatures and donations for who-knows-what in the bus we were on. We did not sign or give her anything, being weary from all the travelling and the never-ending line of people asking, begging and hustling you for money. Suddenly there was a commotion between the young girl and the proprietor of the bus. The girl struggled, but got violently thrown out of the bus, hit in the head and kicked in the chest, and was left crying at the stop as the bus drove off. We later learned from the only other Westerners on board that the commotion was apparently because she had dropped something on the floor of the bus and was trying to retrieve it. That treasured something turned out to be a ballpoint pen.

To counter the sometimes heavy experiences one inevitably had, it seemed reasonable to counteract those with *other kinds* of heavy experiences. The nightlife in Kathmandu was non-existent because of the frequent curfews and shut-downs, and so it happened one night that we were strolling down an empty street looking for a place to have a drink, when we encountered an underground place that seemed to be open. There was a doorman of some kind who smiled and waved us in. As we descended to the floor beneath the ground, we quickly realized what the place was. It was a Nepalese strip joint, or at least it was *supposed* to resemble that, except for the fact that the girls on stage did not actually strip, but simply danced around to weird Nepalese disco music. Never having been ones to shy away from the seamier side of life, we sat down and ordered a bottle of whisky. We were immediately joined by three or four prostitutes, smelling the money, and the whisky bottle was finished in about five minutes. One of the older and less good-looking girls was trying to grab my crotch under the table, her lipstick-smeared mouth slobbering in my ear, *"I want you, English dick"*. As I talked to a young, beautiful Indian-looking girl, I thought of the high prevalence of HIV among female sex workers in Nepal. Having had enough of the whisky, the pushy prostitutes and the somewhat sinister and sordid air of the place, I gave some money to the young girl, and we left for the night and the deserted streets.

A few days later we were supposed to visit the studio of the thangka painter Surendra Bahadur Shahi, a contributor to the book *Shamanism and Tantra in the Himalayas* (by Christian Rätsch and Claudia Müller-Ebeling), but there had been a shooting of several civilians by a soldier, and now there was a general strike. The guesthouse proprietor warned us against going out into the streets, but we went anyway. The mood was tense, fearful and filled with soon-to-erupt violence. Everything was closed; all public transportation had been stopped. People were marching and screaming down the streets, and in places menacing soldiers and army vehicles were gathering. Outbursts of violence against the army by civilians and students had already erupted in other parts in Nepal, so the situation looked grim. As we returned to the guesthouse rooftop, we bumped into a familiar American traveller, sitting by a plastic garden table with books, incense and a small glass pipe for his dope. He was on his way, via Varanasi, to someplace to participate in a course in yoga, meditation or something along those lines. Soon we were joined by another somewhat weary traveller from Australia. He had been travelling for three years straight, was a little paranoid, and later went into a long monologue about ley lines. Indeed it seemed most young Western people in Nepal were into strange theories and esoteric practices in one way or another – the Californian hippy-influence was undeniable. We decided to drink the day away on the rooftop and hence called out for beer and Royal Stag whisky, and I looked at the angry mobs pacing up and down the streets below. As the day slowly melted into night, our little bacchanalia escalated to involve sudden vomiting, lapsing into trance, actions involving cigarette burns, mantras, gongs and more whiskey, much to the bewilderment of nearby neighbours. At one point the American was dangling on the edge of the rooftop and I pulled him violently off to safety, which resulted in yet more broken pottery and legless plastic garden furniture. As night arrived and the restlessness of the streets finally died down, we had managed to create a chaos of our own on the rooftop, and there was something truly reckless and apocalyptic in the air.

Seeking the sacred, one often found death instead. Death, which is so omnipresent and out in the open in much of India and Nepal, is treated in a diametrically opposite fashion to that of the West. There is much less of the sentimentality and taboo associated with death that characterises the Western relationship with it. As a young man said to me in Nepal: "Family don't pay so much emotion here because we believe destruction means creation. So we are not scared of dying, more scared of karma."

In Varanasi, the city of Lord Shiva, the city of death and the eternal city of light, there was a constant smell of shit and incense in the air. A city of thieves and holy men, with its labyrinthine alleys and ancient temples, where people came to die, a restless city that never slept. At night colourful, psychedelically lit parades meandered through the streets as the *Aarti puja*, the ancient fire ritual (puja meaning ritual or worship), was performed by the holy river Ganga (Ganges). And the Ganga, the central vein and holy mother of India was itself the source of all this life and death, being both the perfectly pure and simultaneously utterly contaminated, reflecting the ever-present paradoxes in India. We were sitting at the Manikarnika burning *ghats* ("ghats" being steps leading to a body of water) by the Ganga, watching the bodies burn as the sun rose. As I raised my gaze skyward, the air filled with drifting, floating pieces of ash, while flocks of birds flew somewhere further up. This was one of Lord Shiva's favourite dancing grounds, where they say the fire of the *dhuni*, the sacred ritual fire, has not died out in thousands of years – not to mention the constantly burning funeral pyres. At dawn and dusk a serenity seemed to overtake the ghat, a strange calmness, as the air was warm with the smell of the endless human barbeques. Trampling on a piece of charred human bone amid the golden rays of the dawn, a dark casteless man said, *"burning is learning – all is ash"*.

At the cremation ghats of Pashupathinath in Nepal by the holy Bagmati river, and one of the largest temples to Shiva in the world (in his form as Pashupathi, "Lord of animals"), we again watched bodies burn, wrapped in golden shrouds, as the *pandits* (Brahmin priests) performed the last rites. As in Varanasi, here too they used a special kind of rosewood for the funeral pyres in order for the bodies not to smell bad when burning. Nearby was the tantric Bachhareshwari temple dedicated to Shiva's consort Parvati, with paintings and carvings of dancing skeletons and erotic, copulating figures. In ancient times during the Shivratri festival reputedly human sacrifices were performed here, or at least according to our young guide. We visited the burial ground of the Sadhus (renunciate mystic holy men) in the nearby forest and saw some of their dwelling places, caves and huts in the wall of a cliff. Later we wandered down Ram ghat, again by a river, where the poorer classes are burned. Here, however, there were no temples, no ghats, no pandits, and it looked more like a construction site than anything else. A family had gathered to perform their last rites. Somewhat unceremoniously, the body was laid out and burned, but instead of fine, pleasant-smelling wood, they used car tires, creating a thick, black, acrid smoke.

I woke up before dawn in the only guesthouse of the tiny village of Pharping, Nepal. Here life was quiet, except for each Tuesday and Saturday when the local Dakshinkali temple attracts pilgrims from all over the Kathmandu Valley, and a spiritual and sacrificial frenzy takes over. I curled up in my sleeping bag and had some whisky and a cigarette, while watching the sunrise over the Himalayas. A young woman walked up a path carrying a heavy load on her back. Slowly the sounds of the arriving buses of pilgrims became more and more prevalent in the distance. Dakshinkali temple itself is situated in a cleft between two hills at the confluence of two rivers. The temple is dedicated to the great mother goddess Kali, the Shakti of Lord Shiva, in her ferocious, wrathful form. The main deity in the temple is the black, six-armed, stone figure of Kali, standing on a prostrate figure (Shiva). Twice a week, a steady parade of animal sacrifices are offered to her – chickens, ducks, sheep, goats and pigs. As we wandered down to the temple, the air echoed with hymns to Kali being played from the loudspeakers. Entire families lined up to have a chance for a sacrificial offering that occurs in the main temple enclosure, which we as Westerners, and hence "non-Hindus", had no access to. But as it was an open temple with neither walls nor roofs, we could stand and witness the sacrificial procession in silence. The animals were very unceremoniously and quickly slaughtered by professional butchers, after which the carcasses were taken to be cleaned, cooked and prepared for dinner right beside the temple. After the sacrifices, families gathered in the woods and hills nearby for picnics.

Journeying across India and Nepal, visiting more shrines and holy places than I could recollect here, one began to notice that nature is "marked". The holy places are not random or arbitrary, but situated in conjunction with some natural landmark: a river, a lake, a mountain, a tree. All of nature is considered holy, being the manifestation and dwelling place of gods and spirits. Mountains are gods, the rivers goddesses. Lakes, trees, caves, and indeed all forms of life and creation, are likewise thought of as being embodied with spirits, the personalities of nature, whether benign or malevolent. But all these things seemed connected together by the ever-presence of the three holy rivers of India – the Ganga, the Yamuna and the invisible, mythic Saraswati.

Beyond even the landmarks was something perhaps even more visceral: the real living human beings, far removed from the norms and conventions of modern life and society, still carrying along an ancient esoteric tradition and way of knowledge. I wanted to meet these crazy magicians, these Sadhus, yogis and shamans – *Babas* as they are affectionately called – who still inhabit this ancient land, be they hucksters or miracle men. Emulating their patron gods Shiva or Vishnu, they took on the appearance and attributes of those gods, thereby becoming "living idols". In the case of Shiva, the appearance and attributes were *wild*: with their long, matted *jata* (matted locks of hair) reaching to the ground, wearing garlands made out of the seeds of the Rudraksha tree, skyclad and smeared in ashes, carrying *trishuls* (tridents of Shiva), the Sadhus were an awe-inspiring sight. They were spiritual outsiders, both respected and feared, givers of blessings and throwers of curses. Looking at pictures of them, and later meeting them eye to eye, there was something feral in their eyes, a look of power, fearlessness and pride. They seemed to possess something that could not be taken away, as what can be taken away from someone who has given up everything? Or perhaps it was the case that something possessed them?

And yet, although the sacred was "everywhere", approaching it as a foreigner was never quite as easy as it might seem in theory. One rarely found what one expected. The Sadhus one saw in cities and famous temples were often clearly fakes: thieves, hucksters and criminals on the run, whose ochre robes were just a little bit too brightly orange, having donned the Sadhu-look in order to evade prosecution and con gullible people out of their money.

The first time I met what may have been a genuine Sadhu was at Pashupathinath, Nepal, attending a small Aarti puja at the hut of a local Naga Baba ("naked one", Sadhu belonging to a specific order), which was situated right behind the platforms on which bodies were burning. The Naga Baba, ash-clad and naked save for a loin-cloth and *malas* (strings of beads used for meditation) was shouting at the top of his lungs with

"Burning is learning – all is ash". In Varanasi, with trishuls. Photograph by A.I.H.

an authoritative and somewhat mad voice, constantly taking deep tokes from a *chillum* (a pipe for smoking cannabis and sometimes other plant substances), only pausing to vomit in a bowl. The air in the low-roofed room was thick with smoke from the dhuni, the incense and the *charas* (cannabis). A young priest wearing a Britney Spears t-shirt conducted the puja, and the incessant loud beating of the *ghantas* (bells), the blowing of the conch-shell trumpet and the rhythm of double-headed *damaru* drum in tandem with the intoxicated chants to Shiva was a trance-inducing experience... at least until Baba's cellphone rang. And it was the famous Nokia ringtone, of all things. Having travelled halfway around the planet from the "land of Nokia" to find connections beyond cellphones, hearing that ringtone at the feet of this divine madman, I need not tell you of the surreal irony of the situation. In the end, we put some money under Baba's feet, and he blessed us with smatterings of *vibhuti* ("sacred ash"), on our foreheads. As we left for the night, we were told by our young guide that the Naga Baba in question performs *tapasya*, austerities to get the attention of god, by lifting weights of up to 100 kilos with his penis. *"But only in graveyards"*, our guide continued with a smile. *"You need to have a very strong cock"*.

I took in these experiences, all the life and death, all the heights and depths – perhaps more than could be digested into knowledge in such a short time. Strange rituals on rooftops of empty monasteries, reveries at shrines to unknown gods, revelations of the extraordinary in unexpected moments and places. But I began to wonder – what was the significance of all these things? Beyond the exotic, what did I really think I was going to find as a foreigner in these strange lands?

I was seeking *darshan*, the "beholding", a vision and a direct revealing of the sacred. Rather than information gained from books or second-hand sources, darshan implies being personally touched by this revealing. But sadly, often I felt far removed from such an experience by the often harsh realities of life in India. Even at "holy" places, at natural enclaves, in temples, at spiritual festivals and when meeting supposedly holy men and receiving their blessings, I often felt detached. I heard there was supposed to be 300 million gods in India – and yet I could not find a single one.

Then in another moment, through the dirty window of a bus, I would see a giant statue of the god Shiva standing above all the urban rubble, the smog, shit and suffering, in blissful serenity against an orange sunset. Then, in those moments, something would be stirred within me, and I would remember.

And so, there were times when this great something would reveal itself in small but profound glimpses. It was as if I had suddenly and almost accidentally pierced the veil of some grand illusion and arrived stumblingly at the source of it all. These were unexpected moments of revelation, of ecstasy and joyful wisdom, moments of a *goddrunkenness*. In these moments I sometimes thought of the mantra *"Om Shivoham!"* *("I am Shiva!")*, and pictured I *was* Shiva and could sense all around me as manifest divinity, as *Shakti*.

In the Himalayas of northern India, I made a hike to a *mandir* (temple) at the top of a mountain. The temple had no walls or roof, only pillars and altars supporting hundreds of bells that echoed across the ranges – hence its name, Ghode Khal, which I understood to mean simply "bell temple". Beyond the pillars there were the majestic mountains stretching into all directions. I thought of the line from some gnostic text, maybe the Gospel of Thomas, "god does not live in a building", and never was this more evident than here. The friendly pandit wanted to do a personal blessing puja for me and so we sat at the shrine of a local god, whilst the drummer banged away on his drum and the pandit conducted the puja, blowing the conch-shell trumpet and reciting mantras. As I began my slow descent down the mountain I soon sat down to marvel at the breathtaking vistas surrounding me, realizing why these mountains are thought to be the home of Shiva and the gods, and indeed how mountains are the celestial home of the gods in virtually all cultures.

Beyond the polluted harbour of Mumbai lies the ancient island of Elephanta. There on the island are several caves dedicated to various gods, cut into solid rock some 1,300 years ago. It is unfortunate that many of these ancient and impressive sculptures are in bad shape not because of their age but because of the sabotage and plunder of man: after being ruled by several Hindu dynasties, the Island eventually fell to the sultans of Gujarat and passed from them to the Portuguese soldiers, and the rest as they say, is history. However, the main cave of the seven caves at the island is dedicated to Lord Shiva, and despite being a major tourist attraction, it still echoes with timeless and awe-inspiring beauty and power. It is a complex structure featuring Shiva in his many varied forms, as well as his consort and Shakti, his family and entourage, including his elephant-headed son Ganesha. There is the main shrine guarded on all sides by the protective Dwarapalas, wherein one finds a *Shiva lingam* (a phallus-shaped rock) and *yoni* (a vulva-shaped rock at the base of the lingam) – the self-evident symbols of creation and unity. Despite the thousands of ancient statues and monuments in celebration of sacred sex, where people are copulating in every possible manner, despite the central religious symbols of the phallus and vulva, modern India is still very prudish and moralistic in its approach to sex, and many of its esoteric traditions are still strongly linked with abstinence and renunciation. For a country whose ancient history is so steeped in an appreciation of divine eros, it seems as if something has been forgotten. Standing in the shadows of these ancient structures and laying hands on the Lingam, I was reminded of something I read in the book *Shiva and Dionysus* by Alain Daniélou:

> Shiva is the principle of erotic pleasure, not of fecundity. Wandering in the forest, he spreads his sperm by masturbatory practices and inspires desire and erotic madness. [...] All the beauty and all the joy in the world is manifested by means of an erotic explosion. Flowers cast their pollen to the wind. [...] The creation of the world is an erotic act, an act of love, and everything which exists bears this sign and this message. In living beings, everything is organized in accordance with this expression of pleasure, joy, beauty and happiness, which is the nature of the divine and the secret of all that exists. Eroticism is the bond of attraction uniting two opposite and complimentary poles.

In Goa, intoxicated by the full moon and Royal Stag whiskey, I was dancing under a massive psychedelically lit Shiva-Nataraja statue as the waves of the Arabian Sea crashed ashore. A *bindu* ("point") of blood on my third eye, I was clothed all in white and glowed in the darkness, as did Shiva-Nataraja dancing his eternal dance of creation and destruction. There in the darkness I felt something primordial slumbering and divine madness, drunkenness, desire. Perhaps it was the serpentine *Kundalini*, and I was worshipping its golden skin and flowing like silver on its surface.

Shiva is the god of criminals and cops, artists and outsiders, more so than of householders, businessmen and the status quo. He attracts marginal elements and creatures that live beyond the ordinary, at the edges, beyond the normative rules of reality and society. In this sense I was no exception: not a cop or criminal, but an artist of some kind, and an outsider most certainly. Shiva is the ultimate outsider, and he lives here in these strange lands that I found myself in. Is it any wonder that he spoke to me?

The sign of Shiva – the *trishul* – was very reminiscent of the trident-like rune that I have as a talismanic tattoo on my arm, ever since I was very young. Indeed it seemed to mark and point to similar areas and things, being but one example of how things resemble each other in a deeper way. And what had brought me here was exactly that: resemblances and similarities. There were things in the world that approximated each other, that seemed to be similar or related in mystical ways, that seemed to mirror each other beyond even the cultural differences and forms. For me there seemed to be a common thread running through it all, a current running invisibly through separated streams, connecting them. It was these things that attracted me: the things that instinctually spoke to me, primal images that had always resonated with me, and which alluded to an underlying unity.

There was also a living context and tradition, a way of upholding and obtaining esoteric knowledge, rooted in primeval sources that went back to some of the oldest surviving civilizations of mankind. I saw it as a "pagan" tradition reflecting an as of yet not completely broken, ancient line of knowledge, springing from the dawn of consciousness to the present age. It was something that had withstood, at least partially, the ultimate test: the test of time. And at the centre of all of this seemed to hover the mystical figure of Shiva.

Shiva is pure consciousness. He is Adi Nath, "First Lord", the pure consciousness and ultimate reality at the core of all beings and things. The seemingly endless litany of his different names give form to his infinite qualities and supreme, all-pervasive nature. In his being, Shiva transcends all dualities; in his contrasting qualities he points to the principle of unification.

Shiva is Ardhanarishvara, the hermaphrodite deity, being both male and female, signifying that god is a unity of the masculine and the feminine elements of the universe, as Shiva unites with Shakti.

Shiva is Shankar, the primordial yogi, the great ascetic of the highest mountains, where he resides in isolation and silence, as motionless, non-expansive, still consciousness. Shiva is Nataraja, "king of the art of dancing", the moving, expansive consciousness, engaged in an endless dance of creation and destruction.

Shiva is Rudra, the terrible, the howler, the lord of tears. Shiva is Nandikeshvara, lord of joy, and Pashupati, the wild god of the animals and wild beasts. To redeem the world, Shiva drank the poison of the world, which turned his throat blue, and thus he is Nilakantha, the blue-throated one. To cool the burning sensation of the poison, he was given the moon, which he still wears in his hair. Indeed he is to have said that there is still much poison in this world, which only heroes can drink, wherefore Shiva is the god of all intoxicating substances. Nothing is foreign to Shiva; he is boundlessly merciful and accepts all, and so he is Bholenath, the kindhearted lord, "protector of gawks and geezers".

Shiva is rich beyond rich, yet clothed in tiger skins, ashes, garlands of skulls and serpents, holding horns and trishuls, accompanied by his entourage of heavenly hooligans and rowdy spirits, the *Ganas*. He is the lover of lovers, who copulated with his lady of the mountains, Parvati, for thousands of years. He is the lord of sensual delights and a supreme lover, as well as the lord of death and an ascetic – simultaneously the lord of life and death, creation and destruction.

His third eye, once open, both destroys and creates the world. Shiva is Lord of the Three Worlds and of past, present and future, as his forehead is marked by three horizontal lines of ash. And yet he is without beginning or end, a pillar of fire that penetrates all worlds.

His sign is the *lingam*, the cosmic principle of creation in the form of the phallus, standing erect in the *yoni*, the female receptacle, marking the divine interplay of *Shiva* (consciousness) and *Shakti* (energy, matter and all manifestation), as well as the synthesis of the male and the female, and indeed of all polarities.

Shiva is a god wholly different in nature from those of the other major world religions, or even from those of most modern recreations of some ancient sects. Shiva is a totality, incorporating in his being seeming opposites and even contradictory qualities. He is not a patriarchal or matriarchal figure separate from mankind that one prays to in order to be in his or her favour. He is not a saviour or redeemer – fundamentally, at most times, Shiva does not care. Shiva is pure consciousness, and united with Shakti, points to primal undivided being.

And yet often some of these aspects of Shiva are forgotten, ignored or distorted, even by the followers in his native lands. His essentially *wild* nature is tamed, the fierceness of his being downplayed. The blatantly obvious and often sexual symbolism surrounding him is distorted in favour of some more prudish "interpretation", being a sign of the corruption of the times. Even the Shiva lingam and yoni are reduced to some kind of abstract symbols, when it is blatantly obvious what they represent. But the powerful eternal truths expressed in symbolic language are still there and intact for anyone to read.

My journey was a journey in the patronage of Shiva, reflecting each man's journey to the soul's true homeland. A journey ascending to the highest peaks and descending to the lowest depths, and experiencing and integrating both into one and the same being. This was *yatra*, pilgrimage.

Pilgrimage is to purposefully, intentionally give oneself to experience and momentarily shed one's attachments to one's familiar world, and to enter another where the old rules don't necessarily apply. Perhaps it is only by striving for the lands of primal knowledge incarnate, which simultaneously mirror our own inner depths, that we can truly reach the shores of timeless truth. Perhaps this is the eternal quest of the hero, re-told again and again in myth, legend and story. And perhaps in a world with fewer and fewer heroes, and fewer and fewer things worthy of a quest, this is what is important: to find the magic mirrors worth striving for – mirrors which reflect our own true nature and an undiluted truth.

II: Many Happy Returns

We were in a taxi, my partner and I, as dawn was just breaking in downtown Mumbai. There were still a few hours before our plane would take off for Goa, and we were headed for Chowpatty Beach, the major site of the yearly Ganesh Chaturthi festivals, the birthday of Lord Ganesh. Ganesh, the elephant-headed deity, son of Shiva and Parvati, is the lord of obstacles and new beginnings, who presides over wisdom, prosperity and good fortune, and he is one of the most popular and loved gods of all India, and without question the patron god of Bombay. As Ganesh is always invoked first in any puja, or before any new undertaking, I thought it wise to start our new journey in India with an offering to him. The annual Ganesh Chaturi festival culminates in massive, elaborately constructed, painted and decorated statues of the god being paraded into the sea. As with so many things in India, here too lies a curious paradox: the materials used to manufacture the statues commercially, and the chemicals used to paint them, pose a serious environmental problem for the waters, and the day after the immersion of the statues, massive amounts of dead fish can be seen floating on the surface.

It was surprisingly quiet when we arrived on Chowpatty Beach, save for some families who lived there under the palm trees, and the occasional child or dog strolling by, all equally perplexed to see white people there this early in the morning. The water was brownish and shoreline was literally filled to the brim with garbage, broken pottery and the occasional brightly coloured Ganesh statue, but still several fishermen were silently spreading their nets in the waters. I had brought along a little clay icon of the big-bellied, elephant-headed god that I had found on my last journey, to offer to the sea here in order that he would protect our journey at its beginning and remove all obstacles that might arise. Thrice I spoke silently the Ganesh mantra, before offering the statue for the sea to swallow.

In the taxi on the way back to the airport I felt like life was straight out of a film or comic book, life as fiction. It seemed as though in India everything operated according to some strange, magical logic and narrative, quite different from the way things are perceived in the modern secular world. Here, where rituals are a part and parcel of daily life for most people; where there are altars everywhere, even on highways so that drivers can flip coins at them while driving by; here it seemed like the most logical thing in the world to take a long taxi-ride in an exhausted state in order to throw a little statue in the water, simply to obtain the blessings of an elephant-headed god. If nothing else, it seemed like a poetic act.

When we finally arrived in Goa, we went first to Anjuna beach, a hippy-hangout remnant of the sixties, and got a room with a balcony close to the shore. There we sat and had a drink in the shade of palm trees, and listened to the waves of the Arabian ocean crashing ever ashore. Coming from the deep dark winter of the north, the sun was godly in its brilliance and seemed to light up our sooty spirits, our feet in the sand and sea. In the morning, armies of crows would wake us up, and at night, the sound of waves would put us to sleep.

Equally, some aspects of Goa remained less paradisiacal. The pushy hecklers, merchants and beggars were all there, waiting for you. Walking by the stalls selling statues, t-shirts and psychedelically coloured bric-a-brac, shadowy figures would emerge and recite the menu of dodgy drugs that were available. Even though widely used all throughout India and being rooted in tradition, mere possession of something as innocent as cannabis might land you in jail for ten years – *minimum* – and the police were known to often be corrupt and "plant" drugs on hapless tourists for extortion.

It has been said repeatedly over the ages that magic manifests as an increase in meaningful signs and synchronicities, in seeming coincidences. It has also been said that should one desire a guide along the path, one will appear when the will is strong enough. I sought not theories and ideologies, but a living link to a living tradition of knowledge; I wanted not only to see the Sadhus, magicians and shamans, but I wanted to be able to *see as they saw*. This had, through a series of synchronicities, finally put me in contact with a real Naga Baba, and a very rare one at that, because he had Western roots and therefore a command of the English language. I have also never been satisfied with mere images, but sought direct personal contact, and so there we were, on our way to his house in a taxi.

Hilltop shrine to Dattatreya, the three headed messenger of the gods, and tantric lord of yogis. (Polaroid: Aki Cederberg)

I did not really know what to expect – a wild madman garbed in ashes, a mild-mannered Sadhu in ochre robes, a shaman, or a sham-man, or all of these things rolled into one. When the taxi driver overheard me talking on the phone with "Baba" to ask for directions, he became visibly excited; and as we arrived the taxi driver stopped the car with a quick halt, forgot to ask us for payment (which never happens in India) and almost leapt out of the car to have a chance to talk to – and perhaps receive a blessing from – the man waiting for us outside his house. This epitomized something of how, even in this day and age, Babas still command primal respect and awe.

My initial trepidation vanished as we shook hands with this smiling, bearded older man called Baba Rampuri. We entered the Portuguese-style house and were guided into the living room, the walls of which were lined with pictures of various gurus whom I recognized as being from Rampuri's lineage. There were statues, Shiva lingams and ritual items that formed altars on shelves and tables, as well as a substantial library and oriental carpets on the floor. At one of the main altars I immediately noted two long rare spiral horns, which exactly mirrored ones I had tattooed as talismans on myself.

Baba Rampuri is an American expatriate, the son of a surgeon, who left his home of California in the late sixties at the age of 19 and travelled overland to India, where he has made his life ever since. After travelling across the land, he met a rare English-speaking guru, Hari Puri Baba, and in one, quick, life-defining moment became a *chela*, a disciple. He was given the name Rampuri and received the *Panch guru* initiation, the initiation of five gurus, losing his former self and life and simultaneously gaining a new one, becoming the first foreigner ever to be initiated into India's most ancient order of yogis and shamans, the *Naga Sannyasis*, or Naga Babas. His new name reflected the lineage of Babas of Juna Akhara, the ancient order of the Renunciates of the Ten Names. Despite all the adversity and strife he was bound to encounter as an outsider and foreigner, he received from his gurus the tradition of knowledge, often in the form of stories, passed down from guru to disciple for thousands of years. This mystical tradition included sacred speech, mantra (magical formulae), tantra (philosophy and practice centered around the interaction between Shiva and Shakti, subject and object, consciousness and energy/matter), ayurveda (a system of traditional medicine), astrology, logic, ritual – all of which constitute the ancient tradition of yoga. Rampuri later founded the Hari Puri Ashram in the town of Hardwar at the foothills of the Himalayas, and has since become a high-ranking member in the hierarchy of his order of yogis, a member of the Council of Elders of Datt Akhara, Ujjain. Reflecting his very unlikely life story, he has written a book *(Autobiography of a Sadhu: A Journey into Mystic India)*, which gives a rare glimpse into the world of the Naga Babas.

We sat down on the sofa and his companion Adi Rana Puri, a young German woman, made us some tea as we started talking. Rampuri was a storyteller first and foremost, not interested in proselytisation or dogma, nor in forcing any beliefs on us, or anyone else for that matter. He was *"a local guy, not a universalist"*. Like a grandfather or a bard from a different age, he would weave us into his web of story that he himself had learnt from his gurus, reflecting on some aspect of his tradition, all the while smoking a joint.

Rampuri's initial teachings came not in the form of abstract lessons, but in conjunction with very real and concrete things of the world, such as food. My partner had some problems with her stomach, and so Rampuri gave some herbal medicines and recommendations on what to eat and what to avoid. At the same time he was giving a teaching of the *Gunas*, the three qualities or tendencies of *Prakriti*, of all nature. As students of yoga, ayurveda or of some aspect of the Indian esoteric tradition will know, the *Gunas* consist of *Rajas* (the active tendency), *Tamas* (the passive tendency) and *Sattva* (the balanced tendency). They are found in all of creation, in the five great elements of ether, air, fire, water and earth.

Surely there was nothing on sale here – no ideologies, religions, tricks or quick fixes. What Rampuri seemed to say was, *"Give it all up"*.

When speaking on the question of what relevance Rampuri's experience and knowledge has for the European audience and their lives, he said:

> If one's purpose is the acquisition of knowledge, the acquisition of balance, then it's not important to become a good little Indian, it's not important to do what I have done, to think what I think, to live in a cave, to renounce the world – all these things are superfluous. These things are those cultural elements that have allowed me to go deeper into an Indian tradition, but I don't think this is important for Western people and I

make a very strong point of saying this. I think the important thing for Western people interested in this area is that they have to get in touch with themselves, they have to get in touch with the spirits and deities of their own land, of their own sacred river goddessess, of the spirits of the forest, of the spirits of the sky, their blood, the soil underneath their feet, and this is the important thing. [...]

If we had living traditions in the West, if we had living masters, teachers and gurus who were part of a tradition in the sense that they are passing down what has been passed down to them and passed down to those before them, then I don't think that I would really even have much to say in the West. But the situation is that we don't. So it's my interest that I hold up a mirror to you, and you see yourself, and you see what lies behind you from a different view – but you are looking at yourself, and you are looking at your land and your culture. [...]

And the answer is in the key to hermeticism which is analogy, that my experience in a living oral tradition can be a mirror that reflects one's soil and blood, in another way, an analagous reflection that points towards subtle or unseen aspects of their own lives and locality.

Analogy, therefore, seemed truly to be the key to an understanding of any of this.

When I talked about similarities between signs, such as the Algiz-rune, the trident and the trishul of Shiva, and how they seemed to signify similar things, Rampuri took out a statue of a horned figure and said, *"This is the original trishul"*. The statue was based on a figure found in the Mohenjo-daro, one of the largest and oldest city-settlements (dating back to more than 2600 BCE, depending on the source) that depicts a figure with three faces, sitting cross-legged with bull-like horns, his whole head obviously resembling a trishul. This cross-legged horned figure bore a striking resemblance to various other horned gods (e.g. Dionysus, Bacchus, Pan and Cernunnos) as well as to the archetypal image of the yogi and of Shiva himself.

You see, there is a basic issue here that is very important when you are dealing with magic. The basic issue is: are you using something that is a sign, or something that is a symbol? Are you using something that is marking something of the world, or are you using something that is referencing an idea? Now, ideas are fickle, and ideas change during the course of time, and over geography. So I think that if we are using symbols, which Carl Jung was so fond of and wanted to attribute some sort of universalism to, I think we get stuck in a particular time and place. In magic, we are looking for things that don't mark the fickle ideas of man, but mark things of the world, that we can see reflected in different ways: we can see reflected in the night sky, in the stars, we can see reflected in the topography of the planet, in the mountains, rivers and deserts, we can see reflected in the animal world, we can see reflected in plants, we can see reflected in our faces, our eyes, nose and our physical structure. This is the direction I believe we have to go in if we are maintaining the discourse of magic, rather than the discourse of modern Western philosophy and psychology. So, when we look at something like horns or a trishul, and we say that the trishul marks the three Gunas, or Brahma-Vishnu-Shiva – yes, it's OK for discussion, for entertainment and so forth, but I don't think it gets us into this other space, which is a reflected space, which is a revealed space. The key here is a word that was used again and again in European hermeticism, that Paracelsus for example was very fond of, and the word is resemblance. Resemblance says to us: when something resembles something else, it is a mark that indicates hidden relationships, relationships that exist below the surface.

On the significance of synchronicities, Rampuri said:

Where you have a resemblance, this is not a statement in itself, this is not a symbol in the sense that we immediately start the interpretation. This is not the treasure; this is the mark. On the surface of the world – not the surface of the earth, but the surface of the world – we see a mark, we see a big 'X', and it says to us: 'Dig here'. This is the significance to me.

I told Rampuri I liked his own personal story because he was, in the beginning at least, an outsider. And as a born outsider, I could relate to this, not just in the sense of being the outsider, but also in the sense of a "spiritual" outsider like Shiva. Rampuri interrupted me, exclaiming:

Shiva, the ultimate outsider!
   You said that I have been the outsider, and that I have become an insider. I would disagree with that. I started out as an outsider, and now I am even more an outsider. A lot of this of course is based on circumstance: I am part of an Indian esoteric tradition, but I am a foreigner, and the fact of my foreign birth will always keep me an outsider in the Indian esoteric tradition. And yet, because I am so much a part of the Indian esoteric tradition, it prevents me from ever being an insider in any other tradition. I make a remark in my book when I realize that I am possessed, that I am even an outsider among outsiders. I think it's the outsider that has the ability, or at least has the opportunity, to look at things from a distance, rather than being in the midst of things and assigning some sort of moral values, the good and bad, the good and evil, to things. So I think that many, if not most, of people who have insights, who have particular geniuses in various fields, whether it's music or art or literature or whatever – I think that a requirement is that one is an outsider.

After talking for several hours, we had dinner in a restaurant and lassies in a little juice shop. I was strangely affected by the meeting, feeling both stimulated and disquieted at the same time.

In India, many discussions inevitably lead to religion, magic, spirituality – *spirituality*, a word that always made me cringe in discomfort. *"Are you a Hindu?"*, I was asked many times. Raj, the young man working at the place where we stayed, enthusiastically explained that he was a *"Vishnu kind of guy"*. *"Vishnu is the god for the common man"*, he said. One day Raj brought me a little note on which he had written the popular Gayatri mantra, which he thought I might find beneficial. Later still, he even bought me a gift. It was a book, or rather a booklet, by a wacked-out, starry-eyed Western guy, a Goan regular. On the back cover it said: "You shine without a shadow. Follow the light, and you will never get lost. Let love guide your way, and you shall find peace unto your soul." In the booklet he wrote about angels looking out for him over his shoulder, even when things took a turn for the worse – such as when his friend lost his dentures in the sea. It all seemed hopelessly out of balance, disconnected from the stark realities of life, epitomizing something sadly comical about how spirituality tends to manifest in general: rather than an enhancement of reality, it is an escape from it.

In a Shaivite temple we attended, there was the usual commotion going on in front of the altar when the white-clad pandits were accepting offerings and giving out blessings. When I brought forth my offering, a pandit suddenly approached me and shouted *"From which country?!"*, to which I replied, *"Finland"*. Without blinking, he replied *"Aah, Jumala Shiva!"* (meaning "God Shiva" in Finnish). I was not quite sure what to make of this sudden breaking of language-barriers that one normally encountered from vendors selling souvenirs at tourist hotspots. I received some vibhuti on my third eye, and a red and orange thread on my right wrist.

But on a deeper level, the doors of the temples remained closed to those from outside of this world and its language. I remained a tourist – and perhaps it was for the better. To penetrate the veil in a deeper sense would require a lifetime of effort and dedication. I was and would ever remain an outsider in this world, parts of which I felt a connection to, whereas other parts seemed to instinctually repel me. Not being knowledgeable in either Hindi or Sanskrit, except for some rudimentary basics, and being a foreigner, I was a *mleccha*, a barbarian and an outcast, and despite whatever affinities I had, they would not change this fact.

We moved from Anjuna to Arambol beach, into a little bamboo-shack high on a steep hill overlooking the ocean. At night we would listen to the waves as they roared below. At dawn and dusk, I would sometimes hear the clinging of bells coming from somewhere above mixing in with the sound of waves. I asked about it and was told that there was a little outdoor temple on the top of the hill precisely above our hut, but even the locals didn't seem to know much more than that.

One morning a few days later, my partner and I woke up in our little bamboo shack on the hill and felt like shit. Some days just seem very intrinsically bad, in a deep, troubling way. If I were versed in Indian astrology I could tell you that it was due to this or that negative planetary influence. But be that as it may, this was definitely one of those days. I looked over the seashore and wondered why it was so quiet down there. A little later we were violently vomiting and shitting our insides out, dazed in a fever. During the day we began receiving SMS messages from friends and family asking us if we were all right. Apparently there had been some kind of terrorist attack somewhere in India.

The next day, still weary from the sickness, I wandered down to the bar to get some water and look at the newspapers. In capital letters the panicked headlines screamed: "BOMBAY TERRORIST ATTACKS". A group of young men had attacked several major hotels and tourist hotspots in Mumbai with AK-47s and hand grenades. They targeted Indians and whites, specifically Britons and Americans, but in effect this meant all Western-looking people. A picture of a fiery-eyed twenty-year-old man in a t-shirt wielding a Kalashnikov assault rifle leered from the front page. I felt another wave of nausea building up.

The same young man was later captured at a popular evening destination for locals and the main site for the annual celebrations of Ganesh Chaturi, Chowpatty Beach – incidentally the same place we had visited only a little earlier. They had also had a shooting spree right beside the place where we were supposed to travel to just a day or two later. The newspapers featured pictures and descriptions of the "pools of blood". The siege was still going on, and tourists were advised to avoid train stations and airports. There were also police boats guarding the coastlines of India, especially those areas frequented by tourists.

All this made us feel rather gloomy, and a ominous feeling crept over what was supposed to be a recharging experience. The beaches were unusually silent and an underlying tension was in the air. *"Don't worry"*, the ever-optimistic Raj told me, *"such things always happen in India"*. And come to think of it, they do. In all my travels of India, I have always just barely missed being at the site of a bombing or conflagration. Perhaps Ganesha has been looking out for me after all.

Drawn by the sound of the bells clinging from somewhere above our shack, I finally rose to the top of the hill at dusk. I discovered it was a little shrine to Guru Dattatreya, the lord of yogis and the messenger of the gods. Guru Dattatreya is the primordial yogi, the "original" or "first teacher", bringer of knowledge and giver of initiation, his characteristic being three heads (those of Brahma, Vishnu and Shiva: creator, sustainer and destroyer). He is often shown naked with long, matted locks that merge with the earth, accompanied by a cow and four dogs. He is the one who is called upon to give teachings and initiation while the other earthly gurus stand by as witness-gurus presiding over this process. Dattatreya is the patron of all Naga Babas – including Rampuri. And of all the bamboo huts in Goa, I had chosen this one, directly under Dattatreya's shrine on the hilltop.

The last time we visited Rampuri, we arrived at his house and I was surprised to discover he was playing one my albums I had given him during our first visit. *"I see"*, he said curiously. I had spoken to Rampuri and told him we were feeling weary from the sickness and low in spirits. He had told us to come over as he could help us with traditional medicine and a healing puja. We talked about terrorism as a sign of the Kali Yuga, the fourth and last age in the cycle of ages, characterised by strife and degeneration. Rampuri gave us some ayurvedic medicine and we began the evening puja. As Rampuri and Adi Rana Puri lighted and waved some *ghee* (clarified butter) at one of the altars, they started intoning one of the traditionally most powerful of

Altar at Dattatreya shrine, featuring several murti *(sculptures) of gods, Shiva Lingams, and offerings. In the center is Guru Dattatreya, whose three heads are those of Brahma, Vishnu and Shiva. (Polaroid: Aki Cederberg)*

mantras, the "great death-conquering" Mahamritunjaya mantra:

OM Tryambakam yajāmahe sugandhim pushti vardhanam,
urvārukamiva bandhanān mrityormokshiya māmritām.

We went around the house as he rang the bell and waved burning ghee-lamps above various pictures and statues, starting with a large statue of Ganesh. *"Ganesh is the Lord of Obstacles, so we always invoke him first"*. The puja was conducted at one of the altars, with the traditional blowing of the conch-shell trumpet and the recitation of mantras and singing of bhajans, devotional songs to Shiva and the gods. He offered us sacred water and *prasad*, "that which pleases", sweet food that is first offered to the gods, and then, when the gods are pleased, distributed among the devotees. Lastly, he gave us *Rudraksha* seeds to wear on our necks as malas.

The Rudraksha is the seed of the of the Rudraksha tree, sacred to and named after a form of Shiva. In India many stories are told about the Rudraksha, and a whole magical and medicinal art has sprung up around it. The story goes that Rudra – who is the wildest, fiercest and least compassionate form of Shiva – was high above the world of ordinary men in his celestial abode in the mountains, immersed in deep meditation ("He doesn't give a fuck", in Rampuri's words). One day he opened his eyes and descended down to the world of men, whom he saw hopelessly locked in ignorance, stupidity and suffering. The sight moved him to such a degree that he, Rudra, the fierce, wild, uncompassionate one, shed tears for what he saw. Where his tears fell, there grew the Rudraksha tree with its dark red seeds. Since then the Rudraksha seeds, the eyes or tears of Shiva (*āksa* means "eye", hence "Rudra-eyes") are thought to mark knowledge and health. They are Shiva's gift to man to aid him in overcoming the stupidity and ignorance that lead to suffering. Those dedicated to Shiva have worn the seeds as signs of their dedication to him, and they are a mark of discipleship.

Before the beginning of the puja, Rampuri had said I would feel better afterwards, and I did. While having our last dinner together at a restaurant named in typical Goan fashion ("Bean Me Up"), Rampuri told us about his experiences when he first entered the Naga Babas. He had been expecting to practise *asanas* (yogic postures) and mantras, to delve into a magical world and a rigorous esoteric routine. Instead he spent a lot of time cleaning pots and pans, providing simple service to his gurus and the dhuni, and essentially taking care of cooking and cleaning. While talking about "spirituality" and the hollowness of that word, Rampuri ended by saying:

"... at the end of the day, there is no spirituality ...", and he paused.

"Because you have to make dinner?", I asked.

"Because you have to make dinner", Rampuri said with a little smile.

The last day in India began and ended with a sunrise-puja and sunset-puja at the hilltop shrine to Dattatreya, the messenger of the gods. I bought some offerings and incense to lay at the altar, and rang the bells hanging on trees. Standing at the edge of the cliff, watching a giant bird hover in the air, the scorching sun above and the roaring sea below, I realized I was at an edge of worlds in more ways than one. And as Rampuri would say, that's where the magic happens.

III: INITIATION

It was the height of summer, and I found myself deep in a lush forest adjacent to a lake and river, practically in the middle of nowhere, in the countryside of Sweden. I had made pilgrimage to this remote place that was to be a *tirtha*, a crossing-over place, where the ordinary and extraordinary worlds meet. Surrounded by trees and water, a dhuni had been constructed to serve as the focal point of invocation. This was to be a place of acquiring knowledge in the traditional way, orally, and via participation, revelation and invocation. The very small retreat was organized by two young and beautiful Hatha yoga teachers, Savitri Puri from Sweden and Yogananda Puri from Denmark, and consisted of literally two handfuls of people from different European countries, careers and backgrounds. Sacred speech, which forms the foundation of the esoteric tradition of yoga, mantra, tantra, ayurveda and astrology, was to be the focus of the retreat. This knowledge is not a text or a book but a living oral tradition, resting on the authority of the tradition itself, passed down through the ages from teacher to disciple. Rampuri was such an authority, and an extremely rare one at that because of his

Western background. He was a link to a living esoteric tradition, a foot in the door to a world that would otherwise be totally off-limits.

Havan, the ancient Vedic fire ritual, marked the beginning of the week-long delving into magic, invocation and sacred speech. Rampuri rang the bell outside the little yurt that had been raised in the forest surrounding the dhuni, and with a forceful blow smashed a coconut on a stone on the ground outside of it. The dhuni, which had been extensively decorated with rice, flowers, coloured powders and with symmetrical, geometric symbols, called *yantras* ("seats for the deities"), was ceremonially lighted. Agni, the Fire god, was called upon, along with all the other deities and spirits of earth, water, air and ether. In this ornate and elaborate ritual, the fire was fed with offerings, sacrifices and sacred substances such as incense, herbal mixtures and ghee, along with recitals of mantras punctuated by the chanting of "Svaha!" Water from the Ganga, Yamuna and several European rivers was sprinkled in all directions. And all gods, spirits and plant-deities were invoked to be with us there for that time and give their blessings of knowledge, health and prosperity.

Each morning I would wake up and bathe in the clear lake right beside the dhuni, and every night I would fall asleep to the sound of the adjacent river. In the morning at sunrise and evening at sunset an Aarti puja was performed, those twilight moments being the favourite times of Shiva. Preceding each puja, the altar was decorated with fresh flowers, plants and substances, and in conclusion everyone was offered the sacred fire, as well as water, vibhuti and prasad to eat. Bhajans, the devotional songs to Shiva, were sung. The pujas were anything but quiet meditations: bells rang, conch-shell trumpets pierced the air, horns sounded, cymbals and gongs clashed in loud invocations, as the air filled with smoke.

Rampuri gave *satsang*, teachings, revolving around the revelation of what he called sacred speech within everyone present, identifying speech as *place* rather than sound. We carefully identified each one of the indestructible syllables that form the core of sacred speech, called *matrikas*, the "little mothers" that together form the great chain of resemblances, the totality of speech and knowledge – the "great mother".

What Rampuri taught was completely different from the yoga we think of in the West. It was not about "feel good", not about holding hands and chanting OM, not about some kind of exercise system where you stand on your head; nor was there a New Ager in sight. It was also not about belief systems or wacky ideas that seem so popular these days, but about knowledge that required intelligence and discipline. Yoga, as taught in the traditional way, was more akin to European magic and alchemy than to anything normally associated with it. Even its figurehead, Guru Dattatreya, also called Avadhut (Messenger of the gods), who has three heads (those of the Creator, Preserver, and Destroyer), bore a resemblance to Hermes (Messenger of the gods) Trismegistus (Thrice Great).

The French historian, philosopher, musicologist and Shaivite Alain Daniélou alluded in his works (e.g. *Shiva and Dionysus, While the Gods Play*) that there was a primordial tradition and religion at the root of humanity, from whence sprung several traditions mirroring the original, of which the traditions of Shiva and Dionysus are primary examples. He wrote:

"[...] this early religion is the outcome of man's efforts since his remotest origins to understand the nature of creation in its balanced beauty and cruelty, as well as the manner in which he can identify himself in the Creator's work and cooperate with him. This religion is naturistic, not moralistic, ecstatic and not ritualistic."

In contrast to the moralistic religions and arbitrary ideologies of modern societies, Daniélou suggested that this Shaivite/Dionysian primordial religion expressed more direct, more instinctually pure ways of communication with the creative forces of life, and as its figureheads stood archetypal figures such as Dionysus, Shiva, and similar gods from other ancestral pantheons and cultures.

Whereas the living bacchanalian cults and traditions of Dionysian figures have been largely forgotten in the West and lie dormant in culture, custom, mythology and symbolism, a tradition of Shiva was still alive in India. I was anxious to make a connection to such a living tradition that somehow managed to exist in the modern world. "Yes, Shiva, Dionysus, Pan, and don't forget the Dark Mother, whether Kali, Loralei, or some of yours", said Rampuri.

But Shiva and the Indian gods were not the only ones invoked. All the local gods, the spirits of the place, as well as the ancestral gods that the people present carried within themselves in their blood, were invoked as well. Particularly for the concluding havan of the retreat Rampuri asked me to compile a specific, detailed list of the major gods from different pantheons and cultures represented here by distinct individuals. This reflected something characteristic of India and indeed of its non-dualistic traditions: that there is only One, but the One – in reflection of its own boundless nature – takes on infinite manifestations and forms.

After revealing the matrikas to us, it was time for the concluding havan and initiation for those who desired it. A few people would receive new names according to the tradition. These new names would function as talismans and establish a living connection to the tradition as well as a particular family of Babas. The name is decided upon by the Baba, based on the character, given name and birth star of the person receiving it. My birth star happened to be *Punarvasu*, the same as Rampuri's.

On the day of initiation, I took a long, final bath in the lake under the scorching sun. I swam for a lotus flower growing on the surface of the water, which I was to give to Rampuri at my initiation. As I watched my reflection on the still surface of the lake, I thought of Rampuri's words: "When Shiva looks in the mirror, he sees Shakti."

A red-and-yellow cord was tied around my right wrist. I entered the enclosure, where Rampuri was expecting me, along with Yogananda Puri, who acted as a witness to the proceedings. I paid my respects to the dhuni and to the Baba presiding over it, as is the tradition, and presented him with the lotus flower, as well as a small sum in coins that were put in a *kapala* human skull bowl.

Three times I asked to receive initiation. Thereafter Rampuri pointed to the decorated, three-headed Dattatreya statue at the dhuni and said: "Now you have asked three times for initiation and you shall receive it. Dattatreya, the naked one, the lord of all yogis, is the one who grants initiation, the one who shows the path, as I am merely a witness-guru."

Rampuri called upon the sacred fire, the gods and spirits, as witnesses to the initiation. He smashed a coconut in half with a violent blow, and the broken shell flowed with milk. He took my head close to his and whispered in my ear. From the silence the mantra came as a whirlwind, thrice, syllable after syllable, connected to each other with a bindu in a great chain. This was the *varna mala*, Kali's garland of 51 skulls, mirroring the 51 syllables of the Sanskrit alphabet, the totality of speech and knowledge.

I was given the name Adinath Puri. Puri is the name of the lineage, the family, whereas Adinath, or Adi Nath, or even Adi Natha, means "first lord", the progenitor of all yogis and shamans, i.e. a name for Shiva, pure consciousness and ultimate reality. "A very strong, powerful name that you can grow into", said Rampuri with a smile, while putting a Rudraksha around my neck and giving me water, vibhuti and prasad to eat.

Afterwards, I felt strange, overwhelmed and otherworldly, like I walked just a little bit above the ground. I had just been given a mantra, a new name and made a living connection and relationship to an age-old lineage and tradition of knowledge. Not really being able to communicate this to others, I took a long walk in the woods. Later on, I went and asked Rampuri about this unexpected feeling, and he assured me that the common reaction to initiation is *total confusion*. He told me a story about his own experience of it when he was young. Apparently, just prior to the initiation, the reluctant and apprehensive Rampuri had asked his Baba, "Am I ready for this?", to which the old Baba answered: "You are never ready for this!"

We laughed. With my spirits uplifted, I took my leave.

As I returned to the ordinary world, and watched the changing vistas from the window of the train, I felt lighter. One of the last things said by Rampuri before I left rang in my ears: "... And if nothing else, you have learned how to drink water by the drop and eat ashes."

IV: KUMBH MELA: THE LAST RITES

It was late March and I was on a train again, headed for the Kumbh Mela, the largest gathering of people for a spiritual, magical or religious purpose on planet earth. The train was packed to the hilt, and it was a small miracle that I had been able to secure a ticket the evening before. Unpleasantly hot even in the middle of the night, the train filled with sounds of rattling, snoring and farts. I was on my way from Delhi via night train to Hardwar, a journey of only a little over 200 kilometres, which nevertheless took virtually all night. As I lay awake in the uppermost bunk of three on top of each other in the shuffling train, having arrived in India the previous morning, I sensed something different from my past journeys here. Sometimes all the things one gathers and carries along with oneself can become a heavy load to bear. Perhaps this time I was here to let go of something, to cleanse myself of something.

As the train finally arrived, the bustling city of Hardwar looked surreal in the early morning twilight. Everywhere there were people, so many of them, and I had to step over sleeping bodies scattered on the ground to get anywhere. People from all over

India, as well as from everywhere else in the world, kept arriving here in droves, train upon train, busload after busload, by vehicle or on foot. The roads were regularly closed to public traffic, which meant that you could not get into the city at all. Everywhere there were families, beggars, pilgrims, soldiers and especially Sadhus of all kinds. In the past Sadhus were a relatively rare sight for me to behold, but now suddenly they were everywhere. They sat under trees and stared, with that haunting, otherworldly look that is characteristic to them. But all this was not really a surprise. The Kumbh Mela was after all a gathering of such magnitude that it was actually visible from space. And I, at heart a loner, who often felt crowded even in a room full of people, was now here in the midst of this raging, swarming mass of millions.

The city of Hardwar is situated at the foothills of the Himalayas. From the high mountains the river Ganga runs through it, wide and strong. A giant figure of Shiva guards the city at its entrance, visible from miles away. Indeed, the city is considered a gateway to Shiva and the gods, and its name derives from *Har* or *Hara*, a name of Shiva, and *Dwar*, meaning door. Its other names reflect this as well: Haridwar, (the gateway of the sustaining god, Vishnu, also called *Hari*), Gangadwar (the gateway of the Ganga), (Brahmadwar, the gateway of Brahma, the god of creation) and Mayadwar (the door of illusion, *Maya*), which is said to be its most ancient name. Statues, temples, shrines and signs of Shiva and the gods were everywhere, and indeed the whole city itself seemed to be one gigantic altar between worlds. There was never a moment of silence, as from the early hours to late evening the bhajans and pujas resounded across the shores of the river.

I arrived at my destination by the Ganga at dawn, and had chai while looking over the massive river, ever flowing with offerings of flowers, coconuts and pieces of cloth, as monkeys fished the waters for edible stuff. On the other side of the river, Sadhus and pilgrims wandered and took baths along the banks, and behind them multitudes of tents were set up. As the sun was rising from behind the mountains in an orange halo, bells and songs echoed across the shore. Everyone was here for this river, and everything happened in close conjunction with it.

The origins of the Kumbh Mela festival are steeped in ancient history, going back to mythological events. Kumbh Mela is a composite of two words: *kumbh* from Sanskrit, meaning "pitcher" (as for carrying water), and *mela* meaning "fair" or "gathering". The story goes that the gods and demons came together to churn the primordial ocean of milk for the greatest of treasures, *amrit*, the nectar of immortality, to be distributed to everyone afterwards. However, one of the demons sneaked in line and stole the pitcher containing the amrit. Twelve days and nights (equal to twelve human years) the gods and demons fought over the pitcher. At one point Krishna flew away with the pot, accidentally spilling four drops from it that landed on earth. Those four places are now among the holiest in all of India – Prayag, Haridwar, Ujjain and Nashik – and are the sites of the Kumbh Mela held every four years. At specific dates and times in these places, according to the position of the Sun, Moon and stars, it is said that amrit appears. And on those dates *everyone* comes here to take a bath in the Ganga and to receive a drop of the amrit; millions and millions of people become pilgrims for those brief moments when the heavenly, death-conquering nectar is flowing, echoing a tradition from time immemorial.

Mark Twain wrote of the Kumbh:

> It is wonderful, the power of a faith like that, that can make multitudes upon multitudes of the old and weak and the young and frail enter without hesitation or complaint upon such incredible journeys and endure the resultant miseries without repining. It is done in love, or it is done in fear; I do not know which it is. No matter what the impulse is, the act born of it is beyond imagination, marvelous to our kind of people, the cold whites.

Being a "cold white" myself, I had to agree with Twain: it was pretty marvelous, quite unlike anything I had ever seen. When I arrived to Hardwar, some of the major bathing days were approaching, there was a steady buzz going and you could feel an energy escalating. As all of this, whatever it was, was gathering momentum as a rising storm.

At every moment pujas, rituals and ceremonies were going on. At Har-ki-Pauri, the ghats of the gods, there was a constant swarm of people pushing and shoving to take a bath in the Ganga, and every evening the spectacular Ganga Aarti was conducted there. Equally crowded were the pilgrimage routes to the temples on mountaintops surrounding Hardwar, of which there were three – each dedicated to a different goddess. The streets filled with parades of one kind and another, some streets being closed even for pedestrians, and often it was literally impossible to walk in any other way than the crowds went. And all the time, more and more people kept arriving.

In the middle of this storm of activity, amid the crowds and the hustle and bustle, there was a centre of relative calm (and I use the term "relative calm" in the loosest way possible) – the *Juna Akhara*. The Juna Akhara was the largest Akhara, or division, of the mystical, militant order of Naga Babas, reputedly founded in the pre-historic Treta age by Dattatreya, the naked one. They were finally organized into a proper order by Adi Shankara in the 5th century BCE, in order to protect *Sanatan Dharma*, the "Hindu" religion, but what the Naga Babas themselves view as the natural order of the universe, for which they are the maintainers of the law of nature. This was also the order of which Baba Rampuri was a part. Centred around the Maya Devi temple, the temple of the goddess of illusion, the Juna Akhara was a sprawling encampment of a literal army of Naga Babas – the naked ones, the wild, wandering men, the holy madmen of Shiva. Their encampments consisted of shacks built around the multitudes of dhunis, that were tended by an entourage of ghostly looking creatures. Stepping into the Akhara was like stepping into another time and another world – an extraordinary world, where all previous rules and rationality simply ceased to exist. Instead it was a world of continuous invocation – of spirits, ghosts, freaks and geezers, of wizards and creeps – a storybook world made flesh in the 21st century.

It was evening when I entered the Juna Akhara encampment for the first time. In my hand I had a book wrapped in a red and golden shroud, inside which was my chosen *dakshina* (a traditional monetary gift of honouring) for my patron. I approached the dhuni, surrounded by Rampuri's entourage of Naga Babas, removed my shoes and clasped my hands together, saying, "Om Namo Narayan" to all those present. "OM NAMO NARAYAN!", came the booming chorus in response. I greeted, in the traditional way, first the dhuni and then the Babas presiding over it. The stern-looking Babas eyed me somewhat suspiciously as I paid my respects and received some water and ashes. I had also brought some flowers, which I set decoratively at the sides of the dhuni, after which I sat down in silence. A few of the Babas finally nodded in smiling agreement.

My initial reaction to all of this of course, as I told Rampuri a few days later, was a strong "What the fuck am I doing here?" It was all quite overwhelming and disorienting, suddenly bursting into this alien, foreign fairytale world. Rampuri said it's good I told him, since, he continued, "What do I know – I have been sitting at the dhuni for the last 40 years."

Rampuri offered me an analogy for my situation. I was no longer my ordinary self, but a character, Adinath Puri, in a story written on the surface of the stars. The story was not a new one, but indeed the great story of all times: the story of the quest of the hero.

"It's like in Star Wars when Luke Skywalker first meets his teacher, Obi Wan-Kenobi, who tells him he has a destiny to fulfill, but Luke rejects it saying he must return home to his aunt to help with the cleaning, only to find that it's all been destroyed in his absence. It is the resistance of the call, and the next part of the story would be the conflict."

Oh *great*, I thought: a *Star Wars* analogy.

Be that as it may, the dhuni of Rampuri was the place I made my centre and focus during my stay in Hardwar, attending it daily after dawn and dusk. The dhuni, the sacred ritual fire that never went out, and of which there were hundreds and hundreds, was the centre of all attention. It was the temple, the altar and the deity, and was fed with offerings and mantras. Around the dhuni sits the Baba with his entourage and devotees, surrounded behind them by pictures of gurus from times past, the whole scenario resembling a hall of mirrors stretching into infinity. The square of the dhuni was decorated daily with fresh flowers and purifying cow-dung. It was sprinkled with water, and given offerings of everything that was consumed by its side. It was always kept clean, and no rubbish was to ever be burned in its flames. A trishul raised skyward from its ashes, and a jug of water, a *kamandal*, rested at its rim. The fire is Agni, the Fire god. The outer fire is in turn reflective of the inner fire, and at the dhuni, both are invoked. I was reminded of a line from the *Mahābhārata:* "Fire only exists by destroying the fuel which makes it live, by consuming the oblation. The whole universe, both sentient and insentient, is nothing but fire and oblation."

Each morning I would wander down the street, past the rows of lined-up beggars; over the bridge under which – amongst hoards of wilds boars – a man was, like the animals, searching for valuables in the mountains of garbage; past the ever-swelling crowds; until finally I would arrive at the gates of the Akhara, and be waived in by the soldiers on guard there. Every time I arrived at the dhuni, I made sure I brought something pleasant, some sweet things to eat, some flowers or a small dakshina. Twice daily, around noon and late at night, the kitchen offered food to everyone. The "kitchen" was

The dhuni at the Kumbh Mela. Surrounding the dhuni are portraits of various Babas from the Puri lineage. Adjacent to the central fire are various items, such as the trishul of Shiva decorated with flowers, a damaru double-headed drum, kamandals (water pots), and chimtas (the thongs used to tend the fire). Presiding over the dhuni is Rampuri in the middle, under an image of Dattatreya, engaged in conversation; also visible is the smiling Mangalanand Puri. The narrator is in the far left corner of the picture; to his side is Savitri Puri. (Photograph: Mangalanand Puri)

actually a shack in the corner of a makeshift tent, with very basic cooking utensils on an earthen floor. Despite these conditions, the Baba-chefs managed to make some of what was truly the tastiest Indian food I have ever eaten. One would sit on a thin mat on the ground and be served with as much delicious food as one wanted to eat, and all the while there was a stern-eyed Baba presiding over the meals, having his own food from a skull-shaped bowl. At the recommendation of Rampuri, I did have most of my meals there, and for the very first time during the course of all my travels in India, I remained healthy and free of stomach-problems throughout my journey. There was also constantly tea and coffee being served, not to mention the charas. Consumption of meat and alcohol is forbidden in Hardwar, as it is considered a holy city and these things are traditionally taboo in the Hindu world. On the other hand charas is smoked in unimaginable quantities, literally by the truckloads, from morning to night every day for months on end. Luckily I had some whisky with me, and I would sit late at night by the Ganga, listening to the echoing songs and invocations, and discretely have a few drinks from a coffee cup. I was sure Shiva wouldn't mind – after all, he was often depicted in an inebriated state and was "the drinker of poisons".

Constant greeting-shouts of "OM NAMO NARAYAN!" heralded the arrival of someone at the dhuni. It is said that Shiva is accompanied by an entourage of Ganas, a rowdy and unruly bunch of ghosts, goblins, gnomes, witches, warlocks and other wild spirits, whom Alain Daniélou described thusly (in *Shiva and Dionysos*):

In Shivaite tradition, the god's companions are described as a troupe of freakish, adventurous, delinquent and wild young people, who prowl in the night, shouting in the storm, singing, dancing and ceaselessly playing outrageous tricks on sages and gods. [...]The Ganas mock the rules of ethics and social order. They personify the joy of living, courage and imagination, which are all youthful values. [...] These delinquents of heaven are always there to restore true values and to assist the "god-mad" who are persecuted and mocked by the powerful. They personify everything which is feared by and displeases bourgeois society, and which is contrary to the good morale of a well-policed city and its palliative concepts.

This resemblance to the Ganas could really be seen when one looked at the regular crowd that attended the dhuni. The Naga Babas were ash-covered and sometimes completely naked. These long-haired, fiery-eyed, strange and strong characters carried conch shells and musical instruments, trishuls, swords or other weapons, signifying their status as warriors. Shouting invocations to Shiva, "AALEKH!" or "BOM!", they inhaled the thick smoke from the chillums filled with charas, which they smoked *all the time*. There was the constant choir of wet coughing that went with the non-stop chillum smoking. There were farts and burps, as well as the occasional instruments being played and songs being sung. Indeed at times, especially late in the evenings, nobody talked much, and most in attendance would just sit around stoned, their eyes half-closed, smiling that self-satisfied smile, looking like they are in possession of a big secret. This was the divine stoner party of Shiva's holy madmen.

Sitting by the dhuni, I came to know some of these Babas. There was Mangalanand Puri (formerly Mangalanand Giri), also known as Goa Gil, a world-renowned guru of the techno-trance dance Goa scene. Most of the time sitting to the right of Rampuri, Mangalanand Puri was equipped with a constant, deep smile and an utterly disarming presence. All the time making chillums, he would easily break into laughter, that seemed capable of breaking possible tensions and conflicts. Early one morning, after I had been sitting at the dhuni for a few days, not really talking much to the Babas yet, Mangalanand Puri suddenly exclaimed to me, with his trademark joyfulness:

"Isn't it wonderful?!"

I nodded and he continued: 'It's like when you go to the mountains, camping or trekking, and you lie there under the stars at night, when suddenly you have the realization of the cathedral of nature, the universe, god, the Cosmic Spirit, or whatever you choose to call it, and at that moment you understand how you and every thing fits into that! We Babas choose to give up everything to live in that wondrous moment, in that Oneness of Life always, and that's why we don't have worldly ambitions, families, do work, or live the normal lives of the masses! We choose to remain in that realization and that life under the stars forever!"

And then he punctuated the thought with his easy laughter.

There was Shakti Giri, a flamboyant, middle-aged Baba riding a flashy motorcycle plastered with various trishuls and swastikas, whom I became sort of friends with despite our convoluted conversations. With almost childlike enthusiasm he would take out his little box of treasures to show me his coin collection, to which I contributed a one-euro coin. He would say, "double Shakti!", while pounding on his chest, and I'd say "triple Shakti", and he'd laugh. One day he examined the skin of my right arm, my tattoos and rings closely, and pointing to a trident-like rune he asked, "trishul?". I answered, "my homeland trishul", to which he said the oft-heard phrase pointing to an underlying resemblance: "same same". Going on to read the palm of my hand, he pointed at a line, exclaiming, "Shiva!", and to another, saying, "long life, 80 years".

"Adinath Puri Ji!" I heard someone calling out on the street during my second or third day at the Mela. "Adinath Puri Ji, Rampuri is looking for you!" It was Surendra Puri, one of the rare Babas who spoke English well. He was in his thirties, about my age, and had huge matted locks reaching all the way down to the ground rolled up on top of his head, and a soft, warm but strong and disciplined presence. Like many Babas it seemed, he had been to military school before becoming a Baba. When I asked him something, his reply would be kind and welcoming. "Of course Adinath Puri Ji, this your family, this your home." On one of the first days he took me to the Maya Devi temple for darshan, and we walked around the temple, Surendra Puri narrating on the various manifestations of the goddess.

There were also many Babas actively practicing tapasya of varying severities. Tapasya, physical and spiritual yogic austerities and mortifications which often involve severe vows, ordeals or endurance of pain and suffering of a marked kind, are practiced to cultivate the *inner fire ("tapas")* and to "get the attention of god". The motivation for the austerities lay not in the realms of guilt, sin or repentance, as they would in a Christian context, but in the manipulation of matter for the cultivation of the spirit. Their nakedness is indicative of not some kind of sexuality but their renunciation of the ordinary world. Babas ideally use *kama*, the fire of passion and lust, as a source of tapas, by burning it through austerities. They claim not to deny their sexuality, but to choose to control it, sublimate it and retain it, in order to transform it into spiritual or magical power. As I understood, the tapasya are a form of spiritual machismo, wherein the *tapasvin* (the practitioner), after going through some form of extreme austerity, like climbing a mountain barefoot or living in an icy cave in the Himalayas, becomes untouchable, gaining a kind of divine power from the experience. There was the old Muni Baba, with gray-white matted locks and beard, who had taken a vow of silence for an indefinite amount of time, only communicating with gestures and writing. There was Mahant Amar Bharti Ji, a famous "urdhvabahu" ("arm raised") Baba, who has held up one arm for 32 years, until it has become like a shrivelled stick of bone with the fingernails growing in all directions. "It is like a flag raised in honour of Shiva – and once raised, it does not come down."

Then there were the young boys, definitely more children than young men, who were nevertheless already full-blown Babas, at least on the surface. And as Babas they had already developed a full liking for charas, and the wet, deep and nasty sounding cough that goes along with it. One night a very young boy, a little Baba who had a penchant for posing for photos, sat down by the dhuni and started singing a capella, accompanied only by his little tambourine drum. After the long devotional, beautiful and slightly melancholic song, he burst into a recital of a long series of verses and mantras to the smiling approval of the Babas who threw money and bits of charas in his lap. Rampuri told me that what connects most Babas here is that they became Babas while they were mere kids. Like Surendra Puri, many of the Babas here knew that they would become Babas at a very young age, and neither their families, parents or schools could change their minds. For the little Baba doing the singing – his father had come to see Rampuri one day – it was either that, or becoming a petty criminal.

Like all fairs, the Kumbh Mela had its element of entertainment and performance. Several times a day there would troupes of singers, who would attend the dhuni and perform, and receive some money and some charas as payment. For instance, there were the *Sakhi*, the Gopis of Krishna, who are transvestite-lovers and devotees of him, men dressed as women in order to be as close as possible to their lord and lover.

By the same token, at the Kumbh Mela one encountered both magic invocations and stage magic, both tantra and tan-tricks. There were a fair share of fake Babas, con men, and hucksters claiming to have great magical powers, who were less than impressive. There was an aspect of people trying to upstage one another with ever more amazing and occasionally macabre "magical" feats. Snake-handlers, sword-wavers, and miracle-workers, and everything else you could imagine belonging to the world's biggest magical fair – it was all there, and more. And there were tourist traps aplenty for the spiritual tourist, whether Indian or foreigner. Rampuri's approach to the fake holy men and the people who fell for them was straightforward:

"If somebody was smart enough, they would see that somebody is a fake. And if somebody falls for a fake, that means they're not smart enough to see through it, and they deserve what they get. I hate say it, but this seems to be the reality. Without discrimination, then anything goes. And fools deserve what they come up with."

Sometimes the Babas would turn their austerity almost into an show-off act, to demonstrate their control over their bodies and physique, like tying their penis several times around a sharp sword, twisting the sword behind their feet, and then having someone *stand* on the sword.

In the context of the Mela, and sitting by the dhuni, there seemed to be nothing especially weird in all of this. Things that would normally cause abhorrence, repulsion or bewilderment, seemed to belong in this strange world as "part of the furniture".

Fundamentally, what the Babas do is that they give blessings. People, families, the old and the young, the rich and the poor, from all castes and walks of life, Indians and foreigners alike, all arrived in droves from morning to night, and the Babas would give them blessings. Even many of the high-ranked cops and soldiers were devotees. The Babas would give out their blessings by touching people on the forehead and marking their third eye with vibhuti, which they would also give people to eat. They might also give some prasad, which is often some type of sweet fruit or candy that has been first offered to the gods at the altar, whereupon it is blessed, and is consumed by the devotees.

There is a common notion in the West that knowledge should be "free", and should be equally available to all. In India, this idea does not really exist in practice. There is a tradition of dakshina, of giving wealth or offerings to the guru or tradition as a way of honouring that source of knowledge. That is the way of the esoteric tradition and indeed of Indian culture in general. This tradition is still a confusing issue for many people from outside of India and its traditions, and the subject of much debate. In discussing this with Rampuri, I quoted two passages from the *Linga Purana* about the Kali Yuga: "Masters demean themselves by selling knowledge" [...] "Sacraments and religion are also for sale". Rampuri replied:

"Knowledge has never been free. When a disciple traditionally goes to a guru, the disciple pays a lot for the knowledge. In fact, he pays everything for the knowledge. He brings dakshina, offerings, wealth to the guru, and even much more than that, he pays for the knowledge with his entire life. So in fact, traditionally, knowledge is very expensive. The fact that people attempt to sell and buy knowledge with mere money actually demeans the value of the knowledge; that mere money is only a small price that one has to pay for knowledge. So maybe really an interpretation of that is not that knowledge will be sold, but that knowledge will be sold cheaply.

In the tradition, and even in the tantric text, if you read the text in one way or another, either by reading the book of the world, by reading the tradition or reading the written word, what you will find is that is says "the pleased guru says to his disciple", not "the guru", but "the pleased guru". So it's like anything else in the world: you want something that somebody has, you must please that person. This is the way that it's always worked in the tradition: you must please the guru. You can't be a pain in the ass – the guru doesn't want you around if you're a pain in the ass."

But this is not to say that all the Babas do is to act as conduits of knowledge and to give out blessings. Just as they are givers of blessings, they are also the throwers of curses. Indeed there was an element of fierceness to the Babas and to the dhuni, a violent intensity, that inspired awe and fear in many. In the West, people tend to associate "Eastern spirituality" (whatever the fuck that means) and yogis with peace and love, with starry-eyed pacifism and feel-good harmony, but looking at these yogis of a genuine ancient tradition you could see how deluded that image actually was in reality. These yogis and Babas were not just ascetics – they were warriors. Traditionally and throughout history Naga Babas had been warriors, and even today many of them had a background in the military. There was one Baba, for instance, who enjoyed showing a picture of himself beating a guy with a metal rod who had falsely claimed to be a Naga Baba.

To call the Naga Babas of the Juna Akhara the "Hell's Angels of Indian spirituality" is really not an overstatement at all. There were definite resemblances – the fraternity, the structure and strict hierarchy, the living outside of mainstream society and its norms by their own laws, the exchange of money and the violent commitment to the path. As an outsider, or even a welcomed guest and friend, you had better be on your best behaviour – you did not want to cross these guys. I paraphrase Mangalanand Puri about the results of such misadventures:

"Sometimes when someone does something really bad, they are not just kicked out of the camp, or given over to the police, but they are dealt with and punished very severely here inside the Akhara! Here is one of the examples of how serious transgressions are traditionally dealt with here in Juna Akhara: A number of years ago, at a Kumbh Mela, a young Sadhu did something seriously forbidden and was caught! He was then severely beaten, his head was half-shaved, he was made a mala of shoes to wear, and all of the black soot of the dirty cooking pots were smeared on his face and body! He was then taken around to all of the dhunis in the Akhara, where his crime was proclaimed, and at each dhuni the Babas beat him with their shoes, and some even beat him with their chimtas (the thongs used to tend the fire), after which he was thrown out of the Akhara into the street! He was lucky to have escaped with his life!"

"What did he do?", I asked.

"He got drunk and in a fit of anger pissed on his guru."

And as in all areas of human groupings, not all the Babas were good guys in the least. Simply wearing ochre, matted locks, malas and belonging to an order doesn't make one into a nice person. This was even expressed as a literal warning by Rampuri in a serious tone:

"There are people here who could eat your liver."

I thought, "Why would they, since they are vegetarians?", but refrained from making such a smart-ass remark. Instead I asked:

"Why would anyone want to eat my liver?"

"Because they could. For fun." Rampuri replied.

On certain nights the dhuni also attracted some Aghori Babas. "Ghora" means "darkness", and the "A" negates the word it precedes, so *Aghora* literally means "no darkness". Infamous for their perpetual taboo-breaking and anti-social *sadhana* ("spiritual practice"), such as nocturnal rituals at cremation grounds involving drinking alcohol from kapala skullbowls, ghosts, possession, sex, drugs, meat-eating, sacrifice, and even rumoured cannibalism, they are probably amongst the more extreme of spiritual practitioners in India – kind of like a dark mirror-image of the perpetually smiling, benevolent yogi. As their esoteric practices and doctrines lend themselves to easy sensationalism, they have been a source of many articles and documentaries in the West, as well as in India, where during the Mela they were the subject of newspaper articles in local papers as well as reports on the news channels. On the surface, however, it might be hard to tell them apart from the Naga Babas, which is illustrative of how difficult and bewildering it can be to see the differences between the various *sampradayas* (initiatory traditions) and sects of India, of which there are the multitudes. In Varanasi, I had visited their ashram and temple, and found it little different from other temples. Rampuri explained it thusly:

"Huge difference between Aghori and Naga, but not to do with doctrine per se, as one might imagine. Yes, there are doctrinal differences, but that is not what distinguishes the two from each other. It's more an issue of caste. Aghoris are from non-Brahmin, and usually lower castes, which means that their universe is not intellectual, as it would be with a Brahmin, the magic is not articulated as a Naga might. These are not things to choose between, as one might choose between a working-class bar and a trendy one. These are sampradayas that one would more naturally belong to because of how – in which caste and condition, and in which geography – one grew up. But one does not really choose because it sounds good."

There was an Aghori practitioner there, however, who was now a Naga Baba. Formerly called Ram Nath, he achieved some kind of infamy after a documentary was made about him and his Aghori practices. From what I gather, Matsyandra Giri, as he is now called, apparently got tired of just hanging out with ghosts at the burning grounds, and so he became part of the Naga Babas.

There was also another Aghori sometimes sitting around the dhuni, drinking chai out of his skull-cup. Not a Naga Baba, this particular Aghori had a questionable reputation because of his interest in "helping" Western women with their problems with "boy friend... hasband [sic]". You can imagine that when skull-drinking, ashen-garbed yogis tell you that they will help with "troubles with boy friend", it will usually not involve the boyfriend, but may mean something else entirely, and may not be inspired by entirely altruistic and benevolent thoughts related to their sadhana. And this is illustrative of something else. How much the Babas are really successful in controlling their sexuality to serve their sadhana and generate tapas is hard to say, but the reality remains that when encountering Western women some of Babas get their chakras totally tangled up.

One late night at the dhuni, I met a woman, a fellow Finn, who told me her name was Vishvanath. She had a proud, strong and somewhat crazy spirit that I could recognize as distinct to my homeland. To the amusement of the Babas listening, we talked in Finnish, and she told me her story. She lived in Goa with her children most of the year, but they travelled to many important tirthas, including Kedarnath high up in the Himalayas – and now she was with her kids here at the Mela. She showed me a picture of a painting she had photographed at a Nath temple, which according to her depicted Väinämöinen, the Finnish shamanic storyteller god. Indeed, the figure looked somewhat like the archetypal image of the Finnish god, with fair skin and gray hair and beard, and even the nature and animals in the picture looked distinctly Nordic. According to Vishvanath, she was a Nath. The Naths are again a distinct sampradaya of Babas, founded by Matsyendranath and given further form by Gorakshanath, and Naths could be sometimes recognized by their distinctive thick, black earrings. The Naths do not recognize cast barriers. Indeed, one of the great Naths was a Westerner, Shri Gurudev Mahendranath (1911–1991), who originally got the advice to delve into the Indian esoteric tradition from Aleister Crowley himself. Rampuri once told me a story of his meeting with Mahendranath, or Dadaji as he was called by the locals. They had sat at his dhuni, and Dadaji had offered to give Rampuri his *mahamantra*, his great mantra, and Rampuri had of course accepted. Dadaji had come closer and solemnly whispered the mantra in Rampuri's ear: *"Fuck 'em all"*.

In addition to all the Babas, devotees and seekers one encountered at the dhuni, there were of course the spectators. They were comprised of mostly Japanese tourists watching from a safe distance, with protective surgical face-masks, gloves, and the standard tourist-wear of khaki shorts and hiking shoes. Armed with high-quality cameras – resembling hunters, as Rampuri pointed out – they took shots of the Babas and the dhuni, not desiring anything further than that.

The only way to really learn and understand anything of all of this was to engage and absorb, which in practice meant to sit, watch and participate. Not to make moral, intellectual, or analytical judgements, not to ask what this or that "meant" or "symbolized", as if all things had implicit and deeper "meanings" or symbolic values outside of those directly apparent to them – but to simply to sit and watch how things unfolded. And this is what I tried to do. Not to make judgements on anything one way or the other, but simply to let the experience wash over me, and see what knowledge would grow from that.

And so it was that sitting by the dhuni, I became witness to some major events that took place. After lengthy periods of seeming inactivity and sitting around the dhuni, suddenly there would be a rush of activity, and as if according to some magical logic, these big things would happen. There was a gradual opening up of the Akhara taking place, and part of this opening up included the official recognition of the international element within the Akhara and its connection with the rest of the world. This meant that for the first time in the entire history of the ancient order of Naga Babas three foreigners – Rampuri, Mangalanand Puri and Vasudev Puri from Italy – were given permanent seating in the ruling council of Juna Akhara, and made *Shri Mahants*, which give them considerably more authority than they had before. And also as a part of this opening up, an *Antahrashtriya Mandal*, a "World Circle," was established, as a means of connection between the Akhara and with the world outside of India.

These things were preceded by and took place as a series of events that could be somewhat confusing to an outsider. The governing body of the Juna Akhara met at the dhuni of Shri Maharaj Macchendar Puri to get everyone's signature on the Akhara proclamation made before Guru Dattatreya that these three aforementioned Sadhus would now be known as "Honoured Ones". In a burst of movement, the entourage moved inside the confines of the Maya Devi temple. There, before Guru Dattatreya and Shiva, Juna Akhara secretary Prem Giri Ji made the *Pukar*, the proclamation, in which Rampuri, Mangalanand Puri and Vasudev Puri were each proclaimed *Antahrashtriya Mandal ka Shri Mahant*. The proclamations were marked by the blowing of the snake-shaped *Nagphani* trumpet, as the new Shri Mahants, clothed in huge ochre turbans, were adorned with countless flower garlands so you could barely see their face, looking like crowns of their new status. There was festive mood and everyone present was given garlands of flowers. Finally the entourage sat down at the Puri dhuni of the courtyard of the Maya Devi temple and had a chillum. Although I could not claim to understand all the things connected to this event, I knew I had witnessed something rare, something that had never happened before in the entire history of the order, and perhaps something that marked the changing times.

But everyone was here for the great bath, *Ganga Snaan*. That was the reason for pilgrimage, the moment of culmination, the immersion into the panacea, the elixir of immortality. There were several great baths during the Mela, astrologically significant moments, when ordinary water was transformed into amrit, "that which is immortal". There was a bathing day to happen on the 30th of March, but nobody knew if there was going to be a procession of the Naga Babas or not – not even the Naga Babas themselves. The day before I tried to find out something about what would possibly take place, but everyone seemed to have their own ideas. Babas not of the Juna Akhara would reputedly make a procession, like the Vaishnavas (the followers of Vishnu), some of whom had padlocked their penises away as an austerity; the "locks on cocks" as I called them.

Nevertheless, on the morning of the day of the bath I was sitting at the dhuni, when three Brahmin pandits arrived from Ujjain, Varanasi and someplace else. A small troupe consisting of Rampuri, Mangalanand Puri, Savitri Puri, Yogananda Puri, Surendra Puri and a few other Babas and devotees quickly gathered, and followed the priests through the labyrinthine Akhara towards the river Ganga. We arrived at the secluded Bhairava ghat (Bhairava is a fierce manifestation of Shiva), where only Babas bathe, and here we would take our snaan. I took my dip thrice in the waters of the Ganga, under the watchful eye and guidance of the Babas. As I went under the water, I could feel the strong current of the Ganga and the current of this age-old tradition sweep through me. Emerging from under the water, I lifted my hands in a cuplike salute to the river and the sun, the drips of the water glistening in the radiance of the light.

Under the guidance of the three Brahmin priests, we then took part in a puja by the Ganga while still immersed with our feet in the water, in which an icon of Dattatreya was bathed in the river, and then decorated and showered with offerings of water, flowers, rice, sweets, coloured paste, malas and garlands. Afterwards we sat at the stairs of the Bhairava ghat, taking refuge from the scorching sun. A Naga Baba came up to me, pointing to the ring on his cock put there as an austerity, and smiled proudly.

People from outside of the tradition reacted to these events at the Akhara, and to the Kumbh Mela in general, in very different ways, depending on their perspective, background, intent and cultural discourse. Some people were put off by the big emphasis placed on dakshina at the Akhara, and the all the talk, exchange and counting of it that occurred. Some people thought it resembled a spiritual mafia, which in way, it did. Some people were put off by the sheer intensity of the Mela, the cooky Babas, the endless crowds, the chaos and noise, and the magnitude of it all. A man said to me: "This is not for us. We are Scandinavians, we are forest people."

Some people felt the exact opposite. Having felt the call of the yogic path so strongly for a longer while now, for them all this was like coming home. They had given themselves over to the extraordinary world of the Naga Sannyasis with such abandonment that all doubt went out the window. These people were my friends Savitri Puri and Yogananda Puri, who had organized the retreat I had participated in earlier. Both had been practising and teaching Hatha yoga, and been part of the Western yoga movement, for more than 10 years. Even though they were part of one of the more esoteric approaches to yoga than Pattabhi Jois's yoga which emphasises physical fitness, they had also seen and experienced the limitations to how yoga was presented and understood in the West. To them, the Naga tradition, "however chaotic, insane and seemingly mad it appeared, offered some understanding and sanity in this crazy world and time that we are living in." Both were to undertake the traditional initiation into Naga Sannyasis, the Sacrament of the Five gurus, and the *Virja Havan*, the Heroic Sacrifice.

I saw Savitri Puri the day following her initiation. She had lost her voice in all the excitement, her head shaved, her forehead marked with yellow and red paste, and her face and being gleaming with the aura of a newborn — overwhelmed with joy, bliss, fear and respect. Yogananda Puri was to have his great rite in a few days — the cutting away, the last rites. Going through initiation into Sannyas, an ordinary person becomes transformed into a mythic being of the extraordinary world, where different laws are in effect than those of the ordinary world. The chela, disciple, joins the company of gods and demons, spirits and ghosts. He is no longer part of his biological family, but gains a new family and lineage via the esoteric tradition of which he becomes part, whose progenitor is Dattatreya himself. It is at the Kumbh Mela that the procreation and strengthening of these families occur. In a great chain of succession starting from the progenitor of the lineage himself, the chela aims to become the guru, adopting his knowledge, his personality and sometimes even being possessed by his spirit. It follows that the concept of "individuality", that holds such preoccupation in the West, does not really hold the same position in this tradition, where one aims to become the tradition. To illustrate this, one day at the dhuni Rampuri (himself possessed by his guru Hari Puri Baba) pointed out to me yet another Baba who also claimed possession by the spirit of a long-dead guru.

Indeed, it was getting a little intense for me too at times, and I took off to Rishikesh for a few days to rest and recharge. A few hours' ride by rickshaw, arriving there was a relaxing contrast to the often chaotic hustle and bustle of Hardwar and the Mela. I was also glad to meet my friends Vijaya Puri and Lars there, from Germany and Denmark respectively, who had been ill in Hardwar and needed a respite from all of it. On my first night, I sat on the balcony of the Swiss cottage–style guesthouse and marvelled at the majestic mountains that rise high enough to almost cover the moon. There was a warm breeze in the night air, birds sang and occasionally dogs barked, and it was serene in comparison to Hardwar. The Ganga flowed through the valley below, as it seems to flow through all things in India.

Wandering down into the valley, I could see another chasm of difference between this world and that of Hardwar. Whereas Hardwar was an ancient place of power, and represented a traditional Indian esoteric tradition, Rishikesh was like a spiritual pick-and-choose marketplace, a New Age haven with all the crystals, yoga classes, strange "Swedish" massages, esoteric bookshops, tarot card readers and organic, vegan food shops you'd ever need – if you happened to be into that sort of thing. A shoddily hand-written sign said: "VISIT FOR MEDITATION, PHILOSOPHY, ANSWERS TO SPIRITUAL QUESTIONS, INDOLOGY, GALACTIC CHRONICLES". Rishikesh was also crowded by a particular brand of foreign travellers – the smug neo-hippies that sport a strange kind of hip arrogance, a steady stoned glaze, and who often wander around in inappropriate clothes behaving in an inappropriate manner, giving Western-ers the reputation they sometimes have and affecting how foreigners are treated.

Perhaps it was the unfortunate bastard legacy of The Beatles, and the clichéd "quest to find oneself in the East" that had resulted in this. It was to precisely to Rishikesh that The Beatles famously came looking for that great something. At the behest of George Harrison they came to study transcendental meditation at the ashram of Maharishi Ma-hesh Yogi, located just across from where I was staying, and which now lies abandoned and swallowed by the forest. Although The Beatles composed much of their brilliant *White Album* here, they did not, it seems, find what they were looking for – except maybe for Harrison, whose ashes were scattered into the Ganga river when he died. And that too epitomizes something of the Westerners' quest in the East: often they return to their country even more lost that they were when they first set out on their journey.

Nevertheless, we walked down to the sandy banks of Ganga for the evening Aarti ceremony. A traditional Indian band played devotional music, and from a young boy we bought incense and some floating ghee-lamps made out of leaf and decorated with flowers. I pushed the burning light into the river, and watched it quietly float away among the many others, forming a solemn parade of little lights against the darkness of the night.

The next night, the Dalai Lama was to appear in an evening puja by the Ganga in Rishikesh, and so all traffic was blocked and there was a general buzz going on. But being tired of all the endless ceremonies, and especially the endless crowds, I chose not to go. Instead I had bought some beer outside of the city limits, and stayed on the balcony of my guesthouse drinking and watched the sun set beyond the mountains. The Dalai Lama seemed too far removed from my life to even approach except as a mere curiosity. Besides, the Dalai Lama was never one of my heroes. A doctrine or an idea without force to back it up remains an abstraction; "passive resistance" simply means to let one be trampelled over. Sitting on the terrace overlooking the vast, dark ranges, I wondered where my journeys had taken me, and where they would take me.

Soon I was back in Hardwar. It was early morning and I was at the dhuni when my mother called. I knew instantly, before answering, what it was. After a long illness and a recent fall, my father had died.

I sat down at the root of a tall tree opposite to the dhuni, and listened to my mother's words. Birds were singing in the morning and the sky was a bright blue. The silent Baba walked by and stopped to gesture something to me with a wide smile.

In a detached, surreal state I walked back along the Niranjani Akhara road to the resort by the Ganga where I stayed. I opened a bottle of whisky, and poured the first libation for my father. Then I sat down by the Ganga and drank. Death washed over me as thick and wide as the ancient current of the river by which I was sitting, and I wept.

Around noon I was joined by my friend Christian. He was a Swedish yoga teacher, the same age as me, and we had received the same initiation. He had also lost his mother in a car accident only a few weeks earlier. So there we sat by the shore of the Ganga, listening to bitter-sweet songs, watching the river flow by, and drank whisky. Two men equally overwhelmed by the loss of our progenitors, by the sorrow, the beauty, the magic, by the profundity of life and death. How raw is the fabric of reality when touched by tragedy. Sorrow is a reality, a sobering realization, bound to touch us during our life, no matter how we may wish to hide behind a facade of artifice built to protect us from such unpleasant things.

Rampuri, having heard the news, told me before I could say anything: "Now you take the first flight home. This is what you do." I bought the first ticket I could get. I knew that this was to be the Kumbh Mela for me.

In the evening I wandered down the streets in solitude before visiting the dhuni. How things took on a different, surreal perspective in light of death. I sat down and watched the blinking lights and the people rushing by. On Niranjani Akhara road I bought the best and sweetest things I could find to give to the Babas by the dhuni:

something *gur* ("sweet") for the gurus. Arriving at the dhuni, I gave my offerings and sat down in silence. A few friends and Babas gave me a knowing look.

A week earlier I had talked and smoked cigarettes with an Indian man who had just conducted his mother's cremation, dressed all in white and his head shaved; he said he was here to conclude the funeral rites. Indeed death was something very characteristic of the Kumbh Mela. People, Babas, yogis, and devotees sometimes came here to die. In an act of final defiance and show of divine power, great Babas could sometimes choose their time of death, and would announce it beforehand and then "leave their body" at will. Their bodies would then be carried around, still sitting cross-legged, decorated with garlands of marigolds, with malas in their hands and with money thrown on their lap. It was, so the tradition went, an auspicious time to die. Perhaps because of this death was not a stranger, nor was it treated as such – either with overly visible grief or sentimentality.

Disconnected from the normal talk at the dhuni, I wandered wearily through the alleys of the Akhara. An ash-covered Naga Baba waved me over, and I stumbled toward him. I paid my respects to his dhuni and to him, and sat down. Skyclad in his ashen attire he offered me food and gave me a deep smile. Not conversant enough in Hindi to engage in dialogue, I simply sat there with him, the ash-covered smiling Baba.

Before dawn the next day, just as the sun was slowly beginning to rise, I had my final bath in the Ganga in deep silence, as did my friend Christian. I felt the cold water over my head and body, and the pull of the river. With my feet in the water, I raised my hands skyward, toward the rising sun, and felt the stream of life and death rinse over me, as endless flowers and garlands flowed past. I was at the edge of worlds that was this river – an edge between the ordinary and the extraordinary, between end and beginning. On another level, I was beholding the transformative edge that this time and place represented, and its eventual crossing over. And yet, this here was not an edge for me to cross. I felt the call of my own lineage and lands, rivers and the sea, the call of my own blood and the gods that dwelt therein. I washed my feet, hands and head with Ganga water, filled some containers with it, and said my goodbyes.

As we walked toward the Juna Akhara for the last time, I distributed coins and notes of money to the rows of beggars and Sadhus that gather along the road in the early morning time. This was my day of departure and the last time I was to visit the dhuni. It was also the very day Yogananda was to have his grand initiation into a Naga Sannyasi, a Naga Baba. He was to have his last rites, as I was to have mine. Again I brought some sweets and my last dakshina to the dhuni, and received the blessings and a mark on my third eye with vibhuti, orange and red paste. It was the day of funeral rites, and Rampuri was talking to Yogananda Puri.

"We are cutting away ties. Cutting ties with family, with caste, with the past life, with the ordinary world. Cutting away", Rampuri said, making a scissor-like gesture with his fingers.

Rampuri told me to come and sit close to him and the dhuni. Both he and Mangalanand Puri were talking to me. "Take some water from the Ganga, and bring it home to sprinkle on your father and say a prayer for his spirit to reach the highest heavens. This is why you have come here: travelling all the way to India, to discover that you have to return to your homeland, and put your father to rest. This is your

Kumbh Mela. This is the puja you must perform. The last rites."

And so this I did.

A month later back in Helsinki, there was a heavy downpour of rain when my father's coffin was finally lowered into the earth. I poured a bottle of amrit, the nectar of immortality, on his casket. The celestial waters mixed with the rain and tears, and all that water in turn mixed with the soil on and around my father, as sky met earth.

I once had a dream-vision of death. I was in a large old house, on the shore of a vast ocean, that was made out of a clay-like material, earthen red in colour. The air and ground was warm as I walked barefoot up the stairs to the highest floor, dressed in white. Arriving on top, I saw from the large openings in the walls that it was either dawn or dusk – the kind of liminal state where everything is coloured to a golden red by the sun, and yet the sun itself is not visible. There was no fear, no confusion, no sadness, nothing longed for – only a feeling of a returning to some primal home. I stepped out of the opening in the wall, and simply drifted along with a warm ocean breeze toward the ocean and the purple clouds above it, eventually vanishing there completely, into the mist above the sea. This is how I choose to see my father's death.

A few weeks after returning home I was fortunate enough to meet Savitri Puri who was still gleaming with post-initiatory bliss and power. Because of the eruption of the volcano in Iceland that had effectively shut down all air traffic in Europe, Savitri was on her way over land to Denmark, having arrived in Helsinki via a train from Moscow. She told me about the last, concluding days of the Mela and what had happened on the final major bathing-day on the 14th of April. By that day, vastly surpassing all expectations, approximately 40 million people had arrived at the Haridwar Kumbh Mela area between Jwalapur and Rishikesh. And on that day, 16 million pilgrims took a holy bath in the Ganga. Apparently some Baba had been late with his procession, and in haste had resorted to a shortcut or taken a wrong turn, and as a result his entourage had collided with another procession in progress. Because of this, a barrier had broken and seven people, including a child, had fallen and been trampelled to death. They called it "a karmic tragedy". After hearing of this, the head of the Juna Akhara had announced that the Naga Babas of the Juna Akhara would not take part in the marching and the grand procession, being the only Akhara not to participate. Shortly afterward, the great fair was declared over.

Looking back at the Kumbh Mela, I am aware that I experienced something that perhaps is disappearing in its current form, belonging to an age of the past. How the future Kumbh Melas will take shape is difficult to tell, but I doubt it will be similar to what I experienced much longer. Perhaps then, such Melas will be the source of tale and legend.

And how the Kumbh Mela affected the various participants, how the experience was churned into knowledge, and how the magic manifested itself, is yet another chapter in the ever-unfolding story.

In the end, a magic mirror was found and gazed into, revealing knowledge of the inner and outer worlds, of "self" and "other". And in the end, perhaps even in a more profound sense, the magic mirror broke. While breaking, it revealed an even deeper truth: the merging of "self" and "other", which are not opposites, but a unity reflective of each other.

To truly know something, one needs to be at a touching distance from the thing one desires to know. Insight and knowledge do not require beliefs or ideologies, as those things can indeed just make them even more shrouded. Insight and knowledge can be gleaned from written words, but profound knowledge requires participation in first-hand experience; it requires one to have sense-experience of the object of knowledge, beyond the realm of the mere intellect.

The knowledge I have acquired from delving into the traditional Indian esoteric tradition, I have learnt via personal experience; it has required participation and usage in order for it to become active. It is also nothing I could fully explain in written words, even if I did try. And such knowledge requires pilgrimage. To have knowledge of the source, one has to travel to the source, or be satisfied by the streams that flow from that source, eventually becoming more polluted, more impure, as they get further away from it. To truly know the story, one has to become the story.

THELEMA AND POLITICS

*A talk delivered at the "100 years with The Book of the Law
– Thelema beyond Crowley" Conference, London, April 10th 2004*

Carl Abrahamsson

There is one tricky thing, one dividing line among thelemites who've "accepted" *The Book of the Law*. Not only accepted it as in recognising its existence but as in actually accepted it to become *The* Holy Book of one's own life.

There are many appealing tenets in the book, attractive at a first glance or even a first thorough reading. We find passages of devotion without the need of sacrifice, encouragement of free love, encouragement to do what you want to do regardless of what other people say, etc. It seems like a pretty liberal and youthful appreciation of life as it ideally should be.

The dividing line I initially mentioned runs between those who welcome the message specifically of the third chapter and those who, for some reason, prefer to prefer the two first ones. I do not mean to generalise. I do not intend to become a "centre of pestilence" by indulging in my own interpretations in front of an audience who, I am sure, have their own interpretations of the book – as should be.

What I am going to do though, is allow myself to see if there's a clear political message in *The Book of the Law* and also, more as a matter of discussion and reflection than as distinct statements, if we as thelemites could or should strive to enter a political arena to secure the future existence of the philosophy we claim as ours.

For purposes of propaganda, Crowley developed a simpler version of the message of *Liber AL* in *Liber 77*, also known as *Liber OZ*. We all know it well, some even by heart. It's a declaration of rights that serves as a very good guide to one fairly clear-cut political interpretation. Or, simply, as a way of life.

However, we always interpret philosophical and religious ideas and ideals based on our own cultural background. In many ways we can never escape our cultural imprint, though we can do so slightly more than from the genetic one. A European will interpret the book differently than an Asian or an African.

There have been voices raised within the thelemic community, specifically in the US, that *Liber OZ* not only could but should be practised literally. "This is my farm and I'll defend it until my last breath". Honourable for sure, but the end result may just be that the farm is lost anyway to the foes and the last breath is actually drawn. To what end?

Don't misunderstand me: I do believe that man has the right to bear arms and defend himself and his property with it. The problem is that the proto-cowboy mentality serves no other purposes than mere selfish ones. The reaction against the State as a concept, as presented by, for instance, Jack Parsons, is infantile. A State is needed as long as there are more people than a specifically agrarian culture allows. And I for one don't think it's everyone's will to become a self-serving farmer. The genuine problem is not the concept of the State as such but the fact that the State we know is not based in high, enlightened ideals.

Total anarchy is not, not in my mind at least, compatible with the thelemic ideal. Far from it. However, I'm a spoilt brat coming from Scandinavia. We have minimal bordering on non-existent corruption, a public sector that actually assumes its responsibilities and also a total freedom to move about and initiate endeavours. To those who would raise the question "Oh yeah? What about your high taxes then?", I would answer, "So what?!"

But now I digressed into a polarised point of view bordering on an almost chauvinistic Scandinavian attitude. Let's just say there are many different ways of dealing with the structuring of a society. And this problematic area is essentially what politics should be all about.

Thelemic politics should obviously secure the rights of man according to *Liber OZ*. Meaning securing the rights to freedom of expression and of movement, of love and, simply, of life in general. Section five, "Man has the right to kill those who would thwart these rights", also includes two quotes from *AL*: "the slaves shall serve" (II:58) and "love is the law, love under will." (I:57). It is not really an incentive to actively kill, but rather to seriously value the freedom the law and its politics offers. There can be no freedom without the willingness to defend said freedom, that much is obvious.

The political manifestation of this view of the world would then, for instance, be severe or even capital punishment for active contraforce or misuse or even abuse of the tenets of *OZ* and *AL*. Freedom in itself should obviously be valued higher than letting those who mock or abuse it get away with it. This is certainly a very distinct difference from our liberal Western democracies.

The democratic nivellation of natural differences is decidedly not a part of thelemic politics. Crowley criticizes the notion of this kind of reason and intellectualism in many places when commenting on *AL*. I quote: "Reason is rubbish; race instinct is the true guide. Experience is the great Teacher; and each one of us possesses millions of years of experience, the very quintessence of it, stored automatically in our subconscious minds."[1]

I further quote: "There are no 'standards of Right'. Ethics is balderash. Each star must go on its orbit. To hell with 'moral principle'; there is no such thing; that is a herd delusion, and makes men cattle."[2]

That these specific interpretations of the book smell a trifle Nietzschean comes as no big surprise. "The slaves shall serve". We are accustomed, if I'm allowed to generalise, to interpret slaves as "Those who have not yet found their orbit, their true will, those who are thereby bound to serve the forces of duality". But that is purely a spiritual point of view. If there are actually no standards of right and the moral principles are actually

---

1. Comments for Chapter II, verse 27. *The Law is For all*, New Falcon Publications, Tempe, 1996
2. Ibid. verse 28

destined for hell, then perhaps we could be so bold as to interpret the quote more or less literally: The slaves shall indeed serve. This sounds like a structure where we have segregation based on initiative, force and capacity. "The Law is for all", for certain, but this is also, as clearly declared in row number one of *Liber OZ*, "the law of the strong, this is our law and the joy of the world."

We all know there are many quotes to further accentuate the spirit of *The Book of the Law*: "I am a god of War and Vengeance"[3], "this is the Law of the Battle of Conquest"[4], "Trample down the Heathen; be upon them, o warrior..."[5], "Money fear not, nor the laughter of the folk folly..."[6], "Mercy let be off: damn them who pity! Kill and torture; spare not; be upon them!"[7], "And ye shall be strong in war."[8], "From gold forge steel!"[9], "Them that seek to entrap thee, to overthrow thee, them attack without pity and quarter; & destroy them utterly. Swift as a trodden serpent turn and strike! Be thou yet deadlier than he!"[10], "Success is your proof; courage is your armour; go on, go on, in my strength; & ye shall turn not back for any!"[11]

Etc, etc... These were quotes from the third chapter specifically, but there are poignant ones from the first two chapters too. What we see here is a philosophy of honour and battle, of conquest and strife. This martial focus or resonance could ideally indicate a strong presence of integrated discipline and military life, not only for defense but apparently also for waging wars of attack.

There is a reason why people are shocked when hearing quotes like the just mentioned ones. It is not because they are "wrong" from a philosophical or emotional point of view. That kind of claim, again, is infantile, unintelligent. I think the shock comes from the fact that we experience a so called double commando, where one side of our mind says "This does not resonate at all with what I've been taught at school or at home!", and the other says, or rather feels, "This is an empowering energy that really makes me feel strong and enthusiastic..." Now, what should one go for? Which has a greater value? The intuitive or the imposed? The empowering or the diminishing? As always, ask yourself loudly: "Cui Bono?" Who gains?

Besides *Liber AL*, there's another interesting text in our political research: the constitution of OTO. The structure of OTO is meant, according to Crowley, to be a model for an ideal society and in it we find many hints and concrete measures. But still, how could these be politically translated to an environment outside of the safe and protected haven of a hierarchical fraternal Order?

One concrete mode of division, not only within OTO but in the ideal Thelemic Society, comes, not surprisingly, from *Liber AL*. In the first chapter, we learn that the word of the Law is THELEMA. "For there are therein Three Grades, the Hermit, and

---

3. *Liber AL*, Chapter III:3, *The Book of the Law*, Red Wheel/Weiser, York Beach, 2004
4. Ibid, III:9
5. Ibid, III:11
6. Ibid, III:17
7. Ibid, III:18
8. Ibid, III:28
9. Ibid, III:32
10. Ibid, III:42
11. Ibid, III:46

the Lover, and the Man of Earth. Do what thou wilt shall be the whole of the Law."[12]

Isn't this, in essence, the same kind of division used by, for instance, Georges Dumézil in trying to map the historical, real-political, development of societies and human culture under a specific Indo-European light? Dumézil used the categories "priests", "warriors" and "herder-cultivators" in describing what he had found in essentially all Indo-European historical structures.

The Hermit is the Priest-King, the leader, who leads from the point of view of high standards, genuinely permeated by ideals and religion. The Lover is the Warrior, the segment that secures and enforces the structure and order. After all, "Love is the law, love under will." The herder-cultivators are the Men of Earth, today perhaps a misdirected term as such. But we could possibly translate it with "the creative fundament" or "the base of the pyramid", "the brute manifesting force".

Has this worked in the past, in recorded history? To a greater or lesser extent, one could say that it has NOT worked for any longer periods of time. But this all has to do with the extent of the individual's capacity, of the specific culture's capacity, to understand an ideal and to adjust to the ideal. It says in the constitution of OTO: "With us Government is Service." Our present time, sad as it may seem, is not a great age of service or of ideals. It is an age of infantile regression, of complacency, of abusive States and of emotionally reactive anarchists.

I quote Crowley again: "The principle of popular election is a fatal folly; its results are visible in every so-called democracy. The elected man is always the mediocrity; he is the safe man, the sound man, the man who displeases the majority less than any other; and therefore never the genius, the man of progress and illumination."[13]

The ideal we have chosen to align ourselves with though, is Thelema. And having presented the above mentioned tripartite structure as the actual way of organising society, nothing should really remain but to stir up an immediate and overwhelming enthusiasm for this global instant illumination through Thelema... As they say in America: "A piece of cake, right?"

We see in Thelemic politics a form of enlightened rulership, where Self bows down to the greater good and self-sacrifice is what actually constitutes leadership and brings on the insights needed to lead people and an entire society. A Great Work indeed! That this would mean a tremendous "challenge" for our contemporary democratically elected politicians doesn't even need to be touched upon... Could it be that the contemporary political systems we know, ranging from democracry to totalitarianism, are all subject to corruption because there are no demands of renunciation, no high ideals?

Should political leaders even be paid at all? Wouldn't a strict, well-educated, enlightened academy of sorts, drilled in mental, physical and philosophical fitness, be a better suited structure of leadership than elected (so called) wolves in sheep's clothing all focussed on their own growth, greed and gratification? Isn't there an inherent point of corruption in all the systems we have grown accustomed to? Sooner or later there WILL be temptation to leave the lofty ideals of yesteryear in order to indulge in the pleasures of the private sphere.

---

12. Ibid, I:40
13. *The Equinox*, volume III, issue 10. Weiser/Redwheel, York Beach, 2000.

What we have at hand then would indicate a society structured according to hierarchical principles, but not as rigid as, for instance, the Indian hereditary caste system. Men of Earth should apparently be encouraged to move on, move on up in the enthusiastic energy of reaching towards an ideal. The same goes for the Lovers, to the very best of their abilities. It would be the responsibility of the society to offer the best possible arenas of self development and education. It would seem that the ideal Thelemic society, and hence its politics, would be a synthesis of many "-cracies": a theocratic aristocracy where the main essence is meritocracy, not based on dull and mechanical duties but rather based on individual prerequisites and an encouraged hunger to transcend personal doubts and truly progress... Perhaps the new term, the new doctrine should be "thelemacracy"?

One great difference between reality and ideal though, is that society is not the Order as such and probably never will be. All members of society have not sworn oaths to comply, and this would probably not be the case even if Thelema were to permeate all strata of society. There would still be criminals, opponents, dissent, resistance, as has always been the case in joint human endeavours. But perhaps one way of dealing with this would be to strive for an absolutely intolerant tolerance? Meaning, that if we have a given system that enables freedom to as great an extent as possible for as many serious and devoted people as possible, perhaps there's no reason to tolerate resistance at all, even if we respect that particular expression as one specific will, one specific "star".

You can see where I'm drifting... If there is any chance in the ideal world of securing the existence of a healthy state based on strength, courage, ideals and the encouragement of individual endeavour, then who could argue? The problem is of course that people today are not encouraged to strive for ideals at all – thelemic or other. The overall consensus seems to be to strive, if that's the adequate word, for total complacency. But let's indulge in fantasy for a brief moment... If there were a working structure based on thelemic principles and it were pure in spirit and unpolluted by petty human greed, then the idea or concept of anarchy, as embraced by some thelemic fractions today, would be but a vague memory. No need for juvenile reactive gung-ho, but just the solid, steady building of a brilliant future based on tolerance and human creativity, albeit with a fierce and martial edge.

To say that it would be a paradox to have a thelemic political party because there would be so many different wills involved is a simplification that serves no purpose. A thelemic party would simply make sure there are politically implying forces that secure thelemic rights according to *Liber OZ* and, in extension, *Liber AL*. There are enough guiding lights, hints and comments to make up for one more or less homogenous political direction. What I have touched upon here is merely the tip of the political iceberg.

But then again... Perhaps it is a mistake to interpret the book politically at all? Perhaps it is after all mainly a grimoire for personal spiritual development through the use of the generative force and that's that. It's all symbolic language describing the creative use of sex. But if that's the case, I don't think Crowley or any other interpreter would have gone to the lengths they actually have to more or less present Thelema as a tangible and practical philosophy that's supposed to permeate every sphere of human existence through a highly refined and superior, aristocratic individual – The Thelemite.

To say that Thelema should be exclusively handled by OTO or AA or other groups dealing with the philosophy and magic Crowley and his friends concocted is to tie Thelema's hands behind its own back. These groups were primarily designed for advancing individuals spiritually, to create and refine thelemites. If, however, Thelema should establish itself as the Law of Freedom it claims to be, further measures need to be taken and stronger muscles involved than those used in Temple. Stronger, that is, on the manifested level some would call the Malkuthian.

We all know we can change everything. We all know how potentially powerful magic can be. But, again, if this force is not rooted in an ideal, it is a blind force, a fool's force. Whats sets Thelema apart from many other magical presences today, is that it is first and foremost a philosophy, an ideal. That's actually our greatest advantage today, NOT the fact that Crowley was a great magical and mystical synthesizer.

If we want to share the philosophy of Thelema with the world, we need to rethink and structure those thoughts. If these first 100 years have constituted "Horus' babysteps", then there's no doubt in my mind that we're dealing with very powerful energies. I for one think that these energies could and should be put to more use than mere self help. Politics constitute one very significant arena in which to change the world. That is, really, truly change the world. Now, is that what we want or are we content to be comfortable in our own magical pipe dreams? I raise this question in a celebratory toast to 100 years of *Liber AL*, and to all of you, but my answer remains in silence as I drink.

Someone Is Messing with the Big Picture

A talk delivered at the Equinox-festival, London, June 14th, 2009

Carl Abrahamsson

One doesn't need to go to school to realize that everything around us and in us moves in cycles and regular intervals. Some reference points: breathing, the seasons of the solar year and the overall span of birth-life-death. No one ecapes these fundamental facts: everyone breathes in and out, everyone eventually dies and we are all exposed to the seasonal changes to a varying degree.

These basic but still extremely substantial reference points indicate that life as such consists of beginnings and endings, short or long, and that an ending is always followed by a new beginning, etc. The realization and integration of these fundamental facts both allowed and demanded of primordial man to develop a lifestyle not simply based on chance survival but rather a harmonius adaption to given natural conditions. An adaption to regular movements in synch with nature as such.

As long as nature and nature's cycles were revered and respected, Homo Sapiens was in constant development into an even stronger kind. The safety of belonging to a tribe, a society, a structured gathering of people allowed culture and learning to evolve into arts and philosophy and other manifestations that carried a more distinctly magico-religious respect for the totality, the whole, the big picture. Varying aspects of nature were given different divine names to help man ceremonially as well as actually to strive, defend, defeat, build and re-build.

In all of this, there is a wisdom that transcends religions and cultures: the micro-cosmic, human life should be in harmony with the macrocosmic, natural life force. Inherent in this harmony is the adaption to and, important, reverential respect for the movements and regularities of the whole.

As we now live in something that could easily be described as a garbage heap based on shortsigthed human hubris, it's interesting to note that the fragmentation and dis-turbing noise so predominant nowadays first of all attacked the quintessential cosmic dyad: the perception of time and space (including matter). Once these areas had been soiled by human "progress" (science, industry, etc), the fragmentation of the actual hu-man mind and language was (and still is) immanent.

From having observed changes of the seasons, changes of the days and changes of shorter spans of time, man could organise daily and yearly life accordingly. From solar clocks to mechanical clocks is a big step though. This step was made possible by general fine mechanical skills and aptitude dictated by a desire not only of signifying social status and class but also of greater minute control of others. The step from the pure mechanical perfection to measuring the swinging of atoms to be able to "tell" what time it is was parallel to other atomic developments of equally disastrous proportions. The brute, titanic apprehension and manifestation of "progress" turned time into a commodity mainly used for control purposes.

The never ending, almost perverse, desire of the empirical scientific mind to disintegrate, dissect, catalog and then fragment even more has led to truly horrifying results. While time in its arbitrary form (measured time) is based on the swinging of atoms, the manipulation of this process also releases energy for the ever increasing demand of electricity and also as a devastating weapon. Atomic energy has become a mythical beast that's kept in the silent as long as it's technically possible.

To what end? The progress that science and industry proudly claim are beneficial for the greater good, has, does and will cause harm of unprecendented proportions. The desire to dissect, by some called "scientific curiosity", hasn't really made human beings understand more about life as such at all. Science has become even more abstract and now delves into metaphysical territories – quantum physics, etc – in the hope of penetrating the "mysteries" further. Instead of looking to the whole, one dives ever deeper into minute particles. The main speculated and actual growth areas in science are: atomic energy (now that only a few decades with a supply of oil remain), genetic manipulation (called food production efficiency), effects of overeating (diabetes) and nivellation of the emotionally unbalanced human minds (happy pills). Could anyone really not find the times we're living in dystopic?

The meddling with the minute always carries with it a dear price. I'm certain many scientists agree but am also certain that grants and salaries from "benevolent" pharmaceutical corporations are likely to shut most scientists up. To bring home the bacon, whether it be genetically manipulated or not, seems to be the greatest concern for the majority of people in the Western sphere.

The growth industry of messing about with the human DNA identity code and the totally arbitrary concept of time are future measures for increased control of the individual human being. In fact, all scientific measurements in use today are just arbitrary ways of looking at things, a mere language of classification – the overview needed for extensive control of every aspect. Are the adherents of the metric system really happier than the non-adherents?

Even more bleak are the things going on in the human mind, the last barrier, the last resort of resistance and formulated opposition. Fragmentation seems to be the big thing even here, which is certainly not surprising. Just as most scientific progress uses the justification of medical developments for the greater good, the concept of communication has in just the most recent decade been rammed down our throats like never before. Under the banner of "new", "improved", "faster" and, again not surprisingly, "smaller", we have devices that allow us to communicate in better and more efficient ways. But is this really so? And do people really have more things to communicate now than in 1980? Or even 1990?

Cell phones (an ironically apt name!) and their air borne radiation will very likely be the origin of "epidemics" of new diseases and disorders of the brains. Without enough testing, the small beasts were launched and marketed as "must haves" and now it's almost impossible to get by without them. Wherever you move in urban areas, there are disturbing signals and beeps and people talking about seemingly non-vital things in loud, affected voices. Human noise.

I admit to having both a cell phone and having become an e-mail addict. When the phone is shut off I get weary and when I haven't checked mail in a while I get nervous. For me, that's a terrifying development, as the need to communicate via technology has absolutely nothing to do with whatever it is I at some points wish to communicate. The speed and inexpensiveness – the availability for everyone – is not unlike the cliché we were presented with at school: the dealers and pushers offering the first fixes for free in order to make (and certainly break) new customers.

Once the need is fixed, one has to come up with new and even more unnecessary things – always smaller, faster and cheaper. At the time of this writing, cell phones are now game consoles, telephones, data banks and (video) cameras. Under the banner of total efficiency, entertainment, simplification and technological inspiration, the modern human being is being duped by a concept that could easily be termed "more is less".

Why not also focus on language for a while too? The phenomenon of text messaging through cell phones could become problematic. Instead of language developing into colourful and poetic majesty to facilitate making communications and interactions crystal clear, phonetic abbreviations and sign language take hold. It's a regression to the infantile or, I dare say, moronic. And once the degeneration takes hold of the young, things will be very hard to manoeuvre back to intelligent levels. Slang and generational twists, as well as the effects of migration, have developed and kept language non-static and alive. I seriously doubt that the technological lingo that's already a permeating part of everyday life will have the same effect.

To build life and individuality, a direction based on the Will of the person in question, takes time. It takes a lot of time, emotional and intellectual energy, weighing possible choices carefully against each other and many other things. That's a process that should never cease in the intelligent, open-minded person. The current situation seems to be doing absolutely everything to hamper and hinder that process though. Not only on the macrocosmic level (pollution, noise, manipulated foods, "entertainment", instilling paranoia, etc) but also on the inner, microcosmic level (communications-, work- and technology-related stress). The result is already disastrous. No wonder the ordinary human being of the West feels a (dictated) need of Prozac and other emotional levellers!

One hugely ironic aspect is science's claims of benevolence in the name of medical progress. So much harm has been done in the name of progress that an entirely new growth industry is the "alternative": Alternative health, alternative diet, alternative treatments... Of course, there is nothing inherently wrong in seeking out new ways in the pursuit of happiness and health, but it seems that most alternative options are mere reactive movements. That then turn into similar profit-driven industries once a client segment frustrated with the given (or even a previous alternative) structure has been located and tapped into.

The general obsession with speed is revealing. Speed seems to be the big issue... But what's the hurry? Production lines must move faster, as must sales. The fetish for communicational devices, such as access to the Internet, makes clear that increased speed is of the essence, a goal in itself. I'm only 43 years old, but I feel considerably older when I think back at the time only some ten years ago when most of us communicated in writing via letters and packages – a joy both to receive and send off. I can't recall there being less efficiency around then... On the contrary, I'd say. And my post office box certainly didn't contain 50 or more advertisements a day for pornography, debt consolation, happy pills or potency enhancers. Did anyone say "Symptomatic"?

The generations brought up on TV, computer- and video games, the Internet, cell phones etc seem to be genuinely lost in a maze of technological worship and digital kicks. The attention span needed for proper learning isn't there anymore, something that in itself carries frightening options for their offspring. I'm sure the providers will keep on providing even faster, cheaper, smaller and more moronic gadgets to keep the level of stress up and thinking down in coming generations too... Imagine what kind of children these tech junkies will breed... Down the line, the gene pool will undoubtedly be electric (and wireless)!

Fragmentation is also a threat on a higher level, for instance in regard to life itself. The greatest threats to man used to be so called macroparasitical events such as wars, natural disasters etc. Now, the greatest threats lie beneath the surface, obviously a recoil from excessive lifestyles, environmental abuse and far too high expectations in the name of scientific progress. Microparasitical deaths caused by cellular or metabolic revolts, viruses and other agents of destruction are sweeping the continents, instilling even more fear and even more paranoia. (Wouldn't it be ironic if the current swine-flu originates from genetically engineered steroid monster-pigs?) The unseen, non-tangible, enemies, whether they be viruses or terrorists, are at the mere conceptual level extremely dangerous. They shift the focus from the strong, the balanced, the harmonious and the holistically flowing outlook to a disruption based on fear, negative anticipation and hypocondria. Literally a killer combination!

Needless to say, the fact that death itself has been turned taboo is another crucial fragmentation factor. When death was an integral part of life, and the newly made shells were on display and integrated into the ritual processes of mourning, there was considerably more to relate to on very tangible levels. The apprehension of death as something other than something that's happening at distanced hospitals or elderly people's homes seems to be so terrifying to most people, so ridden with anxiety and fear, it's no wonder they're unable to truly perceive the full generative cycle of life.

Births are relegated to hospitals, as though the mothers were ill. Life is just a series of stress- and anxiety-dripping sets of imposed choices. And death is by vested interests kept in mind as just an abstract and horrifying way out, so that the painfully present void can be safely and comfortably filled with meaningless but costly distractions such as entertainment and medication.

The natural apprehension of justice, as defined in various aspects of Lex Talionis, has been fragmented into "the justice system". Lawmakers are no longer driven by vocation but by the fact that "it's a great job opportunity in a growth industry". The accusers and defenders, the actual interpreters of the various arbitrarily imposed paragraphs dictating justice, are all bred with litigational provisions as centrally fixed carrots. The focus is on the perpetual, minute fragmentation of the interpretation of what's presented as law, not in a clear-sighted simple justice process. Why make things simple when you're paid by the hour?

What then about the economy, the golden calf so especially sacred nowadays? Where previously the focus rested on careful planning and making budgets, to eventually aquire what was really needed, now the fragmentation is complete: By making money invisible and abstract, by granting extensive credits as well as entire systems of "bonus points", and by carefully engineering consumer environments that consciously break down mental clarity and rational defense systems, the celebration of the artificial needs turns into veritable "shopping fests" – a vicious vortex of degrading behaviour. The human being not only is, but is also encouraged to be, a mindless puppet in a spastic Danse Macabre, nowadays on the brink of turning into a full fledged Zombie Rave.

However, we are complex organisms, existing far beyond the rational simplifications of causality. We are omniversal creatures existing far beyond strategies, scheming, soliciting, science, economy, greed, frustration, compensatory oversaturation and politics. They are all results of misdirection and not necessarily an inherent modus operandi at all.

From the smallest genome to the loftiest vision, man's totality is an unsurpassed vessel of potential. One of the reasons being the ability to transcend immediate communication. In every use of communication by proxy lies individual will ingrained. Love charms and jewellery, cave paintings and sympathetic tribal hopes, Luther's German translation of the Bible as an act of monocultural defiance, fairytales as moral education, Picasso's "Guernica" as an act of war against war itself. This desire to formulate emotion and will through generalised expressions, along with the capacity for suicide, may be the most fundamentally human trait. If we, for some reason, are incapable of expressing ourselves, we actively seek out resonance with those who are capable. Their works arouse the spirit of Gemeinschaft, of being a part of the human community rather than a single solitaire grain of sand in a scorchingly hot desert.

One could argue then, that art is a necessary barometer, revealing the present condition in a more precise way than polls, politics, statistics and other kinds of societal soothsaying. What a remarkable phenomenon! One that acts as revealer, evoker, soother, seed-sower, teacher and inspirer, all at the same time.

And just as we communicate with each other in lots of more ways than with words or speech, so does art. Not only is the partaker a differentiating factor, the subjective arbiter of resonance, value, worth, meaning, etc. The artwork in itself changes too, susceptible to the passing of time, surroundings, random givens and environmental erosions. The charming patina of a sculpture or a painting's surface, the fading of a photograph or even the crashed so called hard disk containing so called digital images in so called high resolution, all confront us with inevitable vanitas: everything must eventually go. Existential worth is something we have to create ourselves.

So, what remains? What still affects us? I think it's fair to say that the greater the abstraction from the primordial human condition, the shorter the lifespan of the artwork. And I think that applies to human culture in general too, if I may continue to be slightly dystopic.

The cerebral, intellectual and conceptual art simply reflects a cerebral, intellectual and conceptual era. As such, perhaps enjoyable as tidbits of history in the making, commodified and marketable signs of one way of life or, if we're lucky, of reactions against that way of life.

What about the other side of the coin then? Holistic, natural – I mean that as stemming from nature or longing to nature – communicative art. Art that desires to tell a story of the basic human condition, of cyclical progress and not of steroid-infused linear and neurotic aggression. Art that is rooted in a fascination for life rather than a dissatisfaction or disdain. Simply, art that challenges our life, but respectfully so, and allows a general sentiment that binds together, weaves and affirms rather than evaporates through profitable prodigal putrefaction. I'm sure it's out there somewhere. I hope that you will create that art. I think we need a Prometheus or a Lucifer more than market-trained cynics all too willing to parade as infantile jesters.

Art that sets out to please is merely illustration or design. One could of course argue that, since the creation of art has always been mainly a magical act, ritual creation by sympatehtic proxy, it's not fair to judge someone whose will it is to make money. That said, I think we can agree that it takes more than that to affect substantial change. There needs to be a depth and a height stemming from the creative mind of the artist. Something that originates in pent-up emotions and/or a ritual charging, a primitive release as well as a programmatic act.

As we live in a fragmented world, no wonder the expressions are often fragmented. But that doesn't necessarily imply that they're less releasing or less charging. The scale and level of force can never be greater than the sum of the layers of the artist's mind.

Eliade has written eloquently about the creative phenomenon itself, for instance in "The myth of the eternal return":

"What is important is that man has felt the need to reproduce the cosmogony in his constructions, whatever be their nature; that this reproduction made him contemporary with the mythical moment of the beginning of the world and that he felt the need of returning to that moment, as often as possible, in order to regenerate himself."

Definitions of what art's function is are always very tricky and Zeitgeistishly tainted. And, of course, it may be that there is no function at all. One of the most intelligent attempts I've come across is by the art historian Bernard Berenson. He claimed that it had to do with conveying a feeling of life-enhancement.

> Let me say that by "life-enhancement" I mean the ideated identification
> of ourselves with a person, the ideated participation in an action, the ideated plunging into a state of being, or state of mind, that makes one feel
> more hopefully, more zestfully alive; living more intense, more radiant a
> life not only physically but morally and spiritually as well; reaching out
> to the topmost peak of our capacities, contended with no satisfaction
> lower than the highest.

I know that beauty is a vague, subjective and quite often deceptive term. But still it's one so closely associated with art. Very few complain that the visible remains of ancient cultures are ugly. Quite on the contrary. Could it be that the magnificently beautiful is exactly that which remains, either by divine providence or mere darwinian logic? If so, what does that most likely say about our culture?

First, we greedily destroy our own habitat. Then, to add insult to injury, we initiate an intense uglification process previously unmatched. A rhetorical question: Is it really more expensive to build a house that contains a tangible spirit of life-affirming emotions and harmony than one containing fear-inducing and darkly oppressive delusions of grandeur?

A fragmented mind needs stronger stimuli to respond emotionally. Logically, a fragmented culture needs more extreme expressions to be able to arouse those emotions. The equation could be: Basic stimulus minus the poetic and beautiful qualities. Again, what remains? The simplified, the rapid, the clinical, the explicit, the overt. No more reclining nudes but plenty of genital probing.

The mystery unveiled is a mystery no more. And perhaps that's where we are right now and right here, in this very room? The interest in spiritual things and the re-emergence of mystical and mythical perspectives is surely a common reaction to our retinal and rationalistic hangover?

I can't really see one single interest group responsible for all of this haywire devastation and disruption. It's basically a multifaceted combo effect stemming from the substitution of the holy appreciation of nature with simple infantile greed and it's accompanying stooge – mad and morally morose monotheism. Dualistically soaked reproach could be in order but isn't really. We don't need antidotes as much as prodotes. I hope that your art will be that prodote.

Ultimately though, it's any individual's fault who eagerly swallows without conscientiously chewing first. I offer no solutions or suggested paths but am well content with a couple of insights: To die with at least some dignity means having lived life according to one's own rules, whichever these may be. To develop these rules, one needs to constantly make substantial choices based on cherishing the long term perspective, on continuity and on intelligent interpretations of life as a whole. We need a heterogenic and ethnopluralistic environment to survive. One world made up of distinct parts. I'm still naive enough to believe that art could help balance this mess we're in.

As has been mentioned so many times before, the future belongs to those with the courage and wit to fight for the manifestation of their own vision. For those with their visions set high and far, fragmentational hindrances are just those small things one evaluates and discards on the stimulating road onwards. That said, I wish you all a pleasant journey.

AN ART OF HIGH INTENT?
(WE GET THE CULTURE WE DESERVE)

Carl Abrahamsson

Who remembers or cares about a happy society? After hundreds of years
or so, all they think about is what a society has left. I suppose it's possible
that a society may arise which is so perfect that it will be remembered
for the perfection of its equality. But that hasn't arisen yet, and so far one
remembers a society for what it has created.

– Francis Bacon, *The Brutality of Fact*

The relationship between the hen and the egg is probably one of the most frequent
parables (and false dichotomies) in Western thought. As both empiric and speculative
science has taught us that it doesn't necessarily have to be as simple as "what came first"
(but rather who or what mutated into what or whom), we are left with a vacuum. If
one thing is neither this nor that, nor chronologically fixed, what certainties exist? The
answer, most likely, is "none at all".

Everything around us is malleable, plastic (in the traditional sense), moveable and
adjustable within limits. The butterfly effect is a terrifying yet valid concept for any
mind but those consciously blocking and fighting free thought. What matters is human
initiative, procreative or reactive.

As we live, work, breed and strive to try to mesh with a more or less defined ideal,
we see that change can indeed occur in accordance with will if we are determined and
intelligent. For most people, this means adjustment to given parameters, ie a career
intelligence, a rational and strategic sense of direction.

In spheres more defined by irrational processes and uncontrolled expressions – the
spheres of art – we can see not only a causal process determined more by the "sender"
than those of the "given" parameters in the example above. A sense of possible freedom
in a way. We can also see the effects of that causality affecting the "receiver" in ways that
aren't necessarily visible immediately. Art is an arena of subtle perceptions and messages
regardless of whether sender and receiver are conscious of it.

Looking at art history's earliest phases, this proto-perspective of magical manipulation is a well-known one: non verbal expression as will, with ample examples like painted
cave walls, terrifying totems, tribal dances, embodiments of ancient spirits, altered states
of mind and talismanic weapons. The shaman acted as an ultra-creative guide, and not
always only by proxy. A sacred artist endowed with the trust of an entire community.

Has this magical perspective changed?

It certainly has. One could argue that the means as such, art, has evolved to many different disciplines and categories but that the concept of will has remained, although less and less related to an inner, deeper, essential will. The budding artist may feel an urge or desire to express him- or herself. That will, however, may be more clearly defined in the desired results (ie a career) rather than in the general process of embodying potential. But the causal process is still there and the field of non-rational, emotionally-laden agents, material or not, are there too.

Art's dilemma is not so much the equation of which came first, form or content, but rather a more subtle balancing act between them. A conceptualised form can contain an idea that won't show itself until the matrix as such is there. A strong idea can give an entire universe form.

Let's toy with making the relationship even grander. What actually comes first: The creative idea or concept, or the changes in society and culture around us? The changes in society and culture around us or the ideas and concepts our interpretations engender as reactions?

The history of human ideas contains thoughts from many minds involved in radical and experimental juggling of concepts. Not seldom combined with fields of primitive science or philosophy. One cornerstone has been the classic esoteric dictum: "As above, so below". What goes on inside, goes on outside, etc, sooner or later and always vice versa. This has been the basis of "primitive", sympathetic magic since the dawn of mankind. Given this natural law (if we may be so bold), one could easily apply a change in the small and then watch it manifest in the big.

The challenge of the artist is to go from a mere formalised and formalising "expressionalist" to a seed-sowing magician. This is not easy, as a prerequisite must be that the artist in question knows what he or she wants. Very few people do. Most artists stay on the level of comfortable and controllable form, as it's a safe environment to build a career in and on.

But shouldn't the term "artist" really be more readily associated with "creation", as it once was? The decorative aspects have indeed gone hand in hand with development of bourgeois and post-bourgeois (technological) culture. Instead of digging deep and reaching high, the contemporary artist has been encouraged and taught to remain shallow – and for this he or she is grandly paid.

Again, has our magical perspective changed?

In many ways it certainly has not. The truly creative artist still carries magical status and is exempt from many of the tribe's rules and regulations. Quite often these protagonists help mutation on a much larger scale, or even actively cause the mutation in question. One prerequisite for mutation seems to be radical provocation, benevolent or not, of the immediate environment.

This kind of provocation still occurs but the inherent danger today is that there is simply so much art and things that claim to be art and so many artists on top of this that the mere volume in itself acts as a very noisy silencer. The availability of art through new media, as with music "online" for instance, actually makes it all less threatening. The process of "democratisation" through availability has in fact created nothing more than a digital cesspool of complacency.

Of course, human development is cyclical and what was once radical is now reactionary. Nowhere is this so apparent and clear as in art history. An example: Modernism, followed by cubism, dada, surrealism, et al. Supposed non- or even anti-intellectuals eventually became wrapped up in their own intellectualism. The anti-stance, the found object, the subjectivism of the child are all fair and fine. However, open-minded and detached playfulness as a dogmatic attitude (as it has since become) really leads nowhere and is more likely a sign of immaturity or, perhaps, even retardation.

There are more serious and useable aspects of this point of view though, that also connote the child's attitude: the sacralisation of an apparently simple object, of using fantasy as a solvent for transformation. The process is the same for the child as for the artist-magician. The main difference here is the awareness of intent.

High intent means charging an object or a willed phase with meaning and potential. It means setting content first in a culture or context that generally only accepts form. Form can be alluring, seductive and, not seldom, satisfying. But it should never be allowed in the front seat of the art-as-magic-vehicle. I think it is a sign of illness or at least severe imbalance that our culture is so narrowmindedly immersed in form, design, fashion, as well as in homogenous, rigid and colourless architecture. At the same time our culture fears and resists values and ideas that are not commodified, neatly packaged, two-dimensional, lightly ironic and always for sale.

A schematic view of what the power of art really is could be suitable at this point. Although these are extremely simplified statements, I think they illustrate how the main points of view stand in relation to each other. A classic dialectical model will do:

1. The power of art comes from the maker.

The egocentric point of view containing all kinds of expressions, even mere decorative artworks. Carl Jung has a fine description of this "classic" artist type in his "The Spirit in Man, Art and Literature": "In the artist, the strongest force in his make-up, that is, his creativeness, will seize and all but monopolize this energy, leaving so little over that nothing of value can come of it. The creative impulse can drain him of his humanity to such a degree that the personal ego can exist only on a primitive or inferior level and is driven to develop all sorts of defects – ruthlessness, selfishness ("autoeroticism"), vanity and other infantile traits."

2. The power of art comes from the partaker.

This point of view has become the foundation of the art market and the supposed need of galleries, trade, sales, experts, opinions, institutions, hausses and hypes, etc. Here, a quote from Tom Wolfe's brilliant *The Painted Word* could be illuminating: "(1) The art world is a small town; (2) part of the small town, le monde, always looks to the other, bohemia, for the new wave and is primed to believe in it; (3) bohemia is made up of cénacles, schools, coteries, circles, cliques. Consequently, should one cénacle come to dominate bohemia, its views might very well dominate the entire small town." Wolfe is here talking about the hype of abstract expressionism in the 1950s and the arbitrary creation of new markets, but not much has changed since then.

3. The power of art comes from the interactive energy between maker and partaker, where the artwork *en soi* is but a mere solvent, a grid, a matrix. This point of view constitutes the essence of the magical aspects of art – a psychological, emotional alteration by proxy.

As language as we know it becomes more and more outdated and decomposed due to technologically induced simplifications, new means of communication are needed. In non-rational signs and emotional matrices, new meanings occur. Artists consciously aware of this have enormously powerful possibilities of creating new kinds of talismans for new times and new desires.

Magic in itself, with its rich history intertwined with human development and its relationship to progress in general, has been a never ending source of inspiration for artists. Thematically touching and visually paraphrasing is, for example, the work of Swedish painter Fredrik Söderberg (born 1972). Using powerful images of mandalas, psychedelic patterns and religious symbols from various cultures as stepping stones, he creates an enticing universe of his own. In a way, Söderberg uses magical "sampling" from visual esoteric history and thereby places himself within that living tradition.

Magic as a way of life is another form of art (not quite the same as artform), where the objects, structures, remains, tracks, residues, etc, more act as documentations of a life lived according to will, intent and principle. Of course, these documentations can have imbued intent as well. Another Swedish example is Gustaf Broms (born 1966), who in basically all of his works has used himself as the main agent and principle, leaving a trail of highly interesting works of art around him as talismanic, inspirational "results".

There's a multitude of examples of contemporary artists who are more or less involved in magical art, consciuosly or not. By using primordial agents (blood, seed, saliva) or primordial states of mind (rituals as performances or vice versa, mystery plays, ecstasy-inducing concerts, experiences in nature, etc), as well as thematically integrating "magical" subjects and objects, contemporary spiritual art diligently fights the complacency of the two-dimensional, commodified, decorative arts. Not because there should be a winner or a loser (another false dichotomy) but because that dynamic has always been there in human culture.

Some examples of living magical artists that spring to (my) mind are Genesis Breyer P-Orridge (British, born 1950), Hermann Nitsch (Austrian, born 1938) and Peter Beard (American, born 1938). All use multidisciplinary, psychedelic, "palimpsestic" techniques, often integrating blood and other bodily "expressions", exorcising or encouraging mementoes from their own lives and sometimes setting the ultra-subjective and personal in larger, generalised, almost mythical settings.

Breyer P-Orridge is consciously aware of the magical perspective and uses it to his own benefit. Nitsch, I suspect, has become aware of the power he wields as he has gone along from pure 1960s provocative experimentation to the latter day grandiose ritualistic "aktionen" in his castle courtyard outside of Vienna. Peter Beard, as a psychedelic wizard and shamanic bon-vivant, creates multidimensional beauty that has the power of creating even more beauty as he reuses images and reworks works – a really worthwhile recycling feat in these times of flat impressions and massproduced tapestry art.

Of course, there are many others. However, come to think of it, it really is besides the point whether the magical artist has the status he or she once had in more tribal circumstances. In many ways, this is a colourful gray area that perhaps should remain impenetrable for the sake of potency, at least for the time being. Francis Bacon again: "… It's impossible to talk about chance when you don't know what it is." Whether or not they are seen or even known, the magical artists will always change things around and within us. It's their job and there's nothing we can do about it. For that, and for the related cultural mutations, we should be very grateful.

"I ALWAYS OVERCOME DISAPPOINTMENTS."

A Conversation with Kenneth Anger

Carl Abrahamsson

In the autumn of 2008, I was invited to host an evening with filmmaker, writer and magician Kenneth Anger at Statens Museum for Kunst in Copenhagen, Denmark. In between showings of his key films, we talked, together with other invited Anger fans (Danish director Nicolai Winding Refn, Swedish artist Carl Michael von Hausswolff and Danish journalist Lars Movin). This was followed by a performance by Anger's musical project together with Brian Butler, *Kenneth Anger's Technicolor Skull*. A memorable evening, to say the least.

On the following day, I sat in conversation with Anger at the Danish Film School in front of a small but devoted crowd. Basically, most of Anger's films were shown and we talked in between the screening segments. What follows here is a transcript of that conversation at the film school.

I would here also like to recommend the Fenris Wolf website, which contains a substantial piece on Kenneth Anger and his work, composed of interviews I did with him in 1989 and 2006: www.fenriswolf.se

[Screening of *Fireworks* (1947) and *Puce Moment* (1949)]

Fireworks *was a film that more or less immediately had a big impact. Could you tell us about where it was first shown and what the response was?*

It was first shown at the Coronet Theatre in Los Angeles, which was a small cinema. It was also a theatre where my friend Charles Laughton did plays like *Life of Galileo* by Brecht. That was actually playing when *Fireworks* was first screened at night. The first showing was at midnight. Among the audience was Robert Florey, who was working in Hollywood at that time. He was a very interesting French director who made films like *The Murders in the Rue Morgue*. James Whale was also there, the director of *Frankenstein* and *The Bride of Frankenstein*. I became friends with James Whale and I remianed a friend of his. Since it was a midnight screening, we didn't have any problems with it, like censorship. Then it went on to be shown in San Francisco at the Museum of Modern Art there. Then it gradually spread over the world, I guess.

Tennessee Williams was at the screening in San Francisco, as was Dr. Alfred Kinsey.

Yes, Tennessee Williams also became a friend. Dr. Kinsey came to my screening and he bought a copy of the film for the Kinsey Institute of Sex Research in Bloomington, Indiana. He wrote two famous books that came out in the 50s, *Sexual behavior in the human male*, and also a female version. So the first sale of a copy of my film was to Dr. Kinsey, on 16 mm. That was the available film format that you could get a good result with, 35 mm being beyond my grasp at that time. Later on, I made one film on 35 mm, when I lived in France: *Rabbit's Moon*. I never worked on Super 8. Now, I'm working on digital. I've covered all the bases.

What brought you to France originally was actually a screening of Fireworks *at a festival in Biarritz.*

Yes, the "Festival du film maudit", the festival of damned or cursed films. These were films that had problems with censorship. Jean Cocteau was in the jury and he gave a prize for "poetic film" to *Fireworks*. That encouraged me to come to France and meet Cocteau. I also met Jean Genet and Colette, who was still with us at the time. I wanted to meet André Gide but he died while I was on the boat.

You liked France very much and you were well received by, among others, Henri Langlois, the director of the French Cinématheque.

Yes. One thing that's important to mention about French culture is that they think there's only one language in the world, and that's French. Most of them refuse to speak anything but French. I knew this ahead of time, so I majored in French at the Beverly Hills High School. I arrived in France speaking the language, at least in a rudimentary way. I was fortunate to meet a lot of people, artists like Jean Genet. He saw my film and liked it. I think I inspired him to go on to make *Un chant d'amour*, which was a silent film.

I'm an independent film artist. I've never made a lot of money making my movies but I've managed to get grants and help. With one of the films we'll show here I had a wealthy patron, which is an old tradition in art. Many of the most famous paintings in history could be made because of patrons. Quite often, the paintings were commissioned by the Church. The Church was a big patron of art. Painters could put in their own eroticism if they were careful. There's a lot of nude flesh in historical painting. There was always an undercurrent of eroticism there.

I needed to make more money. I knew a lot about Hollywood history. So I wrote two books, *Hollywood Babylon 1* and *Hollywood Babylon 2*. That became a source of income for me.

We also just saw Puce Moment, *which is a nostalgic view of the silent era. Your grandmother worked in the studios, right?*

Yes, she was a costume mistress for United Artists during the silent period. It's someone who looks after the costumes. She had the idea to make duplicates. In films like *The*

Eagle, Rudolph Valentino had to jump on and off horses and something would always get torn and then you'd have a duplicate ready. For *The Wizard of Oz*, Judy Garland had six gowns ready, just in case something happened.

There were other independent fimmakers emerging at the same time as you. You worked closely together with people like Curtis Harrington and Maya Deren in terms of distribution.

Not with Maya Deren, as she was on the East Coast. But Curtis and I had made little films and we had no way to get them shown, so we founded a company called Creative Film Associates. It was Curtis and me and a few people from San Francisco, like James Broughton. Later on, there was a company called Cinema 16, based in New York, that took over. It was a matter of shipping 16 mm reels back and forth. They're not nearly as cumbersome as 35 mm reels, which weigh a ton. Now everything is simplified with digital.

[Screening of *Rabbit's Moon* (1950) and *Eaux d'artifice* (1953)]

For *Rabbit's Moon*, I was given the negative by the Cinématheque Française. It was a leftover from some documentary project. It was the same stock that Cocteau used to make *Orphée*. I had a professional cameraman who was the son of the silent filmmaker Tourjansky. The actors came from the mime school in Paris. I made the sets and the costumes myself. It was filmed in a studio which I could use during the month of August. France officially closes up then and everyone goes away on vacation. I took advantage of that. I had one month to do everything.

These films were made during your first European stay. You got a great job as Langlois' assistant. How did you work together?

I arrived in France in the spring of 1950. The films that I'd done then were shown at the Cinématheque. That's where I met Jean Cocteau and Genet. Henri Langlois was the director of the Cinématheque and he proposed that I work for him. I was then his personal assistant for 12 years. They had a lot of American films from the silent period in their collection, but under different titles. I helped identify films with Douglas Fairbanks, Mary Pickford and so forth, matching them with the original American titles. I had a background in Hollywood history so I knew all of that. I was able to help them with the collection.

They also gave me the opportunity to edit a film by Eisenstein, *Que Viva Mexico!*, which was an unfinished project. It was actually a tragic story. The producer, Upton Sinclair, was a socialist but yet involved in capitalism. When he saw how much the film was costing in 1930, in Mexico, he pulled the plug on it. The film was never finished. An elaborate sequence of it, on a train with hundreds of extras, was never filmed. I've read the treatment, a very poetic treatment by Eisenstein. This very important piece of the film was never filmed at all. What remained was so wonderful but it had never been put in the proper order. Working from Eisenstein's treatment and a segment called

Death Day in Mexico, and a feature cut of it called *Thunder over Mexico*, which has the beautiful images but not in the right order, I put all of these things together chronologically according to Eisenstein's script. This was shown at the Antibes film festival. It was a project where people were furious that I was allowed to do it. But I don't mind that. It was a very interesting project.

You had also seen Thunder over Mexico *as a boy.*

Yes, it was one of the first films I saw when I was a very young boy. I was taken by my grandmother, who thought it was a travelogue, a documentary about Mexico. She loved Mexico and had been there many times. She was rather shocked to see very sadistic things in it, like the peasants who are revolting against the oppressive government. It's historically correct but cruel. They buried them up to their necks and then the horses ran across the field until the skulls were crushed. Those are images that stuck with me all my life, seeing them as a very young boy. But there were also many beautiful images.

You also attempted to film a ballet by Cocteau?

I was given permission by him to film his ballet *The Young Man and Death*. I filmed it on 16 mm outdoors, because I didn't have any lights. It's a very sadomasochistic story. She is a beautiful model who rejects the man amourously, and she even puts out a cigarette on his chest. He hangs himself, which is a wonderful illusion because he actually puts his arm around the pillar and he's strong enough to hold himself while hanging from the rope. Nurejev danced in the ballet later on. I transposed everything to a garden. The film was basically a study for a 35 mm film in Technicolor that I wanted to make. But even with a letter of recommendation from Cocteau I couldn't raise the money. It was a disappointment but I always overcome disappointments. I don't let them cast me into despair.

How did you come up with the idea to cast a midget in Eaux d'artifice?

By using a midget I completely altered the scale of the film. I was inspired by the etchings of Pirenesi, who was a master etcher. He did etchings of the ruins of Rome and also the garden of Tivoli. Classic famous etchings. He always made things seem bigger by putting tiny people in there. I wanted to find a small person and do what he did. The ruins of the Colosseum are majestic enough but if you double the scale by putting a tiny person there... The midget was a friend of Fellini's. Fellini knew all the freaks and strange people. He said to me that he knew a midget and that she'd be glad to do it. That's how that happened.

[Screening of *Inauguration of the Pleasure Dome* (1954)]

After your initial phase in France, you had returned to the US for a while. Originally, the idea for this film came from a costume party.

Yes. Halloween is the only time in America when we have a festival where people dress up in costumes. The carnival only exists in New Orleans, the Mardi Gras. A party was given in Malibu by one of the actresses, Renate Druks. The theme announced, several months ahead of time, "Come as your madness". Everyone was not to tell anyone else what their personal madness was. I guess it was a sign of the egotism of this crowd, which consisted of bohemian artists mostly, that almost everyone came as a god or a goddess from antiquity. Once I saw the costumes, which were beautifully made, I said that I'd make a film of it, that I'd turn the party into a film. The most famous person in the film was of course Anaïs Nin, who was a well known avant garde writer and poet. Samson de Brier played the main part, or actually several parts. He had appeared in a silent film, *Salome*, in which he plays the slave that committs suicide. I filmed my film over several weekends with the people coming in their costumes. The background is Samson de Brier's house, which was stuffed with his souvenirs.

In this film, you reached a new level of complexity, not only mythologically but also when it came to the technical aspects. For instance, you used a lot of superimpositions. Did you have evrything well arranged and planned before the editing began or was it more like an intuitive process?

I guess you could call it intuitive. I knew that I wanted to do double- and triple-printing. The excuse is that the people in this ceremony take a drink which is probably psychedelic in some way, or hallucinatory, or magic mushrooms, or LSD. I didn't want to make it specific. The patterns of illusions become thicker and more complex. I experimented with LSD years ago and you do get that effect. But I've never tried to make a film while on LSD because it's impossible to focus. You have various layers of depth. I've always been completely straight when I've made my films.

The references to spirituality, magic and even Crowley are more obvious and manifest than ever before in this film. How was Crowley regarded when you found out about him, so to speak, in the mid-1940s?

I was fortunate that Crowley had a magical son in California, in Jack Parsons, who was a famous scientist at Jet Propulsion Labs. He invented the fuel that took the Apollo-rocket to the moon. He was killed in an explosion unfortunately, but his widow, Cameron Parsons, plays the Scarlet Woman in my film. The red hair really was the colour of her hair at that time.

Crowley's work has strongly permeated your own work. How did that develop in the beginning? For instance, to what extent were Crowley's books available at that time in California?

Jack and Cameron Parsons had a collection of those books, most of them first editions and signed by Crowley. I had those books available to me. I found him a fascinating person. He was born in 1875 and he died in 1947, so I never met the man. But I knew various friends of his. I feel I know him, even though we never met face to face.

Why did you want to integrate this kind of symbolism in your films?

Crowley's religion is *Thelema*, which means Will in Greek. The will has to control what you do, but also love. These things were influences but I've always been more of an intuitive artist. I use symbols like others would use colours.

When you shot this film over several weekends, did you give people very specific directions or were they allowed to be free and play around?

It was totally controlled, like a ballet. The movements were controlled.

[Screening of *Scorpio Rising* (1963)]

What was it that was so fascinating for you about these Coney Island youngsters?

They were making their own motorcycles, customizing them. They were like folk artists working on machines. I found that a very fascinating subject. There are some motorcycle gangs that have a bad reputation because they've been involved in drug dealing and murders and things. But this wasn't a group like that. These were mostly Italian-Americans who made their money working in the fish market and then they put all of their money into their bikes. They all had girlfriends but their first girlfriend was their bike. The bike was almost more important than the girlfriend. She just sat on the back. It's a strange kind of innocent fetishism.

The film became famous for its creative use of contemporary pop music.

I think I was the first to use music like that. Now, it's become quite common. In order to show it in public I had to clear the rights, in 1964. At that time I did it through a music lawyer in New York. It doubled the price of the film. The film cost $8000. The music rights cost another $8000. Over the years, I've made back what I spent on it.

How important was it for you, when working with the soundtrack, to have a specific song for a specific segment?

The lyrics are like an ironic commentary on the images. I was the first to use *Blue Velvet*, years before David Lynch. The song is about a girl who wore blue velvet. I used it deliberately on a leather jacket that had blue highlights, and blue jeans. It's an ironic comment on that kind of self narcissism.

It became a very successful independent film. But you also had some problems with it.

When it was first shown in Los Angeles at the Cinema Theatre, which usually showed unusual films, it was denounced by the American Nazi Party, of all things. They denounced it to the vice squad in Los Angeles. If someone makes a complaint, they have to act on it. They came to the theatre and seized the print of the film from the projection booth and arrested the manager of the theatre. Today it seems totally grotesque but at that time they thought they had the right to do that. The case went to the California Supreme Court, where it was declared OK, because it has "redeeming social values". This is a term that would later be used in other legal cases with films and censorship. It has redeeming qualities. It's not technically obscene.

One more thing about Scorpio Rising... *There had been a "stellium" in 1962, during which we shifted from the Age of Pisces to that of Aquarius. Was your film in any way a commentary to that?*

I enjoy the game of astrology. I don't take it terribly seriously. Maybe some of it is true. I use it in a kind of fantastic way. Scorpio is the sign of the zodiac that rules machinery and the sex organs. I'm an Aquarius, like James Dean, Franklin Roosevelt and, unfortunately, Ronald Reagan. I'm an Aquarius with Scorpio rising. An artist has a right to play around with these ideas. I don't have to justify it, whether it has any scientific value. It has a poetic value.

[Screening of *Kustom Kar Kommandos* (1965), *Invocation of my
Demon Brother* (1969) and *Rabbit's Moon* (1971 version)]

Kustom Kar Kommandos *is also about a fetishistic inclination in some young men, with their "Dream Buggies". Have you since then ever come across any similar kind of obsession with machinery?*

Customizing cars is a very Californian thing, making these beautifully lacquered and chromed fantasy machines. If you know Freud... In the interior of the car in the film, the seats are shaped like vulvas. The guy designed everything himself. I couldn't tell him that his seats looked like something from the human anatomy. He made the interior of the car chrome, like mirrored sides. He could see himself reflected on all sides in this mobile box of fantasy. I chose that car because I found it particularly beautiful.

In the mid-60s you lived in San Francisco and started an ambitious project called Lucifer Rising, *with musician Bobby Beausoleil in the leading role. That time, things didn't turn out so well. Could you tell us about the original film you had in mind?*

I had this project of making a film about the fallen angel, Lucifer. It's a metaphor, probably some kind of alchemical metaphor originally, about spirit falling into matter. In this case, I was seeking an actor who could embody this spirit. Bobby Beausoleil was the guitarist ina group called Love, which was an acid rock group. He was 19, very beautiful. I asked him if he wanted to play this part in my film. It didn't work out because there was too much personality involved. When you're casting amateurs in films, the problem is how to hold on to them if you can't have them sign a contract or offer them money. These things become psychological problems. When you pick someone who is a rather difficult personality, it becomes even more of a problem. Basically, we couldn't come to an agreement. I didn't drive myself, but I had a van and he decided to just take it and drive off to Southern California from San Francisco, where we were sharing a Victorian house called "The Russian Embassy". The van broke down in the San Fernando Valley in front of a place called Spahn Ranch. That's where the Manson Family was staying. The girls came out and suggested Bobby move in with them. That's how he became involved with the Manson Family. He ended up killing someone and he's now serving a life term in prison. I absolutely had nothing to do with it but it was an odd way for a kind of Devil figure to end up in real life trouble.

Invocation of my Demon Brother *was made with remnants of that original material.*

Bobby had gone into drug dealing behind my back. I didn't know this, but it was my house. He was a minor and I was an adult. If anyone had gotten into trouble, it would have been me. I found marijuana in the house and said no. When Bobby left after the quarrel we had, he took the van and all the film he could find, just out of spite. But I had scraps left in the cutting room bin. I took that material to London when I went back and did a rough assembly of it. I showed it to Mick Jagger and he said he'd do the soundtrack, improvising on the Moog synthesizer. He gave me that improvisation. I don't think he does that too often.

Your depression even made you place and ad in The Village Voice, stating "Kenneth Anger, Filmmaker 1947-1967".

I said I was finished and that I didn't want to work in film anymore. Everything was going wrong. But I changed my mind after I returned to Europe. I got encouragement from people like the Rolling Stones, Marianne Faithful, Donald Cammell and others.

Rabbit's Moon *in this version from 1971 has a new soundtrack. Going back and retouching and re-editing is something quite consistent in your work.*

Well, *Rabbit's Moon* had a checkered story. I considered it a lost film. It was shot ion 35 mm and stored at the Cinématheque Française. They lost it. It disappeared and was lost for 20 years. The label had come off the can. There are thousands of films there. But I finally got it back after a long time.

[Screening of Lucifer Rising (1981), Mouse Heaven (2004)
and The Man We Want to Hang (2002)]

Crowley took up painting when he was around 40. Particularly when he moved to Sicily. He did some quite interesting work there. It reminds me of the Fauves. Crowley had a very direct way with colour. My film is a tribute to his painting.

Kenneth Anger, Los Angeles 2006. Photo: Carl Abrahamsson

Lucifer Rising *has a subtitle which is "A Love Vision". This was to balance Scorpio, which is so martial. Do you think that the film achieved that balance?*

I hope so. It's a bit like Yin and Yang, the night and the day.

Lucifer Rising *is an elaborate production, with acting and interesting environments. Donald Cammell, who plays Osiris, was well versed in Crowleyan mythology. What was it like with the others – Huggins, Faithful and others? Did they feel that you had to explain things to them?*

I never explain anthing. They have to accept me and what I say. The one person that I began using was Mick Jagger's brother Chris. He went with me to Egypt. He's briefly seen in front of the Sphinx. He kept asking me to explain what he was supposed to do and I said, "Just do it!" I sent him home. He got a free trip back and forth.

In what way does this 1981 version differ from the one you had originally envisioned and shot with Beausoleil?

They're related in subject but with a completely different cast. I was happy to work with people like Marianne Faithful, because she just did what I wanted. She didn't argue with me.

We're going to see Ich will *now. Could you tell us something about that?*

I've always been fascinated by the Nazi period. I worked in the film archive in France for so many years and I was always looking for images from that period. *Ich will* reflects the Hitler Jugend movement, which was the equivalent of the boy scouts. In fact, the Nazis took the idea from the boy scouts in England, which was something invented at the turn of the 20th century by Baden-Powell. There too, the idea was to create a bond with the youth, to prepare them to fight for the empire. People forget that that was the original motivation of the boy scouts, to prepare them for the military. The transition to the military is not that difficult when you've been in the boy scouts.

My brother was an Eagle Scout: a high rank. I absolutely refused to go into it. I was the rebel, totally against joining. My father was a scout master but I said no already at a quite young age. And that's why Kenneth Anger is Kenneth Anger.

I carefully chose a statement or quote from William Shakespeare, from *The Tempest*, as part of the introduction to the film: "Beware of the words that come out of the mouth that transforms men into beasts." That's my only statement about the film. I absolutely cut out all the speeches and I've also cut out all the martial music and substituted it with Anton Bruckner's ninth symphony. That was his last, written when he was dying. He was a brilliant symphonist and, incidentally, Adolf Hitler's favourite symphonist at that time. The other great symphonist, Mahler, was completely rejected for racial reasons.

[Screening of *Ich will* (2008)]

Contributors

Fredrik Söderberg is an artist based in Stockholm. He has had several major exhibitions in Sweden and abroad, and has illustrated a number of books and record covers. www.fredriksoderberg.org

Peter H. Gilmore is an artist, author and composer of music. His most recent book is *The Satanic Scriptures*, published by Scapegoat Publishing in 2007. Gilmore is also High Priest of the Church of Satan. www.churchofsatan.com

Peter Grey is the co-founder of Scarlet Imprint and the author of the acclaimed devotional work for Babalon, *The Red Goddess*. He is an exponent of the antinomian and libertarian strand of the Western magical tradition. His work comes out of physical praxis. His path is one of ordeal, ecstasy, and Love. www.scarletimprint.com

John Duncan is a visual artist who works in the fields of music and sound, film and video, performance and installations. www.johnduncan.org

Ramsey Dukes is a discarnate entity first made manifest around 1970 when it occupied the mind of a Cambridge mathematics scholar with a long standing interest in magic, alchemy, Aleister Crowley and the occult. In return it has channeled a number of books that helped define late 20th century magick - notably *SSOTBME-An Essay on Magic* and *Thundersqueak*, both seminal texts of Chaos magick, and *Words Made Flesh*, proposing the information model of magical reality. In 1977 he performed the Abramelim operation, and he has since worked with a number of ritual groups, including the OTO and IOT, as well as founding the Arcanorium College's Department of Experimental Metaphysics. His most recent book, *How to See Fairies*, is based upon his Arcanorium College course Experimental Clairvoyance for the Non-Psychic.

Timothy O'Neill (b. 1951): Director of the Athanor Institute: Teaching the Esoteric Traditions of West and East through Art and Sacred Geometry since 1986; over 50 articles published in art, esoteric and science books and magazines. www.athanorinstitute.org/index.html Tim O'Neill is also the writer of cheap Lovecraftian horror and sci-fi: www.edenblack.com/Index.html

Thomas Karlsson, Ph.D., is the founder of Dragon Rouge. He teaches Western Esotericism at Stockholm University, Sweden, and is the author of *Qabalah, Qliphoth and Goetic Magic, Adulruna and the Gothic Cabala, Astrala resor ut ur kroppen,* and *Uthark – Nightside of the Runes,* as well as numerous articles in the fields of Esotericism, published in more than ten languages. He holds workshops and seminars on a regular basis all over the world. www.dragonrouge.net

DAVID BETH, born to German parents in Africa, is a gnostic occultist and esoteric philosopher. He has been the main force in the revival of Esoteric Voudon in the past decade and is the founder of La Société Voudon Gnostique. The S.V.G. is a selective group of initiates and artists dedicated to manifesting the more powerful, inner revelations and transmissions of the Gods of Esoteric Voudon, as well as to push evolution and research of Voudon Gnosis and sorcery freely beyond all frontiers of orthodoxy. David is also the head of the Fraternitas Borealis and Ecclesia Gnostica Aeterna. University educated in Germany and the USA, he has travelled and lived all over the world from Nigeria to Hamburg, from Los Angeles to London, studying occult systems and gnosis for the past two decades. David lives and works between Europe and Brazil. His latest book, the revised and extended edition of *Voudon Gnosis*, is available from Fulgur Ltd; he can be contacted via the S.V.G. website at www.voudongnosis.org

PAYAM NABARZ is author of *The Mysteries of Mithras: The Pagan Belief That Shaped the Christian World* (Inner Traditions, 2005), *The Persian Mar Nameh: The Zoroastrian Book of the Snake Omens & Calendar* (Twin Serpents, 2006), and *Divine Comedy of Neophyte Corax and Goddess Morrigan* (Web of Wyrd Press, 2008). He is also editor of *Mithras Reader, An academic and religious journal of Greek, Roman, and Persian Studies:* Volume 1(2006), Volume 2 (2008), Volume 3 (2010). His latest books are *Stellar Magic: a Practical Guide to Rites of the Moon, Planets, Stars and Constellations* (Avalonia, 2009) and *Seething Cauldron: Essays on Zoroastrianism, Sufism, Freemasonry, Wicca, Druidry, and Thelema* (Web of Wyrd Press, 2010). www.stellarmagic.co.uk

HIRAM CORSO is an occult writer/researcher whose writings appear in *Another Mirror at the End of the Road* (an occult zine published by Malachi Gammon). Hiram and Malachi are currently producing a series of occult documentaries encompassing the western esoteric magical tradition as an extension of the articles in *Another Mirror*. For more information: friends_of_gammon_house@yahoo.com or write to Gammon House Publishing, PO Box 6128, Wheeling WV 26003, USA.

JEAN-PIERRE TURMEL created Sordide Sentimental in 1978. A project inspired by the *Do It* book by Jerry Rubin and within the movement DIY (Do It Yourself). It combines Music, Image and Text (MIT) in the same object, the forerunner of Multimedia, and heir to the concept "Gesamkunstwerk" of German Romanticism. Consciously from the beginning he refuses to be associated with the movement of the record labels so called "independents " (because it's an illusion, because to varying degrees everything is under control and that nothing can exist outside the system). He claims on contrary of being a "small trademark" and wanting to stay so (in this he is a pioneer of the movement "small is beautiful" and theories of decay). Finally he bases his approach on the refusal of standardization (especially for the size) and the use of collage as a production process having similar mechanisms to dreams. His first Multimedia project was published in

1979 with Throbbing Gristle, *We hate you (little girls)*. www.sordide-sentimental.com

KENDELL GEERS is an artist, performance artist, musician and film-maker. Geers was born in May 1968. In Venice in 1993, Geers rose to international notoriety when he urinated in Marcel Duchamp's Fountain. He has exhibited globally and participated in numerous exhibitions including Documenta, the Carnegie International, Havana Biennia, Istanbul Biennial, Kwang Ju Biennial, Taipei Biennial, Lyon Biennial as well as presented solo exhibitions in the CCA Cincinnati, S.M.A.K. Gent, Baltic Centre for Contemporary Art, Aspen Art Museum and the CAC in Lyon.

Z'EV is a text/sound artist, sound sculptor, poet and mystic. He is perhaps best known for his performances of acoustic phenomena produced through catacoustic (reflected sound-based) percussion. In 1978 he met Haitian Hougun Rico Joves and was initiated into Vou-Dun drumming. Employed as a researcher for the Society for the Preservation of Occult Consciousness he received initiations into the Western Ceremonial Tradition. In 1979 he began his studies with Rabbi J. Winston, founder of the Jewish Meditation Society. His work is influenced by the Middle Eastern mystical system best known as Kabbalah (although not of the Jewish variety), as well as cultures and esoteric systems world-wide. After studying at CalArts with Concrete poet Emmett Williams he concentrated on visual and sound poetries, and was included in the "Second Generation" show at the Museum of Conceptual Art in San Francisco in 1975. In 1976, inspired by the Punk Movement, he re-entered the musical sphere and was one of the progenitors of the so-called 'industrial' movement in the late 70's. Between the years 1978-1984 he, along with Neil Megson, was fairly responsible for delivering the 'tribal' impulse and esthetic into the Western cultural milieu. In 1992 his first book, *Rhythmajik – Practical uses of Number, Rhythm and Sound* was published by Temple Press UK. With some few exceptions he was retired from artistic endeavors between 1994 and 2003. In 2001 Tzadik Records released his work: *The Sapphire Nature*, five translations of the primal Qabalistic text known as the *Sefer Yetzirah*. While performing primarily as a soloist, since 2003 he has been concentrating on cooperative and collaborative composition and performance. He currently spends as much time as possible in Peckham, England in the company of Conceptual Artist Barbara Stevni, the mother of what is now called Socially Engaged Art.

ROBERT N. TAYLOR (Frater Robert) is half of the seminal musical Neo-Folk band duo Changes. His poetry may be found at: www.theredsalon.com A gallery of his art is at: www.axismundi.tk His writing and art has appeared in: *The Exit Collection, Forty-Five Dangerous minds; Art that Kills; The book Esoterra; Morbid Curiosity Cures the Blues; Another Mirror;* and other alternative and underground magazines. A new book, *Pathway To The Gods*, which collects his heathen art and writing will be released in 2011 by Wolf-Tyr publications. Contact him at: wulfing1@yahoo.com

PHILIP H. FARBER is the author of *Meta-Magick: The Book of Atem – Achieving New States of Consciousness Through NLP, Neuroscience and Ritual* (Weiser Books, 2008), *The*

Great Purple Hoo-Ha: A Comedy of Perception (Mandrake, 2010) the forthcoming *Brain Magick: Exercises in Meta-Magick and Invocation* (Llewellyn Worldwide, 2011), and other books. He is a Consulting Hypnotist, a Hypnosis Instructor, a Master Practitioner and Licensed Trainer of Neuro-Linguistic Programming (NLP), and an author of many articles about magick, hypnosis, consciousness, meditation and popular culture. Mr. Farber has been booked to present lectures, workshops and seminars at conferences throughout the United States and UK (including the National Guild of Hypnotists conference, the International Conference on Shamanism, the Equinox Festival, the Starwood Festival, and many more). His own seminars have filled venues in New York, Los Angeles, Seattle, London, Amsterdam, and many other locations. www.meta-magick.com

THOMAS BEY WILLIAM BAILEY is a psycho-acoustic sound artist and writer on the arts, esoteric phenomena, and technology. Working across multiple media, he aims to construct a body of work that interrogates notions of utopia, anthropocentrism, and "the extreme," while refusing to reject any unpopular cultural manifestation as invalid until its more nuanced aspects have been brought to light. He is the author of *Micro Bionic: Radical Electronic Music And Sound Art In The 21st Century* and has recently completed a second volume, *Unofficial Release: Self-Released And Handmade Audio In Post-Industrial Society*. He has also worked as an educator in Central Europe and Japan, as a radio show host and more besides. In 2011, he will act as 'researcher in residence' at the Sound Archive Of Experimental Music And Sound Art in Murcia, Spain, where he plans to coordinate an exhaustive project dealing with synesthesia's influence on the arts. www.tbwb.net

AKI CEDERBERG is a filmmaker, musician and writer from Helsinki, Finland. Coming from a line of seamen, priests and doctors, his disposition and many of his interests and passions can be derived from these ancestral streaks. Relating to his engagement with various esoteric traditions and realms of knowledge and culture, of which he has sought first-hand experience, as well as his interest in sites of mythological or historical significance both ancient and modern, he has travelled extensively, in Europe, India, Nepal, Russia and America. He has been part of Halo Manash, with whom he has completed numerous released albums and films (the most recent being *Taiwaskivi* on the DVD *Back to Human Nature* by Njutafilms), several exhibitions and tours. He is part of the band Maa, with whom he has recently released an album, *Tuhkankantajat* (www.animaarctica.fi/maa). In the fields of esoterica and various forms of culture, he has written for several publications, as well as appeared as a speaker on many occasions. He has a Bachelor of Culture and Arts (directing and scriptwriting) and currently works in film production.

CARL ABRAHAMSSON is the editor and publisher of *The Fenris Wolf*. He likes to write, take an occasional photograph and at times converse with the audio structure spirits. He also likes vintage pens and mechanical cameras. That's about it. www.trapart.net, www.carlabrahamsson.com, www.patreon.com/vanessa23carl

Editorial Notes

Hermann Hesse's *The Execution (Hinrichtung)*, comes from the collection *Am Weg* (Konstanz/Baden: Reuß & Itta, 1916). Translated by Michael Moynihan.

Peter Gilmore's *Every Man and Woman Is a Star...* is an excerpt from his book *The Satanic Scriptures* (Scapegoat Publishing, 2007)

Payam Nabrz' *Liber Astrum* is an edited excerpt from his book *Stellar Magic* (Avalonia, 2009)

Hiram Corso's *Unveiling the Mysteries of the Process Church* has previously been published in *Another Mirror at the End of the Road* (2009). Timothy Wyllie is the author of *Love Sex Fear Death – The Inside Story of the Process Church of the Final Judgment*, published in 2009 by Feral House. His transcendental artworks can also be viewed on his website: www.timothywyllie.com

Jean-Pierre Turmel's *The Pantheon of Genesis Breyer P-Orridge* is a translation of the outroduction of the French edition (Camion Noir, 2010) of *Thee Psychick Bible*. Translation by Sylvie Walder.

Ernst Jünger's *LSD Again* is a translation of a text from *Annäherungen. Drogen und Rausch*. Translation by Annabel Lee.
© 1970, 1978 Klett-Cotta/J.G. Cotta'sche Buchhandlung Nachfolger, GmbH, Stuttgart.

Carl Abrahamsson's *An Art of High Intent?* has previously been published in the French publication *BC Magazine*, 2009, edited by Kendell Geers.

This book and its cover
was designed by the Editor,
and set in 10 pt.
Garamond.

"Divinity consists in use and practise, not in speculation."
(Luther)

"Knowledge is essential to conquest; only according to our ignorance are we helpless.
Thought creates character. Character can dominate conditions.
Will creates circumstances and environment."
(Annie Besant)

"Godlike is just as the name implies – like a god. Anyone who has learned to take his life into his own hands, by guiding his actions according to his own independent judgement, developing and exercising all his rightful and natural powers, and accepting full responsibility – as well as full credit – for the outcome of all his affairs has eliminated any need for a "god" or "supreme being". If he has accepted all the responsibilities commonly requiring assistance from a divine source, then he has become godlike and should be given due recognition."
(Anton LaVey)

"The religions of the world are the ejaculations of a few imaginative men."
(Emerson)

The Fenris Wolf 10 (2020)

Carl Abrahamsson – *Editor's Introduction*, Carl Abrahamsson – *Onwards to the Source!*, Ludwig Klages – *On the Essence of Ecstasy*, David Beth – *Katabasis and Erotognosis*, Henrik Dahl – *An Introduction to Eroto-Psychedelic Art*, Peter Sjöstedt-H – *Antichrist Psychonaut: Nietzsche's Psychoactive Drugs*, Carl Abrahamsson – *Lux Per Nox – The Fenris Wolf As Libidinal Liberator*, Jesse Bransford & Max Razdow – *Revisiting the Veil of Dreams*, Christopher Webster – *Beyond the North Wind*, Kendell Geers – *A Long Boundless Systematized...*, Kadmus – *Seeking the Three-Headed Saint*, Billie Steigerwald – *The Chthonic Seed: Reflections of an Ancient Death Gnosis*, Fred Andersson – *The Gospel According to the Tomb Man*, Zaheer Gulamhusein – *Sunflower*, Charlotte Rodgers – *The Riderless Horse...*, Craig Slee – *The Occult Nature of Cripkult*, Damien Patrick Williams – *Daoism, Buddhism and Machine Consciousness*, Philip H. Farber – *Thoughts on the Creation of Memetic Entities*, Thomas Bey William Bailey – *Memetic Magick*, Mitch Horowitz – *Is Your Mind a Technology for Utopia?*, Ramsey Dukes – *I'm Gonna Blow Your Mind*, Carl Abrahamsson – *Grasping Reality with Gary Lachman*, Anders Lundgren – *Mike Mignola and the Lovecraft Circle*, Peggy Nadramia – *So It Was Written*, Peggy Nadramia – *Addendum to So It Was Written*, Nina Antonia – *Maya*, Jack Stevenson – *Häxan/Witchcraft Through the Ages*, Andrea Kundry – *The Demonic Cultural Legacy of Antonin Artaud*, Joan Pope – *The Birth of Ideas*, Genesis Breyer P-Orridge – *Idiosyncratic Use Ov Language...*, Vanessa Sinclair – *Try To Altar Everything*, Claire-Madeline Corso – *Cutting Up a New Conversation*

The Fenris Wolf 9 (2017)

Vanessa Sinclair & Carl Abrahamsson – *Editors' Introduction: Looking back at the crossroads*, Katelan Foisy – *Invocation: Homage to the spirits of the land/London*, Sharron Kraus – *Art as Alchemy*, Demetrius Lacroix – *The Seven Layers of the Vodou Soul*, Graham Duff – *Sublime Fragments: The Art of John Balance*, Ken Henson – *The American Occult Revival In My Work*, Gary Lachman – *Was Freud Afraid of the Occult?*, Peter Grey – *Fly the Light*, Val Denham – *Proclaim Present Time Over*, Katelan Foisy & Vanessa Sinclair – *The Cut In Creation*, Claire-Madeline Culkin – *Beds, Bodies and Other Books of Common Prayer – A Reading of the, Photography of Nan Goldin*, Steven Reisner – *On the Dance of the Occult and Unconscious in Freud*, Katy Bohinc – *The 12th House: Art and the Unconscious*, Olga Cox Cameron – *When Shall We 3 Meet Again? Psychoanalysis, Art and the Occult: A Clandestine Convergence*, Ingo Lambrecht – *Wairua: Following shamanic contours in psychoanalytic therapy at a Māori Mental Health Service in New Zealand*, Elliott Edge – *An Occult Reading of PAO! Imagining in the Dark with Our*

Vestigial Shamanism in a Shade, Shadow, Wide, Charlotte Rodgers – *Stripped to the Core: Animistic Art Action and Magickal Revelation*, Alkistis Dimech – *Dynamics of the Occulted Body*, Fred Yee – *Cut-Up As Egregore, Oracle and Flirtation Device*, Robert Ansell – *Androgyny, Biology and Latent Memory in the Work of Austin Osman Spare*, Ray O Neill – *Double, Double, Toil and Trouble: Psychoanalysis Burn and Surrealism Bubble*, Derek M Elmore – *Dreams and the Neither-Neither*, Julio Mendes Rodrigo – *Rebis, the Double Being*, Eve Watson – *Bowie's Non-Human Effect: Alien/Alienation in The Man Who Fell to Earth (1976) and The Hunger (1983)*, Carl Abrahamsson – *Formulating the Desired: Some similarities between ritual magic and the psychoanalytic process*

THE FENRIS WOLF 8 (2016)

Carl Abrahamsson – *Editor's Introduction*, Vanessa Sinclair – *Polymorphous Perversity and Pandrogeny*, Charles Stansfield Jones (Frater Achad) – *Alchymia*, Tim O'Neill: *Black Lodge/White Lodge*, Nina Antonia – *Bosie & The Beast*, Aki Cederberg – *Festivals of Spring*, Michael Moynihan – *Friedrich Hielscher's Vision of the Real Powers*, Friedrich Hielscher – *The Real Powers*, Orryelle Defenestrate Bascule – *Ear Horn: Shamanic Perspectives and Multi-Sensory Inversion*, Zbigniew Lagos – *The Figure of the Polish Magician: Czesław Czynski (1858-1932)*, Gary Lachman – *Rejected Knowledge: A Look At Our Other Way of Knowing*, Carl Abrahamsson – *Intuition as a State of Grace*, Bishop T Omphalos – *The Golden Thread: Soteriological Aspects of the Gnostic Catholicism in E.G.C.*, Kendell Geers – *iMagus*, Johan Nilsson – *Defending Paper Gods: Aleister Crowley and the Reception of Daoism in Early 20th Century Esotericism*, Gordan Djurdjevic – *The Birth of the New Aeon: Magick and Mysticism of Thelema from the Perspective of Postmodern A/Theology*, Tim O'Neill – *The Derleth Error*, Antti P Balk – *Greek Mysteries*, Carl Abrahamsson – *The Economy of Magic*, Stephen Sennitt – *The Book of the Sentient Night: 23 Nails*, Henrik Dahl – *We Ate the Acid: A Note on Psychedelic Imagery*, Jason Louv – *Robert Anton Wilson's Cosmic Trigger and the Psychedelic Interstellar Future we need*, Carey Hodges & Chad Hensley – *New Orleans Voodoo: An Oddity Unto Itself*, Alexander Nym – *Kabbalah references in contemporary culture*, Zaheer Gulamhusein – *Standing in Line*, Carl Abrahamsson – *As the Wolf Lies Down to Rest*, Vanessa Sinclair & Ingo Lambrecht – *Ritual and Psychoanalytical Spaces as Transitional, featuring Sangoma Trance States*, Hagen von Julien – *Listening to the Voice of Silence: A Contemporary Perspective on the Fraternities Saturni*, Erik Davis – *Infectious Hoax: Robert Anton Wilson reads H.P. Lovecraft*, N – *II. Land*, Cadmus – *Neo-Chthonia*, Kadmus – *A Fragment of Heart: A contribution to the Mega-Golem*, Stojan Nikolic – *The One True Church of the Dark Age of Scientism*, Miguel Marques – *The Labors of Seeing: A Journey Through the Works of Peter Whitehead*, Renata Wieczorek – *The Conception of Number According to Aleister Crowley*, Orryelle Defenestrate Bascule – *Fragments of Fact*, Derek Seagrief – *Conscious ExIt*, Kasper Opstrup – *By This, That: A spin on Lea Porsager's Spin*, and Genesis Breyer P-Orridge – *Greyhounds of the future.*

The Fenris Wolf 7 (2014)

Carl Abrahamsson – *Editor's Introduction*, Sara George & Carl Abrahamsson – *Fernand Khnopff, Symbolist*, Sasha Chaitow – *Making the Invisible Visible*, Vanessa Sinclair – *Psychoanalysis and Dada*, Kendell Geers – *Tu Marcellus Eris*, Stephen Sennitt – *Fallen Worlds, Without Shadows*, Antony Hequet – *Slam Poetry: The Warrior Poet*, Antony Hequet – *Slam Poetry: The Rebel Poet*, Genesis Breyer P-Orridge – *Alien Lightning Meat Machine*, Genesis Breyer P-Orridge – *This Is A Nice Planet*, Patrick Lundborg – *Psychedelic Philosophy*, Henrik Dahl – *Visionary Design*, Philip Farber – *Higher Magick*, Kendell Geers – *Painting My Will*, Carl Abrahamsson – *The Imaginative Libido*, Angela Edwards – *The Sacred Whore*, Vera Nikolich – *The Women of the Aeon*, Jason Louv – *Wilhelm Reich*, Kasper Opstrup – *To Make It Happen*, Peter Grey – *A Manifesto of Apocalyptic Witchcraft*, Timothy O'Neill – *The Gospel of Cosmic Terror*, Stephen Sennitt – *Sentient Absence*, Carl Abrahamsson – *Anton LaVey, Magical Innovator*, Alexander Nym – *Magicians: Evolutionary Agents or Regressive Twats?*, Antti P Balk – *Thelema*, Kjetil Fjell – *The Vindication of Thelema*, Derek Seagrief – *Exploring Past Lives*, Sandy Robertson – *The Fictional Aleister Crowley*, Adam Rostoker – *Whence Came the Stranger?*, Emory Cranston – *A Preface to the Scented Garden*, Manon Hedenborg-White – *Erotic Submission to the Divine*, Carl Abrahamsson – *What Remains for the Future?*, Frater Achad – *Living In the Sunlight*, Genesis Breyer P-Orridge – *Magick Squares and Future Beats*

The Fenris Wolf 6 (2013)

Carl Abrahamsson – *Editor's Introduction*, Frater Achad – *A Litany of Ra*, Kendell Geers – *Tripping over Darwin's Hangover*, Vera Nikolich – *Eastern Connections*, Carl Abrahamsson – *Babalon*, Freya Aswynn – *On the Influence of Odin*, Marita – *Runic Magic through the Odinic Dialectic*, Aki Cederberg – *Afterword: The River of Story*, Shri Gurudev Mahendranath – *The Londinium Temple Strain*, Gary Dickinson – *An Orient Pearl*, Derek Seagrief – *Aleister Crowley's Birth & Death Horoscopes*, Tim O'Neill – *Shades of Void*, Nema – *Magickal Healing*, Nema – *A Greater Feast*, Philip Farber – *Sacred Smoke*, Robert Taylor – *Death & the Psychedelic Experience*, Michael Horowitz – *LSD: the Antidote to Everything*, Alexander Nym – *Transcendence as an Operative Category...*, Carl Abrahamsson – *Approaching the Approaching*, Renata Wieczorek – *The Secret Book of the Tatra Mountains*, Sasha Chaitow – *Legends of the Fall Retold*, Sara George & Carl Abrahamsson – *Sulamith Wülfing*, Robert C Morgan – *Hans Bellmer*, Genesis Breyer P-Orridge – *Tagged for Life*, Carl Abrahamsson – *Go Forth and Let Your Brain-halves Procreate*, Anders Lundgren – *Satanic Cinema is Alive and Well*, Anton LaVey – *Appendices*

The Fenris Wolf 5 (2012)

Carl Abrahamsson – *Editor's Introduction*, Jason Louv – *The Freedom of Imagination Act*, Patrick Lundborg – *Such Stuff as Dreams are Made of*, Gary Lachman – *Secret Societies and the Modern World*, Tim O'Neill – *The War of the Owl and the Pelican*, Dianus del

Bosco Sacro – *The Great Rite*, Philip H Farber – *Entities in the Brain*, Aki Cederberg – *At the Well of Initiation*, Renata, Wieczorek – *The Magical Life of Derek Jarman*, Genesis Breyer P-Orridge – *A Dark Room of Desire*, Genesis Breyer P-Orridge – *Kreeme Horne*, Ezra Pound – *Translator's Postscript*, Stephen Ellis – *Poems for The Fenris Wolf*, Hiram Corso – *Mel Lyman*, Mel Lyman – *Plea for Courage*, Gary Dickinson – *The Daughter of Astrology*, Robert Podgurski – *Sigils and Extra Dimensionality*, Frater Nigris – *Liber Al As-if*, Peter Grey – *The Abbey Must be Built*, Vera Mladenovska Nikolich – *A Different Perspective of the Undead*, Kevin Slaughter – *The Great Satan*, Lionel Snell – *The Art of Evil*, Phenex Apollonius – *The Quintessence of Daimonic Ipseity*, Phanes Apollonius – *Infernal Diabolism in Theory and Practice*, Anonymous – *Falling with Love: Embracing the Infernal Host*, Lana Krieg – *Sympathy with the Devil: Faust's Infernal Formula*, Carl Abrahamsson – *State of the Art: Birthpangs of a Mega-Golem*, Carl Abrahamsson – *Hounded by the Dogs of Reason*

THE FENRIS WOLF 4 (2011)

Carl Abrahamsson – *The whys of yesterday are the why-nots of today*, Hermann Hesse – *The Execution*, Fredrik Söderberg – *Black and White Meditations 1-23*, Peter Gilmore – *Every Man and Woman Is a Star*, Peter Grey – *Barbarians at the Gates*, John Duncan – *Hallelujah*, Ramsey Dukēs – *Democracy Is Dying of AIDS*, Tim O'Neill – *The Technology of Civilization X*, Thomas Karlsson – *Religion and Science*, David Beth – *Bloodsongs*, Payam Nabarz – *Liber Astrum*, Hiram Corso – *Unveiling the Mysteries of the Process Church*, Jean-Pierre Turmel – *The Pantheon of Genesis Breyer P-Orridge*, Kendell Geers – *The Penis Might Ier Than Thes Word*, Z'EV – *The Calls*, Robert Taylor – *Dreamachine: The Alchemy of Light*, Phil Farber – *An Interview with Terence McKenna*, Phil Farber – *McKenna, Ramachandran and the Orgy*, Thomas Bey William Bailey – *The Twilight of Psychedelic America?*, Ernst Jünger – *LSD Again/Nochmals LSD*, Baba Rampuri – *The Edge of Indian Spirituality*, Aki Cederberg – *In Search of Magic Mirrors*, Carl Abrahamsson – *Thelema and Politics*, Carl Abrahamsson – *Someone's Messing with the Big Picture*, Carl Abrahamsson – *An Art of High Intent?*, Carl Abrahamsson – *A Conversation with Kenneth Anger*

THE FENRIS WOLF 1-3 (1989-1993-2011)

Carl Abrahamsson – *Editor's Introduction*
Carl Abrahamsson – *'Zine und Zeit (2011)*

THE FENRIS WOLF 1 (1989)
John Alexander – *The Strange Phenomena of the Dream*, Helgi Pjeturss – *The Nature of Sleep and Dreams*, Tim O'Neill – *A Dark Storm Rising*, Carl Abrahamsson – *Inauguration of Kenneth Anger*, Carl Abrahamsson – *An Interview with Genesis P-Orridge*, William S Burroughs – *Points of Distinction between Sedative and Consciousness-Expanding Drugs*, Carl Abrahamsson – *Jayne Mansfield: Satanist*, TOPYUS – *Television Magick*, Anton LaVey – *Evangelists vs The New God*

The Fenris Wolf 2 (1990)
Lionel Snell – *The Satan Game*, Carl Abrahamsson – *In Defence of Satanism*, Anton LaVey – *The Horns of Dilemma*, Genesis P-Orridge – *Beyond thee Valley ov Acid*, Phauss – *Photographs*, Jack Stevenson – *15 Voices from God*, Jack Stevenson – *18 Fatal Arguments*, Tim O'Neill – *Art On the Edge of Life*, Terence Sellers – *To Achieve Death*, Stein Jarving – *Choice and Process*, Tim O'Neill – *Under the Sign of Gemini*, 93/696 – *The Forgotten Ones In Magick*, Tim O'Neill – *The Mechanics of Maya*, Coyote 12 – *The Thin Line*, Genesis P-Orridge – *Thee Only Language Is Light*, Jack Stevenson – *Porno on Film*, Carl Abrahamsson – *An Interview with Kenneth Anger*

The Fenris Wolf 3 (1993)
Jack Stevenson – *Vandals, Vikings and Nazis*, von Hausswolff & Elggren – *Inauguration of two new Kingdoms*, Tim O'Neill – *A Flame in the Holy Mountain*, Frater Tigris – *A Preliminary Vision*, Carl Abrahamsson – *The Demonic Glamour of Cinema*, William Heidrick – *Some Crowley Sources*, Peter H Gilmore – *The Rite of Ragnarök*, ONA – *The Left-Handed Path*, Zbigniew Karkowski – *The Method Is Science...*, Fetish 23 – *Demonic Poetry*, Ben Kadosh – *Lucifer-Hiram*, Freya Aswynn – *The Northern Magical Tradition*, Anton LaVey – *Tests*, Austin Osman Spare – *Anathema of Zos*, Rodney Orpheus – *Thelemic Morality*, Nemo – *Recognizing Pseudo-Satanism*, Philip Marsh – *Pythagoras, Plato and the Hellenes*, Terence Sellers – *A Few Acid Writings*, Hymenæus Beta – *Harry Smith 1923-1991*, Andrew M McKenzie – *Outofinto*, Beatrice Eggers – *Nature: Now, Then and Never*

Genesis Breyer P-Orridge: Sacred Intent
– Conversations with Carl Abrahamsson 1986-2019

Sacred Intent gathers conversations between artist Genesis Breyer P-Orridge and longtime friend and collaborator, the Swedish author Carl Abrahamsson. From the first 1986 fanzine interview about current projects, over philosophical insights, magical workings, international travels, art theory and gender revolutions, to 2019's thoughts on life and death in the the shadow of battling leukaemia, *Sacred Intent* is a unique journey in which the art of conversation blooms.

With (in)famous projects like C.O.U.M. Transmissions, Throbbing Gristle, Psychic TV, Thee Temple Ov Psychick Youth (TOPY) and Pandrogeny, Breyer P-Orridge has consistently thwarted preconceived ideas and transformed disciplines such as performance art, music, collage, poetry and social criticism; always cutting up the building blocks to dismantle control structures and authority. But underneath the socially conscious and pathologically rebellious spirit, there has always been a devout respect for a holistic, spiritual, magical worldview – one of "sacred intent."

Sacred Intent is a must read for anyone interested in contemporary art, deconstructed identity, gender evolution, and magical philosophy. The book not only celebrates an intimate friendship, but also the work and ideas of an artist who has never ceased to amaze and provoke. Also included are photographic portraits of Breyer P-Orridge taken by Carl Abrahamsson, transcripts of key lectures, and an interview with Jacqueline "Lady Jaye" Breyer P-Orridge from 2004.

GENESIS BREYER P-ORRIDGE: BRION GYSIN – HIS NAME WAS MASTER

Brion Gysin (1916–86) has been an incredibly influential artist and iconoclast: his development of the "cut-up" technique with William S. Burroughs has inspired generations of writers, artists and musicians. Gysin was also a skilled networker and revered expat: together with his friend Paul Bowles, he more or less constructed the post-beatnik romanticism for life and magic in Morocco, and was also a protagonist in an international gay culture with inspirational reaches in both America and Europe. Not surprisingly, Gysin has become something of a cult figure.

One of the artists he inspired is Genesis Breyer P-Orridge, who collaborated with both Gysin and Burroughs in the 1970s, during his work with Throbbing Gristle and C.O.U.M. Transmissions. The interviews made by P-Orridge have since become part of a New Wave/Industrial mythos. This volume presents them in their entirety alongside three texts on Gysin by P-Orridge, plus an introduction. This book is an exclusive insight into the mind of a man P-Orridge describes as "a kind of Leonardo da Vinci of the last century," and a fantastic complement to existing biographies and monographs.

CARL ABRAHAMSSON: MOTHER, HAVE A SAFE TRIP

Unearthed plans and designs stemming from radical inventor Nikola Tesla could solve the world's energy problems. These plans suddenly generate a vortex of interest from various powers. Thrown into this maelstrom of international intrigue is Victor Ritterstadt – a soul searching magician with a mysterious and troubled past. From Berlin, over Macedonia, and all the way to Nepal, Ritterstadt sets out on an outer as well as inner quest. Espionage, love, UFOs, magic, telepathy, conspiracies, LSD, and more in this shocking story of a world about to be changed forever…

"It's a thrilling roller coaster ride through psychedelic adventures, juicy romantic interludes, metaphoric dreamscapes, high Himalayan yoga enclaves, telepathic portals, 60's flashbacks, magical constructs, secret government pursuits and many more twists that kept all three of my eyes open. It's a story that you'll definitely want to keep non-stop reading, which I enthusiastically recommend."
 – George Douvris, Links by George

"*Mother, Have A Safe Trip* is a highly entertaining and thought-provoking novel. Chock-full of psychedelia, the book is also a much welcome addition to the far too few fictional works published dealing with psychedelic culture."
 – Henrik Dahl, Psychedelic Press

"The dialogues are great. But it's too short. I wanted more."
 – Genesis Breyer P-Orridge, Artist

"It's a wonderful read. A lovely book."
— June Newton/Alice Springs, Photographer

Vanessa Sinclair (ed.): Rendering Unconscious
— Psychoanalytic Perspectives, Politics & Poetry

In times of crisis, one needs to stop and ask, "How did we get here?" Our contemporary chaos is the result of a society built upon pervasive systems of oppression, discrimination and violence that run deeper and reach further than most understand or care to realize. These draconian systems have been fundamental to many aspects of our lives, and we seem to have gradually allowed them more power. However, our foundation is not solid; it is fractured and collapsing – if we allow that. We need to start applying new models of interpretation and analysis to the deep-rooted problems at hand.

Rendering Unconscious brings together international scholars, psychoanalysts, psychologists, philosophers, researchers, writers and poets; reflecting on current events, politics, the state of mental health care, the arts, literature, mythology, and the cultural climate; thoughtfully evaluating this moment of crisis, its implications, wide-ranging effects, and the social structures that have brought us to this point of urgency.

Hate speech, Internet stalking, virtual violence, the horde mentality of the alt-right, systematic racism, the psychology of rioting, the theater of violence, fake news, the power of disability, erotic transference and counter-transference, the economics of libido, Eros and the death drive, fascist narratives, psychoanalytic formation as resistance, surrealism and sexuality, traversing genders, and colonial counterviolence are but a few of the topics addressed in this thought-provoking and inspiring volume.

Contributions by Vanessa Sinclair, Gavriel Reisner, Alison Annunziata, Kendalle Aubra, Gerald Sand, Tanya White-Davis & Anu Kotay, Luce deLire, Jason Haaf, Simon Critchley & Brad Evans, Marc Strauss, Chiara Bottici, Manya Steinkoler, Emma Lieber, Damien Patrick Williams, Shara Hardeson, Jill Gentile, Angelo Villa, Gabriela Costardi, Jamieson Webster, Sergio Benvenuto, Craig Slee, Álvaro D. Moreira, David Lichtenstein, Julie Fotheringham, John Dall'aglio, Matthew Oyer, Jessica Datema, Olga Cox Cameron, Katie Ebbitt, Juliana Portilho, Trevor Pederson, Elisabeth Punzi & Per-Magnus Johansson, Meredith Friedson, Steven Reisner, Léa Silveira, Patrick Scanlon, Júlio Mendes Rodrigo, Daniel Deweese, Julie Futrell, Gregory J. Stevens, Benjamin Y. Fong, Katy Bohinc, Wayne Wapeemukwa, Patricia Gherovici & Cassandra Seltman, Marie Brown, Buffy Cain, Claire-Madeline Culkin, Andrew Daul, Germ Lynn, Adel Souto, and paul aster stone-tsao.